Ancestors and Anxiety

A

[signature: Philip E. Lilienthal]

BOOK

The Philip E. Lilienthal imprint
honors special books
in commemoration of a man whose work
at University of California Press from 1954 to 1979
was marked by dedication to young authors
and to high standards in the field of Asian Studies.
Friends, family, authors, and foundations have together
endowed the Lilienthal Fund, which enables UC Press
to publish under this imprint selected books
in a way that reflects the taste and judgment
of a great and beloved editor.

Ancestors and Anxiety

Daoism and the Birth of Rebirth in China

Stephen R. Bokenkamp

UNIVERSITY OF CALIFORNIA PRESS
Berkeley · Los Angeles · London

University of California Press, one of the most distinguished university presses in the United States, enriches
lives around the world by advancing scholarship in the
humanities, social sciences, and natural sciences. Its
activities are supported by the UC Press Foundation and
by philanthropic contributions from individuals and
institutions. For more information, visit www.ucpress.edu.

University of California Press
Berkeley and Los Angeles, California

University of California Press, Ltd.
London, England

Library of Congress Cataloging-in-Publication Data

Bokenkamp, Stephen R., 1949–.
    Ancestors and anxiety : Daoism and the birth
of rebirth in China / Stephen R. Bokenkamp.
        p.   cm.
    Includes bibliographical references and index.
    ISBN 978-0-520-24948-6 (alk. paper)
        1. Taoism.   2. Reincarnation—Buddhism.
I. Title.   II. Title: Daoism and the birth of rebirth
in China.
BL.1920.B63   2007
299.5'14237—dc22   2007005167

Manufactured in the United States of America

16   15   14   13   12   11   10   09   08   07
10   9   8   7   6   5   4   3   2   1

This book is printed on Natures Book, which contains
50% post-consumer waste and meets the minimum
requirements of ANSI/NISO Z 39.48-1992 (R 1997)
(*Permanence of Paper*).

To Robert W. Bokenkamp and
Alice K. (Birner) Bokenkamp

Contents

Acknowledgments   ix

Note on Translation   xi

Introduction: The Problem of Rebirth   1

1. Envisioning the Dead   33

2. The Unquiet Dead and Their Families, Political and Agnate   60

3. Questionable Shapes: How the Living Interrogated Their Dead   95

4. Doomed for a Certain Term: The Intimate Dead   130

5. Rebirth Reborn   158

   Postscript   193

List of Abbreviations   199

Bibliography   203

Index   215

Acknowledgments

During the decade that I have worked on this book, I have been the fortunate recipient of comments, criticisms, and suggestions from a large number of friends and colleagues. Among these, my colleague Robert Ford Campany deserves first mention. Rob provided unfailing advice and read uncomplainingly every draft I produced, invariably providing helpful criticisms, sometimes within days. The only passages that he did not critique were those having to do with my use of his own work. For those I bear full responsibility and only hope that I have not poorly repaid his kindness.

The two readers for the University of California Press, Terry Kleeman and Stephen F. Teiser, were equally generous with their criticisms and suggestions, saving me from a number of embarrassing errors. I am also grateful to Reed Malcolm, the Asian Studies editor for the University of California Press, and his wonderful staff for their patience and assistance.

I thank as well the rest of my colleagues and graduate students at Indiana University for providing an exciting intellectual climate and many helpful conversations. Jan Nattier, John McRae, Gil Raz, Clarke Hudson, Stephan Kory, and all the rest of the participants in our weekly Chinese Scripture Reading Group have, over the years, commented on some of the ideas and texts that found their way into these pages.

Portions of this work were presented at conferences and colloquia. In particular, I want to express my gratitude to Carl Bielefeldt, Bernard Faure, and the faculty of the Religious Studies Department at Stanford

University, who helped redirect my early thoughts about this project. In addition, portions of the project, at various stages of development, were presented at the Australian National University (1999); at a conference organized by Florian Reiter at Humboldt University (2001); Harvard University (2001); the Asian Art Museum of San Francisco (2001); the annual meeting of the American Academy of Religion (2003); Sichuan University (2004); Kyōto University (2004); Academia Sinica, Taipei, Taiwan (2004); the Workshop on the Eastern Jin, organized by Michael Puett at Harvard University (2005); and at a conference organized by Donald Harper at the University of Chicago (2005). I am very grateful for all the helpful comments and criticisms delivered by colleagues on these occasions, and regret that I cannot name each of them.

Work on this book was supported by grants from the Committee on Scholarly Communication with China, the American Council of Learned Societies, and the President's Art and Humanities Initiative of Indiana University. I also benefited from three months as a Visiting Fellow of the Humanities Research Centre, at the Australian National University, Canberra, Australia (1999). I am sincerely grateful to these agencies and their staffs for their support and the invaluable time away from teaching duties that they provided me.

I wish to thank my family, whose patience I have at times tried as I struggled with the sometimes dysfunctional families of the past, but who have responded always with love and support. Anastasia Shortridge and Sean Bokenkamp, off on their own now, heard more about this project than about family matters, I'm afraid. Lisa Berkson, Natty Bokenkamp, and Zack Berkson even indulged me by reading and commenting on various drafts of the work. Natty, in particular, provided me with proof that fathers can learn from sons as he bravely faced down seemingly insurmountable challenges to his health, while my granddaughters—Ayley, Jessa, and Samara—showed me again how to find delight in the little things of life. Finally, this book is without irony dedicated to my parents, who have given unstintingly of their support, love, and encouragement throughout my life.

Note on Translation

All translations in this book, unless otherwise noted, are my own. In citing the translations of others, I have silently changed Chinese romanizations to the *pinyin* romanization used in this book. Multivolume works are cited by volume and page, separated by a colon. Premodern Chinese multivolume works such as the standard histories and the Daoist canon, which are often published in varying numbers of volumes, are cited by chapter and page. These two numbers are separated by a period: for example, 23.5. Registers are represented by the lowercase letters *a*, *b*, and *c*.

The Problem of Rebirth

In order to survey the ground we will cover, we begin with two vignettes.

Scene 1

Cai Yong 蔡邕 (133–92) was an eminent official, intellectual, calligrapher, and writer of the Latter Han dynasty.[1] Though born into a powerful literati family, he first came to court notice because of his reputation for filial piety. Historians record that the first publicly recognized instance of Cai's remarkable devotion to his parents came about as follows.

When Cai was young, his mother died. Cai set up a hut beside her grave and ritually served her shade during the mourning period. As a result of his intense devotion, rabbits ran as if tamed alongside his dwelling, and a pear tree planted on the tomb grew two trunks from a single base.[2] These signs of divine approbation were widely known, and many came to view them, bringing renown and eventually offers of official position

---

1. For an English-language biography, see Chris Connery, "Ts'ai Yung," in *Indiana Companion to Traditional Chinese Literature*, ed. William H. Nienhauser Jr. (Bloomington: Indiana University Press, 1986), 787–88.

2. On the increased filiality shown by men of the Latter Han in mourning their mothers, see Miranda Brown, "Sons and Mothers in Warring States and Han China, 453 BCE–220 CE," *Nan nü* 5, no. 2 (2003): 137–69. Brown follows Fan Ye (398–445)*Hou Hanshu* (Beijing; Zhonghua shuju, 1971, 60B.1980) in describing the miracles as "Dodders pressed against the side of the hut and the wood grew into intertwining trees" (163). As all versions of the "Hymn" attest, the graph 菟 (dodder) in the *Hou Hanshu* is a mistake

I

to the filial son.[3] But Cai was not content to accept such praise on his own behalf. He claimed instead that his ancestors were responsible for the prodigies. We do not know what precisely was done with the piece of writing in which he made this assertion, his "Hymn of Praise on the Virtues of My Ancestors," or how it survived to be included in later works.[4] It may have been read as part of the ancestral rituals that Cai carried out in his family hall. More likely it was written out in Cai Yong's distinguished hand, carved into stone, and displayed in the Cai family ancestral hall or at the gravesite and thus preserved for posterity.

The prose introduction to the rhymed "Hymn" reads as follows:

Of old, King Wen [of the Zhou dynasty] first received the mandate and King Wu settled the disordered. Coming to the time of King Cheng [trad. r. 1115–1079], great peace spread abroad. The auspicious omens all descended. How could it have been that the virtue of the descendant was not brought about through gradual influence from [Kings Wen and Wu's] grand deeds? Even so does transformative excellence and the accumulation of goodness provide for lasting blessing. As the ode states: "Sons and grandsons preserve [this good fortune]."[5] And it is not only the way of kings that is so. Worthies and gentlemen who practice benevolence and tread the paths of virtue also possess this power.

Of old my ancestors, down to my father, were recorded through the generations as filial and worthy companions. They planted the seeds of bright virtue, never erring in the various rituals. This is why [their] numinous powers bring down increase and good omen. Wild hares are

---

for the graph 兔 (rabbits). The *Hou Hanshu* line should thus read, "Rabbits were accustomed to roam beside (the grave) and there was, moreover, a tree with intertwined trunks." The type of tree (*gantang* 甘棠) is not mentioned in the prose preface, but appears in the rhymed portion of Cai Yong's "Hymn" (see below), which I have not translated here.

3. Fan, *Hou Hanshu,* 60B.1980. On the social responsibility for demonstrating filial piety and the official rewards that might accrue to one who did so during this period, see Wu Hung, *Monumentality in Early Chinese Art and Architecture* (Stanford, CA: Stanford University Press, 1995), 195–96.

4. Despite the fact that the details of Cai's "Hymn" are confirmed in his biography in Fan Ye's *Hou Hanshu,* it is always possible that he might not have composed it. Cai was a famous political figure and writer, so several texts were attributed to him. Nonetheless, modern scholars who have traced Cai's works have not questioned this piece. See, for instance, Deng Ansheng, "Cai Yong zhuzuo bianyi," *Guji zhengli yanjiu xuekan* 6 (1966): 31–34. The earliest surviving copy of the text is the Tang-period *Yiwen leiju,* by Ouyang Xun (Shanghai: Guji, 1965), 20.374. See also Yan Kejun, comp., *Quan shanggu Sandai Qin Han Sanguo Liuchao wen* (Taibei: Hongye, 1975), 1:874–75. Whether Cai wrote the piece or not, it serves our purposes as representative of the ancestral practice of his day.

5. Ode 269, "Lie wen." Bernhard Karlgren in *The Book of Odes* (Stockholm: Museum of Far Eastern Antiquities, 1974) translates as follows: "Brilliant and fine rulers and princes, you have given these blessings; you have given us favor without bounds. Sons and grandsons will preserve it" (240).

tamed as a manifestation of their benevolence; trees joined at the trunk serve as a symbol of their mutual responsibility. This is the result of the numinous spirits lingering at our ancestral and paternal temples, bestowed by their overflowing virtue. How could I, in my youthful ignorance and solitude, have accomplished it?[6]

Scene 2

In the winter of 453, one of the preeminent Daoist ritualists of his day, Lu Xiujing 陸修靜 (406–477), led his disciples in the practice of the Retreat of Mud and Ash, a penitential ritual meant to rescue one's ancestors from the torments of hell.[7] As part of this ritual, Lu wrote for his disciples a series of five commemorations that they were to keep in mind during their practice so that their thoughts would be properly focused on those who would benefit from the merit of their acts. Following are extracts from the opening portions of that text.

> Father and mother "begat me and reared me. Nourished me and raised me. They thought of me while I was abroad and embraced me at home."[8] . . . They grieved for me and showed concern for me, their hearts as if cauterized or set ablaze. Anxious day and night, they forgot about money and lost sleep. Then, with ever-increasing concern, they became frantic and vexed; their tears poured down in streams. . . . [Thus] have I achieved my present state. Recalling their intense grace, which cannot be measured, I vow in my heart to repay them above. "Before bright heaven, [my intention] is without limitation."
>
> Father and mother saw me to the age of capping[9] and marriage. They collected property so that they might set me up in a livelihood. Perhaps, wanting only abundance for me, they thoughtlessly became covetous and extravagant. . . . Perhaps they became of no account, going against both heaven and earth and harming others. Perhaps they externally transgressed royal law or, internally, the statutes of the unseen world. . . . All because of me they brought upon themselves these disasters. Now they have fallen into

6. Cai Yong, *Cai zhonglang ji,* ed. Sibu beiyao (Shanghai: Zhonghua shuju, 1927–36), 3.22a–22b.

7. On the Retreat of Mud and Ash 塗炭齋, see Henri Maspero, *Le taoïsme et les religions chinoises* (Paris: Publications du Musée Guimet, 1950), 2:156–66; and Stephen R. Bokenkamp, "Sackcloth and Ashes: Self and Family in the Tutan Zhai," in *Scriptures, Schools, and Forms of Practice in Taoism,* ed. Poul Andersen and Florian C. Reiter (Wiesbaden: Harrassowitz Verlag, 2005), 33–48.

8. Both of the quotations in this paragraph are drawn from Karlgren, *Book of Odes* (*Shijing* 詩經), Ode 202, "Lu e 蓼莪," 152–53.

9. The capping ceremony marked a young male's entry into formal adulthood and was usually performed at twenty *sui,* or nineteen years of age.

the three paths[10] and suffer the myriad hardships [of hell]—they climb trees of swords, fall upon mountains of blades, tread burning coals, endure the heat as they are boiled in vats of broth, or sink in the stygian night to freeze in numbing cold. . . . Wishing to escape, they have no means to extricate themselves. Recalling this, I collapse, sobbing. My liver and heart rupture and shatter; my five limbs tremble and collapse; my form and *hun* [souls] slip out of control. Without conscious will, I throw myself to the ground, covered in the mud and ash [of utter societal disorder], I beg for mercy.[11]

While only three hundred years separate these two texts, the conceptual distance between them is vast. Most simply stated: As in ages past, Cai Yong describes his ancestors as providers of grace, while Lu Xiujing imagines his to be in need of grace.

While Cai Yong responds to extraordinary tokens of ancestral blessing, the concepts he expresses are normal for his time and station. Elite, empowered ancestors did provide for their posterity good fortune and worldly blessings, including even such intangibles as virtue—*de,* the moral power to influence other men and the natural world. The cosmic order that made this lineal transfer of merit possible was as reliable in the Latter Han as it had been, at least according to accepted legend, in the Zhou; as true for ritually observant members of elite families as it was for the royal house.

By Lu Xiujing's time, the ancient vision of unbroken lineal continuity had been shattered. Ancestors once seen as source of blessings for their needy descendants still embroiled in the demands of the world prove themselves urgently in need of help. Lu makes no mention at all of any possible benefit that might flow down across generations. Horrifyingly, even the good deeds fathers and mothers performed while alive proved useless in altering their postmortem destinies and might even have exacerbated their present dire predicament rather than alleviating it. There is nothing that they can do to save themselves, much less their offspring.

The stark differences between the conceptual worlds inhabited by these men can, in part, be attributed to the reception of certain Buddhist cosmological ideas. There is no trace of the religion in the writings of Cai Yong. Cai describes his filial services beside the graves of his parents,

---

10. The "three paths" 三塗 is a term adopted from Buddhism, where it generally refers to unfortunate rebirth in the hells, as an animal, or as a hungry ghost. Daoist texts sometimes give the homophonous "three types of servitude" 三徒 , which they explain as three types of slave labor in the hells. See Stephen R. Bokenkamp, *Early Daoist Scriptures* (Berkeley and Los Angeles: University of California Press, 1997), 435–37, fnn. 12 and 14.

11. HY 1268, 2a–2b.

where faint but symbolically powerful signs assure him that the lingering spirits of his ancestors recognize and reward his efforts. These signs were, as his text explains, as much the tokens of orderly rule as they were of the virtuous citizen. In 116, only some thirty-five years or so before Cai's miracle, a distant region of the empire had reported a similar appearance of doubled trees as an omen confirming the emperor's virtue, and books of omens listed such occurrences as evidence of kingly merit.[12] Even the slightly Lewis Carroll–like detail of the "tamed wild hares" that scamper unmolested around the Cai family tombs had a classical precedent in the "tame wild animals" that people of the time believed to be willing familiars of the ancient sage-kings.[13] That the Cai family beasts were small and furry makes them no less potent as symbols.

Cai makes no mention of whether or not his ancestors' spirits inhabited the grave, though the lavishly furnished tombs of his contemporaries indicate that many of them thought so; nor does he even hint that they might be possessed of post-mortem sentience, though arguments on this question too were common in his time. Such concerns were simply not important for proper conduct of the ancestral rituals, nor for numinous grace to arise from such practices.

Lu Xiujing's ritual text, on the other hand, provides precise imaginings as to where the ancestors might now be and just what it is that they now suffer. Here the reliance of Lu's Daoism on the netherworld torture fantasies developed in Buddhist texts shows most starkly. Chinese Buddhist writings describe the punishments he mentions with even greater concern for detail. Lu requires no signs of the deceased ancestors' fate. The new cosmology that asserts the final results of human action are as certain for him as were the mechanisms of ancestral grace for Cai Yong. Even memories of parental love are turned into possible reasons for the torments they now suffer. This seems paradoxical, if not perverse, but within the cause-and-effect-driven cosmos that Daoism adapted from the Buddhist religion, it is not. Lu, like his Buddhist contemporaries, seems

12. For the appearance of this sign during the reign of Emperor An, see Fan, *Hou Hanshu*, 5.224–25. The omen also is listed in a Han-period apocryphal omen-text on the *Scripture of Filiality*, the *Xiaojing yuanshen qi* 孝經援神契; see Yasui Kōzan and Nakamura Shōhachi, eds., *Isho shūsei*, 6 vols. (Tokyo: Meitoku, 1971–78), 5:42.

13. For an excellent discussion of the images of tame beasts that festoon Han-period tombs, see Martin J. Powers, *Art and Political Expression in Early China* (New Haven, CT: Yale University Press, 1991), 271–77. Powers expresses the opinion that such scenes of gamboling beasts "express the improbable freedom of paradise" (276). I would not disagree, but only add that "paradise" was in this period as often an idealized past as a future, otherworldly state of existence.

to have regarded mundane attachment and desire, even the desire that one's children prosper, as causes of suffering.

There are further indications, however, that Lu held this austere causality to be not a normal state of affairs but a condition particularly afflicting a fallen age. The poem from *The Book of Odes* (*Shijing* 詩經) that Lu cites, Ode 202, was traditionally held to have been composed in criticism of King You (r. 781–771 BCE), last ruler of the Western Zhou, whose reign was beset by war. The Mao preface to the odes states that during his reign "the people suffered and filial sons could not support [their parents]"; that is to say, parents died in service to the kingdom while their children were yet young.[14] The stanza Lu cites reveals the filial nature of the persona of the poem; other stanzas register complaints about the persona's parentless state: "If one has no father, on whom shall one rely? If one has no mother, on whom shall one depend? Abroad, one harbors grief; at home one has no one to whom to go."[15] Through allusion, Lu thus presents himself and his disciples as inhabitants of a troubled time but also as recipients of a rare grace—the recent appearance of salvific scriptures that allow them to rescue those who have been lost.

In the final chapter of this work I explore some of the textual sources of Lu Xiujing's ritual practice and say more about the complexities of these ideas. For now, it is pertinent to note that, through his citation of the revered classic, he situates newly integrated notions of purgatories, rebirth, and salvation within the context of his culture's own remembered past. In this way alone, Lu's commemoration, outlandish in all other respects, would have appeared familiar to Cai Yong. Sharing at least an ancestral reverence for the Confucian classics, the two men would have agreed that (to cite the verse Cai used) "sons and grandsons preserve." After this moment of agreement, however, they would simply have stopped talking to one another over the vexed issue of just what it was that posterity was charged to preserve.

And here we come to the crux of the matter. For Cai Yong, "preservation" stands for his participation in the worldly and public exchange in which ancestors might still participate. By raising a monument to them, calling attention to their merits, and reporting the anomalies that betokened their ability to influence the living world, Cai preserves the public personae of his family.[16] The lingering prestige of his ancestors is thus

---

14. *SSJZS* 1:459b.
15. Karlgren, *Book of Odes*, 153.
16. For how this was thought to work, see particularly Wu, *Monumentality*, chap. 1.

made visible and is able to work precisely as it had while they were yet alive. The actual state and true dwelling place of the ancestors could be preserved in privacy. What visits Cai may have had with them in the years following their death, what visions he may have experienced, what hopes or fears he may have had concerning their postmortem state—all belonged to this realm of the private. They are simply not mentioned in Cai's writings. In fact, it would have been a betrayal of contemporary mores for him to broach such subjects, perhaps even a bit like reporting how his father chewed his food.

For Lu Xiujing, knowledge of the otherworld is, on the contrary, precise and public. The fates of the dead can be imagined in grisly detail, and ritual provides occasion for public rehearsal of these intimate details. Like Cai, Lu celebrates the living deeds of his parents, but now that they are dead, there is nothing more they can do for him and everything he can do for them.

. . .

The story scholars have constructed to explain the differences between the approaches of Cai Yong and Lu Xiujing to their respective parents goes roughly as follows. Before Buddhism, the Chinese had no notion of the fate of their dead. Or rather, they had several conflicting and confused notions. At any rate, once Buddhism arrived, with its detailed cosmologies and precise descriptions of rebirth and the afterlife, the Chinese, lacking more persuasive explanations, accepted these. Over the course of time, the Chinese people modified these Buddhist notions somewhat to accord with their cultural predilections, but belief in the existence of Buddhist hells and rebirth became general. The full-scale adaptation into the early fifth-century Lingbao scriptures upon which Lu Xiujing based his practice of what looks very much like the Buddhist cosmology certainly seems to support this characterization. Studies dedicated specifically to this question tend, then, to propose periodizations for the gradual absorption of Buddhist ideas into the Chinese worldview.[17]

Regrettably, in explaining matters to ourselves in this rather simple way, we find ourselves comparing incommensurables—relative silence on the subject of the dead before 200 CE and garrulousness after. We do

---

17. See, for instance, Yamada Toshiaki, "The Lingbao School," in *Daoism Handbook*, ed. Livia Kohn (Leiden: Brill, 2000), 225–55; Russell Kirkland, "The History of Taoism: A New Outline," *Journal of Chinese Religions* 30 (2002): 177–93; and Livia Kohn, "Steal Holy Food and Come Back as a Viper: Conceptions of Karma and Rebirth in Medieval Daoism," *Early Medieval China* 4 (1998): 1–4.

have archeologically recovered records and texts buried with the dead, but these offer nothing like the detailed explanations found in later Buddhist and Daoist Scripture.[18] As a textual scholar, it has long troubled me that ancient Chinese mortuary cults, with their lavish and painstaking care of the dead, apparently left no detailed records explaining why the Chinese did such things. While early Chinese mortuary practice might best be compared with that of ancient Egypt, we have no Chinese *Book of the Dead*. There are, to be sure, pages of careful ritual description for the preparation of the body and for the subsequent ancestral rites to be performed both at the gravesite and in the family shrine. But the received record provides only vague traces of evidence as to what most people thought happened to the dead once the ministrations of the living ceased.

The standard explanation for this silence is roughly this: according to the *Analects*, Confucius had recommended that one sacrifice to the spirits "as if they were present."[19] Later writers, some scholars hold, followed this directive religiously. I have suggested in the case of Cai Yong that we might also be dealing with a division between public and private. What transpired within (and beyond) the grave—like what happened in its above-ground simulacrum, the family home—was part of the private realm. Decorum prevented any public discussion of what precisely was imagined to occur in either place—thus the frequent use of the concessive conjunction "if" 若 in any text that mentions the possible postmortem existence or consciousness of the ancestors. But, like the "Confucius said" explanation, this is but one hypothesis among many.[20] The fact is that we have relatively sparse evidence down to the end of the Han period about what individual fates the elite thought might have

---

18. For Han-period mortuary documents revealing ideas about the dead that became part of Daoist views, see Terry F. Kleeman, "Land Contracts and Related Documents," in *Chūgoku no shūkyō, shisō to kagaku: Festschrift in Honour of Makio Ryōkai* (Tokyo: Kokusho kankōkai, 1984), 1–34; and Anna K. Seidel, "Traces of Han Religion in Funeral Texts Found in Tombs," in *Dōkyō to shūkyō bunka* [Volume in honor of Professor Akitsuki Kan'ei] (Tokyo: Hirakawa, 1987), 21–57; and "Post-Mortem Immortality; or, the Taoist Resurrection of the Body," in *GILGUL: Essays on Transformation, Revolution and Permanence in the History of Religions*, ed. S. Shaked, D. Shulman, and G. G. Stroumsa (Leiden: E. J. Brill, 1987), 223–37.

19. *Lunyu*, "Bayi 八佾," in *SSJZS* 2:2467.

20. David N. Keightley, who has thoroughly studied the origins of the ancestral cult during the Shang, argues that "an inverse relationship exists between the degree to which an ancestor cult is articulated and the degree of attention paid to the actual, personal circumstances of the soul in the afterlife"; see his "Clean Hands and Shining Helmets: Heroic Action in Early Chinese and Greek Culture," in *Religion and the Authority of the Past*, ed. Tobin Siebers (Ann Arbor: University of Michigan Press, 1993), 47. More recently, in a carefully nuanced discussion, he presents evidence that Shang, Zhou, and Han ancestral

awaited their sainted ancestors. For the non-elite majority, the silence rings even more loudly in our ears.

We are left, then, at an impasse. Since few works beyond later, triumphal Buddhist accounts—together with a few alarmist anti-Buddhist tracts—survive, there seems to be no way for us to catch even a glimpse of what might have happened on the ground as the society at large was adopting ideas of rebirth.

As I pondered this dilemma, trying to make sense of the changes in views of the afterlife that occurred between Cai Yong and Lu Xiujing, I came to realize that a number of the texts I was reading—descriptions of the lands of the dead, accounts of those who returned to tell of life beyond the grave—while they contained little specific reference to Buddhism, in fact provided evidence on the way ideas of rebirth came to be contested, modified, and later accepted in China. In fact, precisely because these were not Buddhist texts, they provided insights that self-identified Buddhist writings could not. The views that Chinese Buddhist writers, quite naturally, included in their writings and collected into their canon tend to portray the inexorability of the growth of their faith and the power of its ideas. Buddhist works do include, for instance, records of court debates on the religion that provide at least edited voices from outside the faith. "Apocryphal sutras," Buddhist scriptures composed in China, are another rich source of information on the doctrinal modifications that their priestly authors deemed necessary to adapt Buddhism for their Chinese audience. But such evidence can only present, to a greater or lesser extent, "insider" perspectives on the spread of Buddhist ideas among the Chinese populace. The texts I treat here reveal outside perspectives on the religion.

----

practice served to create order in dealings with the ancestors precisely by assigning them roles in the otherworldly bureaucracy and the ritual cycles that reinforced these roles: "In the ideology of the early Chinese elites, the depersonalized dead were the ordered dead. There was no need to tell their individual stories, for the 'quirkyness' of the individual personalities would, precisely, have threatened the good, impersonal order that was desired"(David N. Keightley, "The Making of the Ancestors: Late Shang Religion and Its Legacy," in *Religion and Chinese Society: Ancient and Medieval China*, vol. 1, ed John Lagerwey [Hong Kong: Chinese University of Hong Kong Press and École française d'Extrême-Orient, 2004], 3–64, esp. 34–45). Despite the necessary circularity of some of his claims, Keightley's argument explains much. It may well be that the closely guarded, personal nature of interactions with the dead in family ritual stemmed from the ancient impulses to order that Keightley demonstrates. As we shall see, however, that ideal system fell apart with the fall of the Han in the early third century. The "quirkyness" of the dead provides the stories upon which this study is based. And, with the Lingbao initiative to reestablish a "good, impersonal order" in relations with the dead, we may well have the parallel case that confirms Keightley's hypothesis.

To foreshadow somewhat my findings, what I came to understand was that, just as they were for Cai Yong and Lu Xiujing and others of early medieval China, accounts of the dead and their interactions with the living were "good to think with" (to borrow Lévi-Strauss's phrase), or perhaps more aptly "good to work with." The writings I survey provide evidence that Buddhist accounts of rebirth and the afterlife did not come to be accepted in China by default, or through ideological poverty, or by fiat. Instead, they were gradually adapted into preexisting Chinese conceptions of how to deal with the dead because they helped to solve particular problems among the living.

That is to say, I want to take the focus off of karma and rebirth as an evolving "system of belief" or "doctrine." The texts I have assembled show clearly that the conversations with and among the dead in early medieval China were not finally about belief systems at all, but about other sorts of concerns, some religious and some not. It was, of course, these concerns that Buddhist doctrines of rebirth would have to successfully address in order to be accepted in Chinese society. I do not, however, explore here how Buddhism came to deal with these challenges.[21] My survey ends with Lu Xiujing and the adaptation within his Daoist sources of the doctrine of rebirth. My focus, throughout, is on the individuals involved in these conversations with the dead—their anxieties, concerns, and aims in making the dead speak as they did—and on how ideas of rebirth came to seem apposite in solving these problems.

I could not hope to explore such questions for every instance in which the dead are mentioned. The reader, beset with a welter of unfamiliar names and historical detail from the outset of the next chapter, will soon understand why this is so. Instead, I have chosen to focus on a relatively small sampling of texts. Since the dead of early China were, like the living, members of large extended families, and any competent exploration of the issues involved must trace these family connections, there is simply no other way to proceed. For those unused to reading about China, the sheer number of unfamiliar names and places necessary to this kind of study will prove daunting enough. I apologize at the outset, hoping

---

21. For studies of Buddhist adaptations to accommodate aspects of Chinese ancestral practice during the fifth and sixth centuries see Stephen F. Teiser, *The Ghost Festival in Medieval China* (Princeton, NJ: Princeton University Press, 1988); Hou Xudong, *Wu, liu shiji beifang minzhong fojiao xinyang* (Beijing: Zhongguo shehui kexueyuan chubanshe, 1998); Alan Cole, *Mothers and Sons in Chinese Buddhism* (Stanford, CA: Stanford University Press, 1998); and Bret Hinsch, "Confucian Filial Piety and the Construction of the Ideal Buddhist Woman," *Journal of Chinese Religions* 30 (2002): 49–76.

that the patiently assembled detail will allow at least some of the fascination I find in these accounts to show through.

Several concerns remain to be addressed before we begin. The most direct evidence for Chinese adaptations of Buddhism appears, not surprisingly, in Buddhist scripture, ecclesiastical histories, and other documentary records, many of which were gathered in Buddhist literary collections. Such materials provide the data for a host of studies that inform my analysis at several points, but I draw my primary data from different sources. With the exception of the didactic tale presented just below, not one of the texts I study in this work is in any way "Buddhist."

Nonetheless, throughout these pages, I identify passages in the texts I treat that cite or invoke traditional Chinese ideas or Daoist ideas and—again, explicitly or implicitly—contrast them with "Buddhist" ideas. When our authors do so, they sometimes label the way of the Buddha a "foreign" intrusion on the Chinese scene. Thus, I would like to counter two common misconceptions from the start. The first is that these adaptations of "Buddhist" ideas are the result of "influence." In reading them, we must first of all take care to see these Daoist texts as *responses* to Buddhism, rather than evidence of the *influence* of Buddhism.[22] That is to say, we must guard against what Michael Baxandall has characterized as the "billiard ball" image of causality.[23] In the case of Buddhist ideas such as rebirth, we too easily imagine the agent of change (Buddhism) to be the cue ball and the recipient, or locus, of change (Chinese systems of thought) to be the billiard ball struck by the cue ball and driven in certain predestined directions by its trajectory. This common mental image obscures the true mechanisms of change, which reside fully with the receiving parties, the only true actors in the transaction.[24] My focus, then, is on how the texts I survey engage, deny, or appropriate Buddhist ideas, rather than on how those ideas influenced these texts.

22. As Stephen Teiser has helpfully pointed out to me, it is also true that Buddhist scriptures composed in China, Buddhist polemical essays, and even Buddhist translations might equally be seen as "native responses to Buddhism." While this is quite true, my aim here is to show how these particular texts, which align themselves in opposition or contradistinction to Buddhism, can tell us things about the Chinese reception of the religion that self-identified Buddhist texts cannot.

23. Michael Baxandall, *Patterns of Intention: On the Historical Explanation of Pictures* (New Haven, CT: Yale University Press, 1985), 58–60. Baxandall also provides a helpful list of verbs (59) that might be employed to describe the actions of the true institutor of change.

24. For more on how such views of "influence" have obscured the true lineaments of Chinese adaptation of Buddhist ideas, see Stephen R. Bokenkamp, "The Silkworm and the Bodhi Tree: The Lingbao Attempt to Replace Buddhism in China and Our Attempt to Place Lingbao Daoism," in Lagerwey, *Religion and Chinese Society*, 317–39.

The second, related, misconception is that, despite the claims of some of our early medieval authors, the "Buddhism" to which they responded was "foreign." Now, it is of course true that Buddhism, or rather a number of "Buddhisms," were imported into China and that Chinese Buddhist monks adopted modes of speaking and appearance (transliterated Sanskrit terms and shaved heads, for instance) that continued to mark them as "other." This easily leads to the simplistic mental model that Robert Sharf, in his *Coming to Terms with Chinese Buddhism,* calls the "encounter paradigm," whereby two distinct religious cultures, one Indic and the other Sinic, are imagined to have come into contact and borrowed from one another. As Sharf helpfully reminds us,

> It is . . . difficult to speak in simple terms of a Chinese dialogue or encounter with Indian Buddhism. Chinese functioned as the sole ecclesiastical language from the inception of Buddhism in the Han on down through the medieval period, and given the paucity of bilingual clerics, whatever "dialogue" transpired took place largely among the Chinese themselves. Their encounter was with a Buddhism already sinified if only by virtue of being rendered, through an often convoluted process of translation and exegesis, into the native tongue.[25]

I will, of heuristic necessity, continue to speak in these pages of "Buddhism," especially when it comes to the distinctive complex of ideas surrounding karma, retribution, and the hellish fates of some of the dead, but the reader should understand that I refer to what was by this time a fully Chinese discourse taking place among people who describe their own religious affiliations in diverse ways. Neither should my choice of "non-Buddhist" texts—that is, texts that position themselves in opposition to Buddhist claims—to explore the Chinese reception of rebirth be construed to mean that this is the whole story, but only that this is the part of the story that has been under-represented in the scholarly record. And, as I have argued, they tell a story to which we have not always attended in our attempts to understand the growth of Buddhism in early medieval China.

In part, my choice of data has been suggested by my own scholarly concerns. For some twenty-five years, I have been engaged in the study of the Lingbao scriptures that began to appear in the earliest years of the fifth century CE. The Lingbao scriptures were composed to replace all previous spiritual knowledge with higher and more enduring truths. To

---

25. Robert H. Sharf, *Coming to Terms with Chinese Buddhism: A Reading of the "Treasure Store Treatise"* (Honolulu: University of Hawaii Press, 2002), 19.

accomplish this task, the authors rewrote or recontextualized pieces of earlier scriptural texts, Buddhist texts among them. Most striking is the fact that, while earlier Daoist texts make little mention of Buddhism or its doctrines, the concept of rebirth proves central to the salvific concerns of these scriptures, as we saw in the case of Lu Xiujing.[26] The question motivating my initial interest in the issue of the Chinese reception of the idea of rebirth, then, was "How was it possible that such a thorough-going acceptance of the idea could suddenly make its appearance in these texts written at the beginning of the fifth century?"

Analyzing the Lingbao texts to determine specific Buddhist and Daoist sources of the scriptural pastiche could not answer this question, for such a procedure left in abeyance the issue of why any Chinese author would feel that his productions might be well received by his Chinese audience (and we know that they were). But phrasing the question in this way did open new possibilities for exploration because it precipitated a shift in focus to something for which we have an abundance of evidence— evolving literary portrayals of familial relations with the dead during the period from the third through the sixth centuries.

The problem that then presents itself is that we often know so little of the precise social contexts that produced Daoist scriptures. Decades of research into the texts of the religion have allowed us to date a few texts, sometimes to within the decade, and even on occasion to propose plausible authorship, but in most cases we are still far from knowing the precise human situations to which authors of revealed material responded. This is a matter of no small moment for this project, since my primary interest is in the familial dynamics of ancestral practice and how these were reconfigured to account for concepts of rebirth.

Only one point of entry presented itself. The *Declarations of the Perfected (Zhen'gao* 真誥), a collection of visionary transcripts and autograph materials related to them collected by Tao Hongjing 陶弘景 (456–536), includes not only compelling descriptions of the fates of dead individuals, but also high family drama. The author of the revealed materials Tao

26. The earliest mention identified to date of Buddhism in texts emanating from the first Daoist movement, the Celestial Masters, appears in the *Commands and Admonitions for the Families of the Great Dao*, dated to 255 CE; see Bokenkamp, *Early Daoist Scriptures*, 158, 169–70. When scholars look at Celestial Master compilations of materials ranging in date, they find that Buddhist elements appearing in the texts are couched in Lingbao terminology and so postdate the appearance of the Lingbao texts. For an excellent example of this, see Franciscus Verellen, "The Heavenly Master Liturgical Agenda According to Chisong zi's Petition Almanac," *Cahiers d'Extrême-Asie* 14 (2004): 291–344.

collected was the Daoist Yang Xi 楊羲 (330–86?), who received these texts in visions between the years 363 or 364 and 370.[27] During that time, Yang was employed as a spiritual advisor by a southern gentry family in the county of Jurong, just southeast of the Eastern Jin capital Jiankang (modern Nanjing). Yang's principal patrons were Xu Mi 許謐 (303–73), a minor official at the imperial court, and his son Hui 翽 (341–ca. 370). Among the materials that Yang received were accounts of the underworld, Fengdu, of such specificity that they listed the ranks and fates of the inhabitants—ancestors of men Xu Mi would have known—much in the manner of Dante Alighieri's *Divina Commedia*. We even have fragments of letters between Yang Xi and Xu Mi questioning certain features of this news from beyond the grave. Moreover, the scholarly thoroughness of Tao Hongjing led him to collect further accounts of the underworlds and to compare these with the revelations granted to Yang.

The material collected in the *Declarations* thus offers a rare window, not only into changing descriptions of the afterlife, but also into the precise familial and social uses to which these tales of the individual dead were put. The tales Tao collected provide the road map I have followed into this *terra incognita*. In the final chapter, I consider another corpus of Daoist texts, the Lingbao scriptures. Traditionally held to have been composed by Ge Chaofu 葛巢甫 and released to the world around 400 CE, these scriptures were collected and edited by Lu Xiujing. By this time, scant decades after Yang Xi's revelations, a distinctive Chinese concept of rebirth appears for the first time in a native Chinese religious tradition.

While the project might thus seem tightly focused, the tales prove wonderfully anfractuous, leading into a number of fruitful lines of inquiry involving genres of literature—anecdote, religious writings, history, ge-

---

27. The *Zhen'gao* is HY 1010 in the Daoist canon. On the Shangqing revelations granted to Yang Xi by a new, higher class of deity, the Perfected, who descended from heavens higher than those known in previous Daoist scripture (the Shangqing heavens), see primarily Michel Strickmann, "The Mao-shan Revelations: Taoism and the Aristocracy," *T'oung-pao* 63 (1977): 1–63; "On the Alchemy of T'ao Hung-ching," in *Facets of Taoism: Essays in Chinese Religion*, ed. Holmes Welch and Anna Seidel (New Haven, CT: Yale University Press, 1979), 123–92; *Le taoïsme du Mao chan: Chronique d'une révélation* (Paris: Collège du France, Institut des Hautes Études Chinoises, 1981); and Isabelle Robinet, "Les randonées extatiques des Taoistes dans les astres," *Monumenta Serica* 32 (1976): 159–273; *Taoist Meditation: The Mao-Shan Tradition of Great Purity*, trans. Julian F. Pas and Norman J. Girardot (Albany: State University of New York Press, 1993); and *La révélation du Shangqing dans l'histoire du taoïsme*, 2 vols., Publications de l'Ecole française d'Extrême-Orient, no. 137 (Paris: École française d'Extrême-Orient, 1984).

nealogical records—too often kept distinct in modern studies of China's past. The resulting picture of early medieval Chinese ideas of the afterlife is just messy enough, to my mind, to approximate some strands of the complex texture of social change as Chinese resisted, modified, and co-opted elements of the various ideologies brought in with Buddhism concerning the fate of the dead.

Fortunately for me, as I was preparing this book, a research group at Kyōto University began publishing a preliminary translation of the *Declarations*.[28] Yet, even with international help, problems of understanding remain, for these are intimate family documents. Reading the *Declarations* is often a bit like listening to the conversations of a family counselor when we do not know the family involved at all and must listen through a thick wall that obliterates some of the voices (especially the higher voices of women!), and when the voices we do hear clearly speak a family idiolect, sometimes referring to one another by pet names or referring to people and events of which we can have no knowledge. Add to this the circumstance that we cannot even listen through the wall directly but must depend on transcripts assembled by someone else for an audience of his own. To make matters even worse, the transcribed fragments have somehow become jumbled, so the dates and times appended to each item are a matter of guesswork even for our informant. Grasp all this and you will begin to divine the difficulties we face.[29] The words we overhear in these transcripts are muted and fragmentary, and their once-familiar references are now unclear in the extreme. Still, the urgency of the tones, the accents of panic, anger, despair, and relief, are palpable. And some of the subplots are recoverable. We want to listen.

HOW TO PROCEED?

Readers may wonder why I did not simply trace the Buddhist textual antecedents of the Lingbao scriptures in order to understand the uses to which they put them in constructing their distinctive notions of rebirth. I may yet write that book, but it is not this one. Here, I want to explore

28. This work was eventually published in book form; see Yoshikawa Tadao and Mugitani Kuniō, *Shinkō kenkyū: Yakuchū hen* (Kyōto: Kyōto daigaku jinbun kagaku kenkyūjō, 2000). All references to the work of the Kyōto group refer to this final product of their joint collaboration.

29. Given the impediments, in using the accounts in the *Declarations*, I have tried to note levels of probability clearly and have indicated where readings are my own and not shared by the Kyōto group.

another avenue of discovery. As I began to follow the documentary trail left by Tao Hongjing to isolate sources for the concepts I found in my Lingbao texts, I immediately learned two things. First, not all the inter-related texts I found were claimed by Yang Xi or the Lingbao writers as contributing directly to their Dao; rather, they extended to a variety of other religious and nonreligious stances on the issues. They thus speak to concerns extending beyond our imagined Buddhist and Daoist "monasteries"—never so closed off from society as their walls might in-dicate. And second, while I did notice an increasing reference to Bud-dhist ideas of rebirth in these texts, other concerns were often the focus of the authors' attention. In tracing these, I came to the conclusion that anxieties concerning family relations with their cherished dead and aris-ing from the prevalence of disease, warfare, and societal dislocation in the third to fifth centuries formed for many one context for Daoist de-ployments of the Buddhist doctrine of rebirth.

While it might at first seem perverse in a book dedicated to analyzing texts about the afterlife and rebirth, I make no claims about the beliefs of the authors I treat. Not only is belief unavailable to the scholar as an object of study, it is arguably not central to the practice of religion, as Donald S. Lopez Jr. has recently shown.[30] What we can examine are the words—written words in the case of this book—that the religious use to describe, explain, and justify their acts.

For this purpose, I find useful the distinction made by Robert Ford Campany between "internalist" and "externalist" descriptions.[31] Dis-cussing the culinary choices of certain religious groups in China, Cam-pany writes,

> Internalist . . . rationales for dietary regimes . . . explain and justify them in terms of the intrinsic benefits, properties and functions of the foodstuffs they feature or the preparations they prescribe. Often such explanations explicitly link a dietary choice to a larger theory, set of beliefs, ideology, cosmology, cosmogony, or myth. . . . Externalist meanings or functions pertain when dietary choices have the effect, whether by intention or not, of associating eaters with certain clusters of values in a culture and disso-ciating them from others. Here, culinary regimes are a way of making statements about a wide range of other matters (and often other groups of eaters).[32]

30. Donald S. Lopez Jr., "Belief," in *Critical Terms for Religious Studies,* ed. Mark C. Taylor (Chicago: University of Chicago Press, 1998), 21–35.
31. Robert F. Campany, "The Meanings of Cuisines of Transcendence in Late Classi-cal and Early Medieval China," *T'oung Pao* 91 (2005): 1–6.
32. Ibid., 2.

We can adapt this insight more generally to statements and rationales given by the religious for any of their practices. *Internalist* explanations or statements are general statements that pertain to the inner logic of a religious system, meant to reaffirm "beliefs, ideology, cosmology, cosmogony, or myth." *Externalist* explanations or statements, by their nature, are situational and make claims concerning the relations between specific religious persons and groups and the society in which they operate. They often make explicit distinctions between one way of viewing the world and another. Of course internalist statements can draw such contrasts as well, but they are addressed to the religious group for whom they are made and do not seek to establish claims beyond that group. Externalist statements do. The distinction Campany makes, as I understand it, does not concern the semantic contours of the statement itself but the rhetorical situation in which the utterance occurs and the function it is intended to perform.[33] Externalist statements are, to some extent, challenges thrown into the world that are meant to effectuate the distinctions they claim. While the precise rhetorical situation might not be fully available to us, it is explicitly or implicitly indicated in the nature of the statement itself.

Take, for example, the case of a son who sets out to describe the postmortem rank of his father in the otherworldly hierarchy at a time when his contemporaries, "once they consider the limiting factors of [Buddhist] samsara (cyclical rebirth) and retribution, [have] all succumbed to panic" at the fate that awaits them and their families.[34] If the writings of that son show that he was aware of Buddhism and its views on rebirth, and yet he pointedly ignores these, we may analyze his claims as externalist, associating him "with certain clusters of values in a society and dissociating [him] from others." It is my burden, then, in the chapters that follow to demonstrate in each instance when and how each writer expresses such alterity and what it might indicate of societal resistance to, accommodations to, or modifications of the idea of rebirth.

Stimulated as well by the recent work of Michael Puett, I see the texts that Tao Hongjing isolates, the passages of the Lingbao scriptures, and

33. Notice, for instance, that Campany ("Meanings of Cuisines," 2, n. 3), while noting the differences, claims as one source of his internalist/externalist claims J. L. Austin's distinction between "locutionary acts" and "perlocutionary acts."
34. Yuan Hong (328–376), *Hou Han ji jiaozhu [Records of the Latter Han]*, ed. Zhou Tianyou (Tianjin: Tianjin guji chubanshe, 1987); translation modified from that found in Tsukamoto Zenryu, *A History of Early Chinese Buddhism: From Its Introduction to the Death of Hui Yüan*, trans. Leon Hurvitz (Tokyo: Kodansha, 1985), 476.

other writings I discuss as arguments, though not arguments over abstract concepts such as "transcendence," "cosmos," or "afterlife"—as Puett tends to do—but over quotidian details of the survival and significance of specific persons.[35] These more immediate concerns, often familial in nature, were what prompted medieval Chinese to make their dead speak and constituted the reason they attended to those voices from beyond the grave. While the resulting arguments often tell us something of doctrine and ideology, the reasons for their being lie elsewhere. The arguments attributed to the dead present, in short, externalist arguments that .can tell us as much about society and its discontents as about evolving religious ideologies. As will become apparent, I am guided in this analysis by the way in which Tao Hongjing and Lu Xiujing read the texts that came before them, though I often highlight social details they want to suppress or redefine.

As the title of this book indicates, I have frequently found that the statements I analyze express certain "anxieties" concerning the fate of the dead and the threats that Buddhist notions of rebirth initially posed to traditional ancestral practice. Certainly, sons claiming exalted postmortem rank for their fathers can be shown to be expressing certain anxieties concerning the fate of their cherished dead. But this is not the only sort of anxiety I mean to highlight. Sometimes, our authors betray an anxiety concerning the authority of other, prior texts whose claims they must either confront or avoid. Harold Bloom dealt with such anxiety in his *Anxiety of Influence*. Bloom was writing of poetry and of "learning to read any poem as its poet's deliberate misinterpretation . . . of a precursor poem."[36] Yet I find his reading strategies enlightening when applied to other sorts of texts as well—say, for instance, when that son, writing of the otherworldly status of his father, feels that he must also mention the current status of persons placed in the otherworld by prior writers.

My deployment of the term *anxiety,* then, sometimes finds its basis in the understanding that prior works of cultural imagination serve to motivate religious writers in ways that prove unavoidable. This entails that,

35. See Michael J. Puett, *The Ambivalence of Creation: Debates Concerning Innovation and Artifice in Early China* (Stanford, CA: Stanford University Press, 2001), esp. 16–20; and *To Become a God: Cosmology, Sacrifice, and Self-Divinization in Early China,* Harvard-Yenching Monograph Series, no. 57 (Cambridge, MA: Harvard University Press, 2002).

36. Harold Bloom, *The Anxiety of Influence: A Theory of Poetry* (Oxford: Oxford University Press, 1973), 43.

in encountering strong alternative explanations, such as those the Buddhists introduced, the predominant response might be to reinterpret (a process Bloom calls "misprision") the "fathers," so as to counter or accommodate the new, potentially disruptive vision.

It may well be that all religious change results in part from the sorts of anxiety and misprision that Bloom finds in responses to literary "forerunners," but that is not the claim of this book. Rather, I want to argue that Buddhist views of the afterlife, along with imponderable societal pressures resulting from disease and dislocation, prompted Chinese writers to reconfigure (misprise) the words of the "fathers" in ways that led to new conceptions and helped foster the positions of the Lingbao scriptures.

The field from which I draw my data extends beyond bibliographically classified religious writings to encompass ghost tales, private and official histories, poetry, and memorials. In casting such a wide net, I respond as well to "New Historicist" approaches. Their insistence on a widened scope of inquiry allows us to extrapolate social concerns from what might seem the slenderest of threads, the anecdote. As Stephen Greenblatt writes,

> The anecdote was not merely background: it demanded attention; it threatened to take over the whole enterprise. . . . It offered access to the everyday, the place where things are actually done, the sphere of practice that even in its most awkward and inept articulations makes a claim on the truth that is denied to the most eloquent of literary texts.[37]

Since the tales that form the majority of my evidence are anecdotes, I too found myself cast into the realm of glowing detail, where both true and untrue things were written about topics that concerned the authors and their audience. Fictionality, when we are dealing with accounts of—and the voices given—the dead, cannot be a determining concept, and we can seek "authorial intention," like belief, only in the personal circumstances of the living.[38] I want instead to recover the ways in which certain persons of the third to the sixth centuries in China made their dead speak, with due attendance to the ways those voices might have resonated for those accustomed to hear the voice of authority from beyond the grave.

37. Catherine Gallagher and Stephen Greenblatt, *Practicing New Historicism* (Chicago: University of Chicago Press, 2000), 48.
38. While the tales I treat in the following chapters were not classified as *zhiguai* (roughly "tales of the strange"), they come mostly from a cognate literature, private histories. For a lucid analysis of how such tales were received in medieval China, see Robert Ford Campany, *Strange Writing: Anomaly Accounts in Early Medieval China* (Albany: State University of New York Press, 1996), especially 156–59.

Given perduring Chinese notions of the powerful dead, this is a matter of some consequence for the evolving social constructions that finally allowed the incorporation of selected Buddhist notions into the mix.

YANG TIAOHUA

Certainly, I could focus my analysis on a different array of texts (and voices). For example, the extremely diverse range of genres found in the Buddhist canon *could,* with caution, be used to construct another account of the personal and familial negotiations involved in the Chinese reception of rebirth. By way of illustration, I offer here one example.

The following tale, purportedly dating from around the time of the appearance of the Lingbao scriptures, is drawn from the *Traditions of Eminent Monks,* composed by the Buddhist cleric Huijiao (497–554) early in the sixth century. The *Traditions* was a didactic work, meant to demonstrate for the elite audience of medieval China the excellence of the teachings and the noble deeds of Buddhist monks.[39]

Through a close reading of this particular biography, we stand to learn something of how the ideals of Buddhist monasticism clashed with traditional Chinese notions of family cohesion and filial duty. In addition, the story illustrates how even the conventions of Chinese literary tradition might pose impediments to authorized Buddhist practice and notions of death. It thus stands as a suitable prologue to the grislier—and even more immediate—accounts of the following chapters.

> Zhu Sengdu 竺僧度, whose lay surname was Wang, given name Xi, byname Xuanzong, was a person of Dongwan.[40] Although he lost his father when young, he was well endowed by heaven and developed a flourishing talent. When he reached the age of sixteen, he was exceptionally spirited and brilliant, had a warm nature, and was the envy of the neighboring families. He lived alone with his mother, whom he served with a filiality fully in accord with the rites. She sought for him in marriage the daughter of Yang Deshen 楊德慎, who was also of an official family. The daughter's name was Tiaohua 苕華. She was comely, skilled in the classics, and matched Sengdu in age. The marriage was agreed to on the same day that the engagement was first proposed.

39. See John Kieschnick, *The Eminent Monk: Buddhist Ideals in Medieval Chinese Hagiography* (Honolulu: University of Hawaii Press, 1997), 6–8, for the goals of Buddhist biographers.

40. Dongwan is present-day Juxian of Shandong Province. A "byname" was the name commonly used in social intercourse. Zhu Sengdu will be referred to by his adopted name in religion, Sengdu, throughout the remainder of the biographical notice.

Before the ceremony could take place, however, Tiaohua's mother died. A little later, her father died as well. Then Sengdu's mother died. Observing the impermanence of human life, generation upon generation, Sengdu was enlightened. He thus abandoned the profane, "left the family" [i.e., became a monk], and changed his name to Sengdu. Wishing to perform lofty deeds transcending the dusty realm, he left [his home] region to travel and study.

Having completed her mourning, Tiaohua thought to herself "the three obediences [owed by a woman to her father, husband, and son] contain no provision that one live alone," so she sent Sengdu a letter, saying: "Even the hair and skin [received from one's parents] must not be harmed;[41] the ancestral offerings should not be cast aside even for an instant. If you were to pay attention to the teachings of the generations and alter your far-flung aspirations so as to let shine your stature of lofty brilliance in the world of fulsome brightness, in the distance the spirits of your ancestors would flourish and nearby the wishes of human nature would be fulfilled."[42]

She further sent him five poems. One of them reads,

> The great Way is endless;
> Heaven and earth extend and endure.
> Massive boulders thus will not dissolve;
> Mustard seeds are also innumerable.
> A human life is but one generation;
> Passing as swiftly as a steed before a window.[43]
> Are the flowers at fullness not lush?
> Yet at close of day they wither and stiffen.
> While mournful chants yet linger over the river,[44]
> In the slanting rays you think of "drumming on a pot."[45]
> Pure sounds can delight the ear,

41. This is a citation from the *Scripture of Filiality:* "One's body, hair, and skin are received from one's parents. Not daring to harm them is the beginning of filiality"; see *SSJZS*, 2:2545.

42. This follows the variant 人情 for 人神; see Tang Yongtong, ed., *Gaoseng zhuan* (Beijing: Zhonghua shuju, 1992), 175, n. 8.

43. The original wording is simply *guoyou* 過牖 "passing before a window." Just what is passing by is not specified. The same image was used somewhat later by Zhang Shuai 張率 in his "*Duan ge xing* 短歌行," in Guo Maoqian, comp., *Yuefu shiji* (Beijing: Zhonghua, 1979), 30.449, but again what is passing by is not indicated. I suspect that the image derives from the widely cited line of the *Zhuangzi (Zhi bei you)* that the length of human life is like "a white colt passing a chink in the wall, in a moment it is gone"; see A. C. Graham, *Chuang-tzu: The Seven Inner Chapters and Other Writings* (London: Allen & Unwin, 1981), 133.)

44. The term *yuyin* 餘吟, "lingering chants," is not, to my knowledge, attested in earlier literature. The more usual term is *yuyin* 餘音, "lingering sound," a term that refers to the lingering resonances of music and, by extension, to the enduring echoes of tradition. *Yin* 吟 denotes a choked-off sound, whether of textual recitation, soft singing, or, on occasion, funeral plaints and sighs. I believe that the latter is intended here, especially given the reference to the river—a universal image for the passage of time. If I am correct, the line means "While the mourning chants for our parents have still not died away (how can you think of reclusion)"?

45. The reference is to Zhuangzi: "When Zhuangzi's wife died, Hui Shi came to console. As for Zhuangzi, he was squatting with his knees out, drumming on a pot and singing" (Graham, *Chuang-tzu*, 123).

Luscious flavors may suit the mouth;
Gauzes and crepes can adorn the body,
A floriate crown may bedeck the head.
For what reason, then, do you shave your hair and whiskers,
Indulging in emptiness to the detriment of what exists?

Do not say that I am insignificant—[46]
If only I bring you to pity posterity.

Yang Tiaohua's letter and verse reveal a remarkable woman—perhaps an imagined one. Clearly well-educated, she cites in support of her plea the most revered works of her tradition—the *Analects,* the *Classic of Filial Piety,* the *Book of Odes,* the *Zhuangzi,* the *Daode jing,* and the *Nineteen Old Poems.* Her letter, for instance, alludes to lines from the *Scripture of Filiality* that "One's body, hair, and skin are received from one's parents. Not daring to harm them is the beginning of filiality." This was a passage commonly turned against Buddhist monastics, with their regrettable habit of shaving their heads and leaving behind wife and family.

Yang Tiaohua even seems to be aware of the *Vimalakīrtinirdeśa-sūtra,* popular among the gentry of the time for its portrayal of a householder able to best the spiritually superior bodhisattvas in Buddhist argumentation. At one point in that scripture, the layman Vimalakīrti amazes Śāriputra, the Buddha's disciple most renowned for his wisdom, with his ability to magically fit thirty-two thousand massive lion thrones into his modest dwelling. When questioned, Vimalakīrti responds that the transcendental powers of a Buddha or bodhisattva are such that he could make all of Mount Sumeru fit into a mustard seed. Tiaohua's couplet, "Massive boulders thus will not dissolve; mustard seeds are also innumerable," can be read as a response to this miracle, implying that the Buddhist dharma will not fade away before Sengdu completes his familial responsibilities and that, at any rate, nuggets of eternal truth are not confined to a single Buddhist mustard seed.

Yang Tiaohua's poem presents some of the issues that concern us in the chapters that follow. Still, given its deployment of currently popular *carpe diem* themes, it seems from our vantage point not the most useful

---

46. The term *insignificant* 區 區 also carries the connotation of dogged devotion on behalf of a subordinate. Both meanings are apparent in poem 17 of the *Nineteen Old Poems,* addressed from the persona of a woman to her lover or husband. She speaks of a letter she received from him, the words of which are still legible though she has carried it inside her garments for three years. The final couplet of this poem reads, "My whole heart holds to my insignificant service [區區] to you. I fear only that you will not recognize it" (collected in Xiao Tong [501–531], comp., *Wen Xuan,* [Hong Kong: Shangwu yinshu guan, 1974], 29.636).

strategy to convince her errant fiancé. Sengdu left her, after all, precisely because he came to recognize the vanity of his role in the reproductive march of generations. What good could arguing that "a human life is but one generation / Passing as swiftly as a steed before a window" possibly do her? We should remember that this is a Buddhist story, retold by a Buddhist for prospective converts as a proselytizing tool. Is Yang Tiaohua, then, but a "straw woman," an opponent constructed so as to be easily vanquished?

Whether Yang Tiaohua existed or not, whether she was possible or not, I would argue that this entry into the realms of Chinese poetic discourse was absolutely necessary to Buddhist writers as they sought to clear space for their message in a crowded literary scene. Yang Tiaohua, in repeating the themes of currently popular poetry, set the stage for what Harold Bloom, following Jacques Lacan, has characterized as a "tessera":

> In his *Discours de Rome* (1953), Lacan cites a remark of Mallarmé's, which "compares the common use of Language to the exchange of a coin whose obverse and reverse no longer bear any but worn effigies, and which people pass from hand to hand 'in silence.'" Applying this to the discourse, however reduced, of the analytic subject, Lacan says: "This metaphor is sufficient to remind us that the Word, even when almost completely worn out, retains its value as a *tessera*." Lacan's translator, Anthony Wilden, comments that this "allusion is to the function of the tessera as a token of recognition, or 'password.' The tessera was employed in the early mystery religions where fitting together again the two halves of a broken piece of pottery was used as a method of recognition by the initiates." In this sense of a completing link, the tessera represents any later poet's attempt to persuade himself (and us) that the precursor's Word would be worn out if not redeemed as a newly fulfilled and enlarged word of the ephebe."[47]

Buddhist scholiasts, in composing literature that would appeal to their Chinese audience, necessarily drew on the work of earlier poets and writers. The weight of the "fathers" hung heavily on the brushes of anyone who would write in early medieval China (heavier yet in later ages), so that all Bloom's strategies of misprision, and more, were called into service. Not only were citation and allusion sanctified to the literary tradition, but themes that Buddhists found central to their scriptures—death, separation, pain, illness, and so forth—had already found compelling expression in a literary tradition spanning nearly a thousand years. There were established figures of speech, styles of discourse, and strategies of

---

47. Bloom, *Anxiety of Influence*, 66–67.

engagement dealing with the very realizations that were, by the Buddhist account, to stimulate one to abandon the world. Even more to the point, the traditional answer had not always been renunciation.

Through the agency of the so-called Music Bureau myth—the idea that government agents of antiquity collected poetry from the realm to gauge popular sentiment and the success of rule—the poetry of the third to sixth centuries, while still tenuously connected to its didactic and political roots, had come to deal with a wide range of personal emotions. Among the newly allowable topics, in the words of David Knechtges, were "sorrow at separation from friends, grief at the death of a loved one, . . . the complaint of a wife who longs for her husband away on a distant journey, and despair at the swift passage of time."[48] To these themes, we might add another mentioned later by Knechtges, the "summons to reclusion," and poems countering the eremitic option. Such poems deal forthrightly with the problem of those who abandoned the cares and worries of official positions to live a life of ease outside of society.

Yang Tiaohua's poem echoes all of these. Indeed, it might be seen as a palimpsest of Music Bureau–inspired poetry in which themes from all these types, perhaps hundreds of poems, show through from beneath. Her invocation of Laozi in line two ("Heaven and earth extend and endure") leads to what seems the commonsensical, if not nonsensical, observation that "massive boulders will not dissolve." But this echoes lines from poem 11 of the *Nineteen Old Poems* to the effect that "A human life is neither metal or stone—Who can achieve extended longevity?"[49] Since human beings stand between heaven and earth and yet, unlike other elements in this intervening matrix, do not endure, the transition makes sense. A medieval reader would then recall the closing lines of that earlier poem: "Since we so swiftly follow all things in their transformations, a glorious name is our [sole enduring] jewel." Only through praiseworthy action (like the filial performance of Cai Yong) can humans truly hope for the longevity of metal or stone.

To take another example, Yang Tiaohua's "while mournful chants yet linger over the river" 川上有餘吟 recalls a poignant scene from the *Analects* that finds Confucius on a river bank, meditating on the passage of time: "The Master, standing by a river, said: 'It passes away like this,

48. David Knechtges, "Culling the Weeds and Selecting Prime Blossoms: The Anthology in Medieval China," in *Culture and Power in the Reconstitution of the Chinese Realm, 200–600*, ed. Scott Pearce, Audrey Spiro, and Patricial Ebrey (Cambridge, MA: Harvard University Press, 2001), 227.
49. Xiao Tong, *Wen Xuan* 29.634.

not ceasing day or night.'"[50] While this passage does not mention sighs, the tradition supplied them. As Yang Tiaohua's line demonstrates, Confucius's plaint prompted a "lingering sound" 餘吟 on the theme of impermanence. Contemporary readers would have been well acquainted with the lingering literary echoes of the *Analects* scene. Among them, they might have counted the closing lines of Zhang Xie's (fl. 307) "Miscellaneous Poem #2": "One sighs over its passing away on the riverbank 川上之嘆逝 / One prepares ahead of time in order to urge oneself on."[51] Or perhaps they might have recalled the lines of Zhang Hua's (232–300) "Inciting My Determination": "It passes away like this, never distinguishing day from night—Alas you common man, do not be content to cast yourself aside!"[52] Or they might have remembered the more resigned final couplet of Guo Pu's (276–324) "Roaming in Transcendence, #4": "Looking down at the river, I mourn the passage of years 臨川哀年邁 / Stroking my heart, I can only shout out in grief."[53] Most likely, the line would have called to mind all of these passages and more that are lost to us.

The "lingering" sound of traditions' enduring response to loss is paired in the couplet with a reference to another, more transient, sound—Zhuangzi's drumming on a pot and singing after the death of his wife.[54] Few, if any, of the poetic fathers had signaled their approval of this image. Still, in its euphuistic balance of lasting and evanescent sounds, allusive resonance, and poetic poverty, the couplet coheres to present a stark picture of the respective choices of Yang Tiaohua and Sengdu.

Examples of this sort of superscription might easily be expanded to the point of tedium. We moderns must labor to reconstruct associations that were natural to the literate people of early medieval China. For our purposes, we need to recognize how this textual depth, through calling up literary traditions for dealing with loss and recommitment, represented

---

50. *Lunyu*, "*Zihan* 子罕," in *SSJZS*, 2:2491; see also James Legge, *The Four Books: The Great Learning, The Doctrine of the Mean, Confucian Analects, and the Works of Mencius* (New York: Paragon Book Reprint, 1966), 237–38.

51. Xiao Tong, *Wen Xuan* 29.651.

52. Xiao Tong, *Wen Xuan* 19.412. For Zhang Hua's biography, see David Knechtges, *Wen Xuan or Selections of Refined Literature*, vol. 3, *Rhapsodies on Natural Phenomena, Birds and Animals, Aspirations and Feelings, Sorrowful Laments, Literature, Music, and Passions* (Princeton, NJ: Princeton University Press, 1996), 399–400.

53. Xiao Tong, *Wen Xuan* 21.462. For Guo Pu's biography, see David Knechtges, *Wen Xuan or Selections of Refined Literature*, vol. 2, *Rhapsodies on Sacrifices, Hunting, Travel, Sightseeing, Palaces and Halls, Rivers and Seas* (Princeton, NJ: Princeton University Press, 1982), 356–57.

54. See Graham, *Chuang-tzu*, 123–24.

an insurmountable challenge for Buddhist writers. Confronted by the novel situation of a fiancé who proposed to abandon her at the death of their parents—just when the reproductive imperative was most extreme— Yang Tiaohua was most assuredly not without resources. In the remainder of this tale, Zhu Sengdu will take this well-used coin and return it as a "tessera" in a creative act of misreading that seeks to renew the Chinese poetic tradition through his Buddhist message.

> Sengdu's letter in response said "Serving one's ruler to bring to order a single kingdom is not so good as spreading the Way in order to succor the myriad countries. Bringing comfort to one's relations through marriage is not so good as exalting the Way to succor the three realms. That hair and skin should not be injured is but a common saying among the profane. But were my virtue not to spread afar because I could not lose them—this would cause me shame! Moreover, though it be building a mountain by the basketful, I would wish to accomplish it even by these slender means.[55]
>
> As for wearing the *kaṣāya*, brandishing the tin staff, drinking from pure currents, and chanting the *Prajñāpāramitā,* I would not exchange them even for the garments of a Minister or Prince, banquets of the eight delicacies, the sounds of official gongs, or resplendent beauty.[56] If we are able to make an engagement at all, then let us plan to meet in *nirvāṇa*.
>
> But peoples' hearts are each different, as much so as their faces. Your lack of love for the Way is just like my lack of regard for the mundane. Miss Yang, we must part forever. Our ten thousand-generation karmic destiny is now broken. "The year is drawing to a close."[57] Time is not given to me. Those who study the Way should set their wills on daily diminution, while those who reside in the world must labor for timeliness. Your years and virtue are now both in full flower. You should soon achieve that which you desire. Do not belabor your heart over a gentleman of the Way and thereby waste your productive years!
>
> Further, Sengdu sent her five poems, one of which said:

55. Though this sounds modest, it is not. One possible reference is to the *Analects,* "*Zihan* 子罕," where Confucius is recorded as saying: "If in building a mountain there lacked only a basketful [of earth] and I stopped, it would be me stopping." (*Lunyu,* in *SSJZS,* 2:2491). Another possibility is the legend of the foolish old man who moved a mountain, found in the *Liezi,* "Tang wen" chapter; consult A. C. Graham, *The Book of Liehtzu: A Classic of the Tao* (New York: Columbia University Press, 1960), 99–101. In either case, the point is that unstinting effort pays off in the end.

56. *Weiye* 暐曄 "bright resplendence," in Zuo Ci's *Wu Capital Rhapsody,* refers to a brilliant palace that shone like the sun; see David Knechtges, *Wen Xuan or Selections of Refined Literature,* vol. 1, *Rhapsodies on Metropolises and Capitals* (Princeton, NJ: Princeton University Press, 1982), 397, 1.336.

57. This line is from *Shijing,* Ode 114, "Xishuai 蟋蟀". The first stanza of this ode reads, "The cricket is in the hall, the year draws to a close. If we do not now enjoy ourselves, the days and months will be passing by. But may we not be too joyous, may we only think of our positions. In our love of pleasure, may we not go to excess. The good gentleman is circumspect" (Karlgren, *Book of Odes,* 74).

The cycles of destiny do not stop,
And swiftly pass with the years and seasons.
Massive boulders will meet with depletion;
And who can say mustard seeds are many?
Good opportunities pass away incessantly,
Thus we sigh by the riverside.
Have you not heard of Rong Qiqi,
Who with white head issued forth a pure song?[58]
Cloth garments can warm the body,
Why discuss decorating it with crepes or gauzes?
Though this age might be said to be joyous,
What of later lives?
Transgression and merit originate in the self.
Need one add that one pities others?

Sengdu's will was firmer then stone—it could not be moved. Tiaohua was enlightened by his response and also came to have a deep trust in the dharma. Thereafter, Sengdu devoted himself steadfastly to the Way of the Buddha and studied many scriptures. He wrote the *Guide to the Abhidharma,* which was widely circulated.[59] His end is not known.

Lacking knowledge of the poem to which Sengdu's verse responds, we would be at a loss as to how to read it. Knowing the poetic depth of the verse that prompted Sengdu's, however, we recognize his misprision of the tradition. He returns to Yang Tiaohua a tessera, rubbed bare of content, bearing only vague traces of recognizable images, and creatively reinscribed.

Note that while Yang Tiaohua's poem begins with an invocation of the classical trinity formed by heaven, earth, and humans, Sengdu opens with cycles of time and fate. There is no transition to, and no classical precedent that I can discover for, the boulders and mustard seeds that appear in his second couplet. These inhabit the space created by Yang Tiaohua's palimpsest of the poetic tradition and have no other function here than denial. In fact, there is no independent textual depth to be found anywhere in Sengdu's poem. Had this been a standard "response" poem, the poet would be compelled to skillfully resituate any images drawn from the cor-

58. The reference is to a story recorded in the *Liezi;* see Graham, *The Book of Lieh-tzu,* 25. Confucius encountered Rong Qiqi, an old man, roughly dressed, playing the lute and singing a happy song. When Confucius asked the reason for his joy, Rong replied that he had three: He had been born human, was a male, and had, unlike many others, survived to old age. Sengdu's reference to the story seems, though, to draw on Rong's closing statement rather than these "three joys." Graham translates as follows: "For all men poverty is the norm and death is the end. Abiding by the norm, awaiting my end, what is there to be concerned about?" In the succeeding couplets Sengdu lists his "concerns." He is concerned for his own later lives and for the merit-making activities that will succor others.

59. This work survived into Tang times. See *T* 2149, 55:245a and 330a.

respondent's verse and, at best, to draw in new classical references to deepen the resonances of the poem. Something very different is going on here.

In Sengdu's response poem, the boulders and mustard seeds, "sounds by the riverside," the "pure song," and the reference to fine raiment are all borrowed from Yang Tiaohua's verse and thence from the poetic tradition. Here, however, they do not serve as allusions to the rich poetic tradition of sorrow and recommitment. Instead, they specifically deny such appeals. Boulders *do* wear away—no need to lament that human beings lack the longevity of "metal and stone." The fact that we miss out on good opportunities again and again causes *all* to sigh by the riverside— Confucius's response need not be specifically privileged; still less need it be compared with other classical responses to passing. "Pure songs" arise from the self, and coarse garb serves its purpose—there is no need to appeal to the traditions of reclusion poetry.

Into the space created by his erasure of these allusions, Sengdu inscribes a constant message: The cycle of death and loss cannot be accepted. It must be bypassed. Where Yang Tiaohua, with her predecessor poets, spoke of human life as "a single generation" and yet as having elements of transient joy, Sengdu alludes throughout his verse to the frustration of all hope in endless cycles of rebirth.

Tiaohua had reminded Sengdu of his duties to both family and kingdom. Ancestors were to be served with offerings and progeny. Fine raiment, good food, and the clang of metal drums and gongs connoted not merely pleasure, but high office of the sort that Sengdu could have made his own by virtue of his family background and education. In the China of this time, such a post, bringing good fortune and fame to the family, represented the highest kind of filial service. Skin and hair, which we think of as ultimately personal, are shown here for what they were in that time and place, part of the integument tying one to the family and, through the family, the state.[60] The personal was not only political but also familial. None of these associations finds acceptance in Sengdu's lines.

---

60. The history of hair in China remains to be written. For a fascinating initial foray, based primarily on early medical texts, see Lin Fushi, "Toufa, jibing yu yiliao—yi Zhongguo Han-Tang zhijian de yixue wenxian wei zhu de chubu tantao," *Zhongyang yanjiuyuan lishi yuyan yanjiusuo jikan* 71, no. 1 (2000): 67–127. Lin surveys the multiple ways in which hair was implicated in the causes and cures of disease, as well as its deployment in apotropaic and spirit-summoning magic. In addition to indicating personal health, long hair was a symbol of social status and cultural identity. As Philip A. Kuhn has engagingly demonstrated for a later period in China's history, loss of hair threatened not only the self, but also the kingdom; see his *Soulstealers: The Chinese Sorcery Scare of 1768* (Cambridge, MA: Harvard University Press, 1990).

Most noteworthy in this regard are the final couplets of Sengdu's poem. He avoids the charge that he is going into reclusion because governance has failed and the times are bad—the standard explanation given by hermits for withdrawal from society since Confucius's time—with this assertion: "Though this age might be said to be joyous, what of later lives?" And he answers Tiaohua's final implication that he does not "pity posterity" with the claim that his new merit-making persona will actually benefit later generations more than would his socially ordained role as official and father.

At a deeper level of imagery, free of the poetic tradition, Sengdu's defense of his revolutionary act becomes even more interesting—and revealing. In his letter, he allows that Tiaohua might pursue the same ideals and eventually meet him in *nirvāṇa*. *Nirvāṇa*, or "extinction [of the illusory notion of self]," understood in terms of Indic Buddhism, is not a place where one might meet another. In this respect, Tiaohua's understanding of Buddhism seems to exceed Sengdu's. He does indeed seem to "indulge in emptiness" to the detriment of what he has and is. But Sengdu's focus is not on his personal religious development. He is engaged in saving those who are destined to be reborn. He will "succor the three realms," and his compassion is focused on "later lives."

He easily reminds his importunate intended that his compassion is not diminished, but greatly increased, by his choice of a more fundamental and enduring ground of merit-making endeavor.[61] To accomplish these acts of merit, Sengdu, by implicitly comparing himself to Rong Qiqi, imaginatively transports himself from his apparent status as a young, virile male to that of an old man, well past the years of social involvement and reproduction. In counterpoint, he reminds Tiaohua forcefully of her own youth and reproductive capabilities, though they are in fact the same age.

Strangely for us, the social role Sengdu imagines for himself is that of elderly sage, one permitted to exist outside of familial and political realms of action by virtue of age and, we might add, the experience that he does not yet possess, since, according to his biographer, only later did he peruse the countless scriptures. It is, in some respects, the image of the recluse, though Sengdu has erased most of what traditionally characterized and privileged that status. He specifically denies, for instance, one

61. Still, from the Chinese perspective, there is a jarring note of personal willfulness in his admission—surely meant to excuse Tiaohua's wrong-headedness—that people's hearts might be as different as their faces.

of the primary themes of the recluse ideal—*carpe diem,* the idea that recluses seek simple personal joy in the face of the futility of human pursuits—with words that emphasize loss rather than gain: "Those who study the Way should set their wills on daily diminution, while those who reside in the world must labor for timeliness." Yet still he lays implicit claim to the status of elderly recluse. The contradiction draws our attention.

From this deeper level of analysis, we come to realize something of the times during which Sengdu lived and Huijiao wrote—or was imagined as having written. In fourth- and fifth-century China, Buddhism was beginning to work long-lasting and profound changes on society. But these changes were gradual and subject to countless permutations and negotiations before achieving anything like a standard form. Sengdu could confidently be portrayed as responding to the fact of rebirth, since by the end of the fourth century the idea had firmly—though not universally—taken hold, but his great endeavor could only be accomplished were he to represent himself as what he clearly was not—an elderly man. He had, in short, to inhabit a different sort of body, one suited to coarse garments, a staff, and disregarded hair.

Those non-Buddhists who left the elite family in this age were largely recluses, mages, and fortune-tellers. They were uniformly portrayed as wise old men, whatever their actual chronological age. Almost unconsciously, Sengdu, or whoever crafted this story (for we have no independent verification), cast the young monk as this accepted social persona, while denying the identification. The power—and utility—of the image is visible in centuries of painted and verbal depictions of the Buddhist monk.

Even in a Buddhist text meant as normative, then, we discover strong, nearly inescapable presumptions concerning proper social roles. The social network constructed around the concept of family fails to fully unravel even here in the imaginative space of Buddhist hagiography.

•   •   •

As an extended, externalist argument, the Sengdu story must enumerate in detail the objections that contemporaries leveled against Buddhist monks who would leave the home, ignore marriage and procreation duties, and "abandon" their ancestors. Through the voice of the cast-off fiancée, Yang Tiaohua, the story more than accomplishes this aim through providing, as I have tried to show, something of the traditional canonic and poetic resonances that gave force to such criticisms. This allows Sengdu to reconfigure these resonances in creative acts of misprision, whereby "sorrow over the passing of time" is transformed into concern that this opportunity to save others might be missed, "abandonment" becomes a loving commitment to saving the three realms, and the endless turning of time is revealed to be empty cycles of rebirth. But, as I have also tried to show, through entering into this necessary dialogue with the tradition, Sengdu must take on at least some elements of the socially accepted role of recluse.

One more attempted erasure deserves comment. Neither Yang Tiaohua nor Sengdu mentions in their verses their specific familial losses. Their dead disappear among the countless millions awaiting salvation through the spread of the dharma. In the Chinese tales we encounter in the following pages, the dead have names—and voices. The externalist arguments presented in those stories are told from a position outside the Buddhist fold, but always with the intent of positioning their representations of the dead against the new alternative of rebirth that Buddhism had newly made available.

STRUCTURE OF THE WORK

Chapter 1, "Envisioning the Dead," begins our exploration of the record that Tao Hongjing has discovered for us. Through the story of Su Shao, who returned to his son to tell of the underworld, we begin to explore the environs and staffing of the underworld bureaucracies. We shall learn from the best of authorities, one of the dead, about the obligations of memory and how changes in mortuary practice problematized them.

Chapter 2, "The Unquiet Dead and Their Families, Political and Agnate," departs from the records mentioned in the *Declarations*. The central text of the chapter is an imperially sponsored ritual debate of 318 concerning what the emperor regarded as deviant mortuary practice. To understand how an emperor came to be concerned with the spiritual constituents of the person, we begin with a different landscape, that of the human body. In the end, we come to see how even the intensely personal might become political.

Returning to the stories Tao Hongjing collected, chapter 3, "Questionable Shapes—How the Living Interrogated Their Dead," introduces more of the ways that the living of the mid-fourth century came to envision, and to question, their dead. The imagined answers to these imagined questions were not always comforting and never final. In this chapter, I explore three sorts of witness to the fates of the dead. (1) The story of the shade Guo Fan, who, like Su Shao, appeared to his living son, displays yet another way that interfamilial politics might be continued beyond the grave. (2) With Yang Xi, we encounter a new type of interlocutor, someone from outside the family who offers professional services as a medium between the living and the dead. Juxtaposing his concerns with those of Guo Fan's son allows us to gauge the differences. (3) Finally, we look at the resources of our guide, Tao Hongjing, who interrogates the dead as do we, through scholarly methods. While the specific intellectual strategies that Tao employed differ little from ours, his very different emotional commitments deserve exploration.

This attention to the stances of our witnesses prepares us to comprehend more fully the Xu family records from the *Declarations* that form the substance of chapter 4, "Doomed for a Certain Term: The Intimate Dead." Yang Xi's negotiation of his own and the Xu family concerns finally brings to the surface silenced voices—those of the Xu family women. In telling this story, I have implicitly compared it to Shakespeare's *Hamlet*. As in that play, so in this story, we encounter evil mothers and faithful sons, while the words of the Ophelias go unheeded.

Finally, in chapter 5, "Rebirth Reborn," we return to the question that set this study in motion. The Lingbao scriptures' wholesale adoption of the theory of rebirth, in a form that looks at first glance very much like the Buddhist idea, has prompted modern scholars to speak of "Buddhist influence." We shall see that the scriptures in fact contest Buddhist ideas of samsara, and respond directly to the third- and fourth-century changes in native Chinese views of the afterlife that we have traced. Finally, while the Lingbao scriptures are notably misogynist in their concerns, we shall see how a woman who wanted to be emperor employed their mortuary ritual in pursuit of her personal goals.

CHAPTER I

Envisioning the Dead

The living and the dead form a single moral community,
divided by visibility and frequency of contact perhaps, but
not by obligation, affection, emotion, or even aesthetic taste.

—Robert Campany, *Strange Writing*

One of the most intimate descriptions of the underworld abode of the dead in all of Chinese letters is to be found among the visionary transcripts of Yang Xi (330–86?), as assembled and annotated by Tao Hongjing. In book 5 of his *Declarations of the Perfected (Zheng'gao)*, Tao has transcribed for us the revelations Yang received, both from his celestial informants and by other, unknown means, concerning the six palaces of Mount Luofeng, or Fengdu, as the administrative center of the dead was known.[1]

Located on and under a massive mountain in the far north, the direction of winter, darkness, and seasonal death according to five-phase thought, the six palaces of Fengdu are all under the control of the Northern Thearch.[2] Under his imperial oversight are a number of functionaries, men of remote as well as recent memory, who enjoy titles and func-

---

1. For previous descriptions of Fengdu that inform this one at many points, see Peter S. Nickerson, "Taoism, Death, and Bureaucracy in Early Medieval China" (PhD diss., University of California, Berkeley, 1996), esp. 537–612; Sandrine Chenivesse, *Le Mont Fengdu: Lieu saint Taoïste émergé de la géographie de l'au-delà* (Paris: École Pratique des Hautes Études, 1995); and Matsumura Takumi, "Shinkō ni mieru Rahōdo kikai setsu," in *Rikuchō dōkyō no kenkyū*, ed. Yoshikawa Tadao (Tokyo: Shunjūsha, 1998), 167–88.

2. According to the cosmology fully developed by the Han dynasty, all existence was composed of and governed by five phases that had the following major associations: wood (east, green, spring); fire (south, red, summer); metal (west, white, autumn); water (north, black, winter); and earth (center, yellow). For more on the system and its importance in Daoism, see Bokenkamp, *Early Daoist Scriptures*, 15–20.

tions similar to those they held in the sunlit world. Indeed, when Yang's informants do not reveal the offices to which underworld titles correspond, Tao Hongjing sometimes does.

Much of the administrative work of Fengdu seems to consist of judging new arrivals and assigning them to appropriate positions in the teeming land of the dead. We hear, of course, only of the elite. For Yang, as for Dante, the common folk are invisible. Presumably they are subject to the administration that forms the sole concern of Yang's informants. Like Dante, too, Yang is quite aware of the political and social stakes involved when someone is assigned to this or that position in the underworld. Placement might be higher or lower than the rank that person achieved in life. Postmortem promotions and demotions, too, are possible. Yang differs from Dante, however, in that, given Chinese ideas of clan responsibility and ancestor cult, the living prove to be even more closely implicated in the fates of the dead than were the citizens of fourteenth-century Italy. Then, too, Yang's material was not meant to be simply allegorical. He presents his revealed material as factual, and Tao Hongjing takes the information Yang provides as an accurate record of the underworld. In his annotations he compares what Yang reports with earlier revelations, allowing us to trace to some extent the tradition within which Yang worked.

That tradition, composed of reports on the underworld—by ghosts, usually family members of the person receiving the revelations, or by those who had died and somehow been resuscitated—is known to us from as early as the fourth century BCE.[3] Because such reports from the underworld were, by their nature, oral and not the sort of anecdote regularly recorded for posterity, we have no way of judging just how widespread or early the phenomenon might have been. The documentary record that does survive suggests that from the third century CE on, either the number of returnees increased dramatically or the impulse to record and circulate such stories became much stronger.[4] As we saw in the introduction, the tendency among modern scholars is to attribute this apparent new interest in the structure and denizens of the underworld to the influence of Buddhism and the consequent changes in attitudes toward the dead. As we shall see, Yang Xi's account of Fengdu does not easily support this hypothesis.

3. Donald Harper, "Resurrection in Warring States Popular Religion," *Taoist Resources* 5, no. 2 (1994): 13–29; Nickerson, "Taoism, Death, and Bureaucracy," 97–100. I discuss the evidence Harper presents in the section entitled "Moderation in Burial" in this chapter.

4. See Robert F. Campany, "Return-from-Death Narratives in Early Medieval China," *Journal of Chinese Religions* 18 (1990): 91–125.

FENGDU AND BUDDHIST "HELLS"

Among the gifts of religious imagination brought to China with the Buddhist religion was a distinct vision of hell as a place—or rather a network of places—where the dead were held for a period of brutal punishment in retribution for the sins that they had individually committed during their lifetimes.[5] The term coined to designate these infernal regions was *diyu,* "earth prisons," a term some have suggested should be translated as "purgatories," since the damned were confined there for set terms.[6] But even my preferred translation—"earth prisons"—is not quite accurate, since the *yu* of ancient China were not penal institutions, but rather courts of inquisition where complaints were lodged, the accused questioned, and punishments determined. Suspects were incarcerated in the *yu* during this process, usually in shackles, but the administration of punishment was often carried out elsewhere.[7] Nonetheless, the use of torture to extract true information made the ancient *yu* similar to Buddhist hells (*naraka* in Sanskrit), where the dead underwent hideous retribution and were tortured over and over as they recalled the transgressions of their previous lives.[8]

These ideas, introduced at least by the second century CE, found fertile ground for acceptance because the Chinese already entertained several roughly compatible notions concerning lands of the dead. There was

5. My account of the curious mixtures of Buddhist with traditional Chinese descriptions of the underworld owes a particular debt to the following works: Nickerson, "Taoism, Death, and Bureaucracy"; Sawada Mizuho, *Jigoku hen: Chūgoku no meikai setsu* (Kyoto: Hōzōkan, 1968); Stephen F. Teiser, *The Ghost Festival in Medieval China* (Princeton, NJ: Princeton University Press, 1988), esp. 168–95; Xiao Dengfu, *Han, Wei, Liuchao Fo Dao liangjiao zhi tiantang diyu shuo* (Taibei: Taiwan xuesheng, 1989); and Michihata Yoshihide, *Chūgoku Bukkyō shisōshi no kenkyū: Chūgoku minshū no bukkyō juyō* (Kyoto: Heiryakuji shoten, 1979), esp. 200–224.

6. Stephen F. Teiser, in his survey of Buddhist scriptural accounts of the underworlds, argues against this translation; see "'Having Once Died and Returned to Life': Representations of Hell in Medieval China," *Journal of Asiatic Studies* 48, no. 2 (1988): 435–37. In his *The Scripture on the Ten Kings and the Making of Purgatory in Medieval Chinese Buddhism* (Honolulu: University of Hawaii Press, 1994), however, he allows that this "vision of the hereafter and its social realization are sufficiently analogous to the medieval European situation to merit the label of 'purgatory,' which may be defined as the period between death and the next life when the spirit suffers retribution for past deeds and enjoys the comfort of living family members" (1).

7. A. F. P. Hulsewé, *Remnants of Han Law* (Leiden: E. J. Brill, 1955), 74–155.

8. On the suffering of those incarcerated in the hells, see Sawada, *Jigoku hen;* Michihata Yoshihide, "Tonkō bunken ni mieru shigō no sekkai," in *Tonkō to Chūgoku Bukkyō,* ed. Makita Tairyō and Fukui Fumimasa (Tokyo: Daitō, 1984); Donald E. Gjertson, *Miraculous Retribution: A Study and Translation of T'ang Lin's "Ming-pao chi"* (Berkeley: Centers for South and Southeast Asia Studies, University of California, 1989), 132–44; and

the subterranean Yellow Springs, where commoners were believed to labor, as they had in life on the banks of the Yellow River, governed by
those who had governed them before. This labor was not punitive, but
rather a continuation of their lives above ground. Another account finds
the underworld administrative center ruled by the Lord of Mount Tai, a
mountain in Shandong province, while those who managed to avoid
death altogether enjoyed an equally bureaucratically organized existence
on mysterious isles floating in the seas off the east coast of the Chinese
mainland.[9] The extent to which these traditional, otherworldly geogra-
phies were seen as suggestive of Buddhist concepts of hell is evident in
the fact that early translators sometimes used the term "Offices of
Mount Tai" to translate what must have been "hells" in their sources.[10]

Since Fengdu, as we shall see, arrived on the scene rather later than
the Yellow Springs or Mount Tai, we might expect to find traces of Buddhist conceptions, but we do not. Compared with the postmortem de-
lights that Yang Xi had to offer those who followed his way, Fengdu is
not entirely pleasant, but it is not a place of punishment.[11] Instead, those
who serve there, the "lords below the ground" 地下主, occupy administrative posts similar to those they held in life. They may even, through
hundreds of years of study, advance in the bureaucracy to the point where
they are transferred to more attractive afterlife destinations. Yang Xi was
aware of the notion of *diyu*, for the Perfected beings mention the term
once in a series of poems they recite at a gathering in the heavens on the
autumnal equinox.[12] But this is Yang's sole mention of *diyu* in the *Dec-*

Teiser, *Scripture on the Ten Kings*. For a comparative study of descriptions of hell found
in Lingbao and Buddhist texts and their basis in Chinese legal practice, see Amy Lynn Miller,
"Doing Time in Taoist Purgatory: Annotated Translations, Dating, and Analysis of Punishments in Two Six Dynasties *Ling-pao* Texts on Purgatory" (MA thesis, Indiana University, 1994), 176–202.

9. On the antiquity of this bureaucratic image of the otherworld and the construction
of orderly channels of communication with the dead, see David Keightley, "Shamanism,
Death, and the Ancestors: Religious Mediation in Neolithic and Shang China" *Asiatische
Studien* 52, no. 3 (1998): 763–828. For some of the many interesting means by which a
practitioner might hope to avoid death, see Campany, *To Live as Long as Heaven and Earth*,
18–85.

10. See, for instance, Kang Senghui's use of the term in *Liudu ji jing, T* 152, 1:1a24ff.;
3:13b19; 3:15a20; 3:16a7ff.; 4:20c12ff.; 4:21b26ff.; and 5:30b24ff. for just a few of the
grislier descriptions.

11. On this point, see Christine Mollier, "La méthode de l'empereur du nord du mont
Fengdu: Une tradition exorciste du Taoisme médiéval," *T'oung Pao* 83 (1997): 341–42.

12. *Zhen'gao*, HY 1010, 3.9a9–9b1. The series of poems deals with Buddhist concepts. For instance, the term *miedu* 滅度, an early translation of nirvana, appears in one
of the verses. They also mention physical punishment in the afterlife.

larations of the Perfected.[13] He does not use the term in referring to Fengdu. It is likely, then, that Yang and many of his contemporaries believed concurrently in several postmortem destinations. Yang Xi's description of Fengdu and the several accounts of his predecessors identified by Tao Hongjing actually deal with different postmortem destinations. Nonetheless, Tao treats them as if they were all part of the same system.

It will thus not serve us here to attempt a history of these Chinese abodes of the departed—they are at any rate poorly documented for the earliest periods, and what is known has been ably presented and analyzed by a number of scholars.[14] Our focus on the roles of ancestral practice in traditional Chinese religion does, however, require that we keep in mind the highly moralistic, personal, and retributive character of the Buddhist afterlife. As we shall see, the underworld presented in the stories we examine first features none of the punitive elements so common in Buddhist descriptions of the hells. These Chinese underworlds are, despite some signs of conflation with the hells, desirable destinations.

EXPLORING THE UNDERWORLDS

The earliest story that Tao Hongjing mentions in his annotations to Yang Xi's revelations of the underworld involves the return of a dead ancestor who appeared to one of his sons both to report on the afterlife and to request a certain disposition of his physical remains. Receiving visions of deceased ancestors was as common in China as elsewhere in the world. Indeed, there is evidence that such visualizations formed part of normal ancestral practice.

The *Records of Ritual (Liji)*, a Confucian compendium of practice compiled ca. 50 BCE from ancient materials, provides a touching description of the procedures by which ancestors were to be visualized, nourished, and thus made a living presence in the quotidian life of their families. The text begins with recommendations for the period of purification preceding the feeding of the ancestors and moves on to the actual day of the sacrifice:

13. Another reference to suffering in the earth-prisons appears in *The Upper Scripture of Purple Texts Inscribed by the Spirits*, a scripture likely to have been composed by Yang Xi. See Stephen R. Bokenkamp, *Early Daoist Scriptures* (Berkeley and Los Angeles: University of California Press, 1997), 364.

14. See Nickerson, "Taoism, Death, and Bureaucracy"; Poo Mu-chou, *In Search of Personal Welfare: A View of Ancient Chinese Religion* (Albany: State University of New York Press, 1998), 157–77; and Xiao, *Han, Wei, Liuchao.*

On the day of the purification ritual, one thinks of the ancestors seated, thinks of their smiles and speech, thinks of their will and intentions, thinks of that which pleases them. On the third day, one will see those for whom he is conducting the purification ritual. On the day of offering, when one enters the chamber, the images [of the ancestors] will indeed appear on the seats provided. As one makes his rounds and is about to go out, with a sense of reverence one will hear the ancestor's voices. When one has gone into the front hall, one will hear their faint sighs.[15]

This passage is important for the evidence it provides of the ubiquity of the visualization of spirits in early Chinese society, but it reveals only one part of how ancestor rites were meant to work. Proper ritual offerings to the ancestors fostered correct remembrance on the part of descendants. But Confucian family rituals also enacted remembrance on the part of the ancestors for their descendants.[16] The voices of the ancestors were heard through the mouths of lineal male descendants, as in the story we discuss below. In traditional ritual, at least as hallowed in the approved ritual corpus, the voices of the dead were scripted, issuing from the "personators" (*shi* 尸; literally, "corpses") in time-honored cadence and in terms that invariably announced the ancestors' "enjoyment" of the sacrifice.[17]

Significantly, while our story's vision of a dead ancestor occurs outside of this tightly controlled ritual context, familial sacrifice does play a prominent role in the tale. And, for all their evidential weight, visions of the dead can be doubted. When this happens, memory is again foregrounded.[18]

15. *Liji*, chap. 47, *SSJZS* 2:1592c; see also James Legge, *Li Chi: Book of Rites, An Encyclopedia of Ancient Ceremonial Usages, Religious Creeds, and Social Institutions*, 2 vols. (New York: University Books, 1967), 2:210–11. The translation is mine.

16. For a fascinating study of one performance text, see Martin Kern, "*Shi jing* Songs as Performance Texts: A Case Study of 'Chu ci'(Thorny Caltrop)," *Early China* 25 (2000): 49–111. Kern argues that such performance texts are "constitutive"; that is, "(a) they generate and semanticize the very situation in which they will play a part, (b) they enforce social hierarchies, . . . (c) they circulate collective messages within the ritual community, (d) they contribute to the sensual efficacy of the performance proper, (e) they emblematically express authoritative control over the tradition, and (f) they instantaneously confirm the success of the ritual efforts" (66–67). While Kern's primary concern in this article is with cultural memory, we shall see that many of these features operate as well in the discontinuous and ad hoc ritual texts we analyze below.

17. See Kern, "*Shi jing* Songs," esp. 103–6; and Lothar von Falkenhausen, "Reflections on the Role of Spirit Mediums in Early China: The *Wu* Officials in the *Zhou Li*," *Early China* 20 (1995): 297–99.

18. The following account is based on the citation in Li Fang, *Taiping guangji* (Beijing: Zhonghua, 1961), 319.2528–30, of Wang Yin's 王隱 (fl. 318) now lost *Jinshu* 晉書. Other sources that cite the tale are (1) Tao Hongjing's annotations to the *Zhen'gao* (HY 1010, 15.4b, 15.7a, 16.4a, and 16.11a); (2) Li Fang, *Taiping yulan* (Beijing: Zhonghua,

SU SHAO 蘇韶

Su Shao, byname Xiaoxian, was a person of Anping.[19] His highest rank
was that of Governor of Zhongmou[20]. He died early in the Xianning 咸寧
reign period [275–280].[21] Shao's paternal uncle was Cheng 承, who died
holding the title Southern Palace Attendant and Military Adjutant
南中郎軍司].[22]

When all of Shao's sons were escorting [their father's] body home
for the funeral and had reached Xiangcheng 襄城,[23] the ninth son, Jie
節, dreamt he saw the armed retinue of an official procession, its ranks
extremely regal. Then he saw Shao. An outrider[24] called to Jie, saying,
"You are encroaching upon the procession! For this crime, your head
should be shaved." Jie lowered his head and accepted the tonsure. Then,
startled awake, he rubbed his head. It was in fact bereft of hair in spots.[25]
The next evening, he was sleeping together with others when he dreamt
that Shao said to him, "Not all of your hair has been cut." Then he was
again shaved as on the previous night.

The next night, Jie made diligent preparations. He lit a lamp and
arrayed talismans and interdictions. Again, he dreamt of Shao, who had
him shaved as before. This went on for five nights. Originally, Jie had
beautiful hair, but after five nights it was all gone. Then, for six or seven
nights, he had no further dreams.[26]

The tale of Su Shao's return begins by drawing on traditional Chinese
methods of mediumistic communication with the dead and on the emerg-

---

1960), 883.3b–4a, 554.7a, and 373.4b; and (3) Xu Song *Jiankang shilu,* ed. Zhang Chenshi (Beijing: Zhonghua, 1986), 188–89, citing the now lost *Sanshi guo chunqiu* 三十國春秋).
All of the latter sources cite the tale for specific reasons and delete parts of it that are not
pertinent to their arguments. The encyclopedia *Taiping yulan,* for instance, cites the Su
Shao story under "spirits and ghosts" (883), "funeral processions" (554), and "hair" (373),
citing in these chapters only the parts of the story that fit the category. Tao Hongjing mentions only the ranks of the dead, and Xu Song (or his source) severely abbreviates the story
but confirms its general outlines. I give only the meaningful variations among these sources
in the following footnotes.

19. Southeast of Linzi County 臨淄縣 in modern Shandong Province.

20. The eastern part of Zheng County 鄭縣 in modern Henan Province.

21. The date of Shao's death appears in the citation of Wang Yin's book found in Li,
Taiping yulan, 373.4b.

22. Su Cheng is otherwise unknown to history. Li, in *Taiping yulan,* 883.3b, has only
a portion of this sentence and skips to "ninth son," making it look as if Jie were Su Cheng's
son. This seems to be the slip of a copyist's hand, since all of the other available sources,
except for Xu Song's *Jiankang shilu,* which claims that Jie was Shao's younger brother, list
Jie as Su Shao's ninth son.

23. Present-day Xiangcheng County 襄城縣 of Henan Province.

24. Li Fang, in *Taiping yulan,* 373.4b, reports that Shao himself made this
pronouncement.

25. Li Fang cites the passage to the effect that a "finger's breadth of hair" was found
to have been cut off (*Taiping yulan,* 373.4b).

26. Li Fang, in *Taiping yulan,* 883.3b, elides both of these paragraphs, but they do appear at 373.4b–5a of the same work.

ing prestige of Buddhism. In addition to visions of the dead made possible through family ritual, there were also established liturgies that allowed the dead to respond. This was effected through selecting a younger male member of the family, usually the grandson of the deceased, as impersonator of the dead. The *shi* passively allowed the ancestors to animate him. He accepted the offerings meant for the ancestor, eating and drinking the deceased's portion. His utterances, generally involving a recital of the blessings to be granted in response to the ritual feeding, would then be interpreted by a ritual specialist.[27]

In China, possessions by spirits that occurred outside of this ritual scenario often involved younger members of the family as well. As in instances of mediumism around the world, the youthful and illiterate were regarded as more reliable conduits to the dead, since they could hardly be suspected of having fabricated their utterances and writings themselves.[28] This fact brings to the fore questions of power. Women and junior male members of a family frequently found that mediumism was a way to bring attention to their own, otherwise easily ignored, concerns.[29] Given that Jie was the ninth son of Su Shao, we suspect he might have harbored such motives himself. Though the tale naturally provides no evidence of this, it is likely that the messages Su Shao brings to the brothers through Jie represent Jie's own views.

Jie's period of preparation and his assumption of the role of family medium might thus be fruitfully analyzed in psychological and sociological terms. For our purposes, however, it is more important to note the role played by the image of Buddhism (though not the actual religion itself). Jie's gradual hair loss, while it may have been a hysterical response to the grief of losing a parent, serves to transform him into a

27. Patricia Ebrey, *Chu Hsi's Family Rituals: A Twelfth-Century Chinese Manual for the Performance of Cappings, Weddings, Funerals, and Ancestral Rites* (Princeton, NJ: Princeton University Press, 1991), xvi, xviii.

28. On the prevalence of mediumism among women and the "powerless," see I. M. Lewis, *Ecstatic Religion: An Anthropological Study of Spirit Possession and Shamanism* (Harmondsworth, UK: Penguin Books, 1978), 66–126. Glen Dudbridge, in *Religious Experience and Lay Society in T'ang China: A Reading of Tai Fu's Kuang-i chi* (Cambridge: Cambridge University Press, 1995), provides many Chinese examples, especially of female mediums.

29. Of the possession of one young girl, Glen Dudbridge writes, "Young girls, of course, would not enjoy conventional access to . . . polite male society. . . . But trance made all the difference. The first possession . . . came unexpectedly, perhaps involuntarily, but now it rewards the girl with a place of honour and respect as the centre of attention in the local official's social circle" (*Religious Experience*, 4). For parallels in medieval Japan, see Doris Bargen, *A Woman's Weapon: Spirit Possession in the Tale of Genji* (Honolulu: University of Hawaii Press, 1997).

simulacrum of a Buddhist monk. This hint that a knowledge of Buddhist practice might somehow lurk in the background of these events is underscored by the fact mentioned later on that Su Shao, when he causes Jie to write the language of the dead, produces only the incomprehensible horizontal writing of the *hu* ("western barbarians"), the pejorative ethnic designation regularly applied to foreign Buddhist monks at this time.[30] Since these hints are never made explicit in the account and there are no further references to the religion, Buddhist claims to control the fate of the dead figure as little more than a backdrop, lending an air of prestige and believability to the visual and auditory hallucinations (if such they were) of Jie.

Despite these odd, foreign embellishments, Jie responds to the appearance of his father in traditional Chinese fashion—he prepares "talismans and interdictions" to rid himself of the demonic vapors that accompanied death. Nonetheless, the hair-cutting continued, and the visions became even more vivid:

> Later, Jie was boarding a carriage in broad daylight when Shao came riding in on a horse from outside the gates. He was wearing the black headwrap of a civil official, an unlined robe of brown brocade, white stockings and silk slippers. He drew near to the axle of Jie's carriage. Jie said to his brothers, "The Governor is here." They all looked around in astonishment, but saw nothing. So Jie asked Shao why he had come, to which Shao replied, "I want you to rebury me." Then he took his leave, saying that he would come again. When he went out of the gate, he could no longer be seen.[31]
>
> After a number of days, Shao came again. The brothers sat together with him. Jie said, "If you want to be reburied, you will have to order it yourself." Shao replied, "I will write a letter." Jie gave him a brush, but Shao was unwilling to take it, saying, "The dead write differently than do the living." Then he caused Jie to draw some characters—they were like the writing of the Western barbarians 胡. At this, Shao smiled and ordered Jie to write at his dictation as follows:
>
> Of old, the Martial Marquis of Wei 魏武候 [r. 387–72 BCE] was floating along the Western River. When he came to the middle stretches, he looked over his shoulder and said to [his general] Wu Qi 吳起, "These fastnesses between the river and the mountains are truly beautiful! This is the treasure of the Wei!"[32] Now, by nature I love the eastern capital and the Lo river.

---

30. For more on the script of the dead, see Michel Strickmann, *Chinese Magical Medicine* (Stanford, CA: Stanford University Press, 2002), 12, n. 52.

31. The final sentence of this paragraph does not occur in Li, *Taiping yulan*, 883.3b.

32. This event is recorded in Sima Tan and Sima Qian, *Shiji* (Beijing: Zhonghua shuju, 1972), 65.2166; and Sima Guang, *Zizhi tongjian* (Beijing: Guji, 1957), 1.28–29.

Each time I left or returned, I looked up at Mount Mang with pleasure.[33] There are the tombs of ten-thousand generations![34] To the north, the Meng ford backs them—the river so vast; to the south, they look out on the Celestial Citadel, with its throngs so bustling. Even though I never spoke of this aspiration, it has been inscribed in my heart. I did not count on life's brevity and so I was not able to realize my sentiments. In the coming tenth month, I would like to be reburied. Buy several *mou* of land next to the Adjutant [my uncle, Su Cheng]—that should be enough.

Our account began with Jie and his brothers returning home for the burial of their father. The tomb must have already been prepared, but now Jie learns that his father wishes to be buried instead at Mount Mang, the imperial burial grounds north of the eastern capital Luoyang.[35] The reasons Su Shao gives for his preference are telling. In his "letter" he cites an exchange during the Warring States period between the Wei monarch and his general Wu Qi, known to all literate men of the time from its inclusion in China's first universal history, the *Shiji*. But Su Shao cites only the monarch's praise of the mountains that were to become the resting place of later rulers. Wu Qi's response, which he does not mention, but which would have been in the minds of all who heard this, concerns the greater importance of a ruler's charismatic virtue over such trifling strategic considerations as the selection of easily defensible ground. The implied message for those who would oppose Su Shao's burial next to his military relative at Mount Mang is that such an act overweighs any consideration as to who might or might not be interred on this specific piece of real estate, since the burial expresses both the virtue of the Jin rulers, who would inspire such loyalty, and of Shao himself, who could respond to it. The question of loyalty resurfaces later in the tale.

When Jie would talk to Shao, those beside him could only see his mouth move, as if he were speaking clearly and loudly, but nothing could be heard.[36] [Jie] led Shao into a room where a seat had been set out so that they could sacrifice to him. Shao would not sit, nor would he allow them

33. Mount Mang lies north of the eastern capital, Luoyang, and is the site of imperial graves.

34. Li Fang, in *Taiping yulan* (554.7a and 883.4a), records this line as "This is the foundation of the ten-thousand generations!" and leaves out the detail concerning Shao's wish to be buried next to the Adjutant.

35. For the practice of rewarding meritorious service with burial near the imperial graveyards, see the case of Wen Qiao 溫嶠 (288–329; reported in Fang Xuanling et al., *Jinshu* (Beijing: Zhonghua shuju, 1974), 37.1795–96). In Wen's case, the move to rebury him north of the imperial mausolea was blocked when Tao Kan 陶侃 (259–334) produced a letter detailing Wen's last wishes.

36. Li, *Taiping yulan*, 883.4a, does not have this sentence.

to feast him. Jie said to Shao, "All your life, Governor, you loved ale and fish. You can have a small drink!" Shao, holding the cup, drank it down, then said, "Fine ale!" Jie saw that the cup was empty, but when Shao left, it was full again.

Shao came some thirty or more times and the brothers began to be disrespectful in his presence.

Jie asked Shao about things he wanted to know. Shao said, "The affairs of heaven and the underworld cannot all be known. Yan Yuan 顏淵 and Bu Shang 卜商 are today Gentlemen of the Imperial Gates 修門朗.[37] There are eight gentleman-attendants in this department. Among the sages here is Xiang Liangcheng 項梁城 and among the worthies, Wu Jizi 吳季子.[38] Yang Xiong 揚雄, Zhang Heng 張衡 and others are the Five Thearchs."[39]

Like Jie's audience, we modern readers expect a bit of legerdemain, some small miracle, to provide a sense of verisimilitude. Su Shao could no more actually drink human liquor than could the ancestors to whom it was regularly offered in family sacrifice. The mysterious emptying and refilling of the beaker demonstrates this nicely. The report on the official status of the dead in the otherworld, however, represents a sort of proof that no longer figures prominently in Western culture, our nearest analogue being the visions of Dante Alighieri. Sometimes medieval Chinese reports on those in the underworld did, as we shall see, adopt the monitory tone of Dante. Often, though, the figures in such accounts are doing quite well for themselves, as are the men Su Shao mentions here.

Yan Yuan 顏淵, better known as Yan Hui 回, and Bu Shang 卜商, or Zi Xia 子夏, were both well-known disciples of Confucius. Wu Jizi 吳季子, also known as Ji Zha 季札, was the uncle of King He Lü 闔閭 of Wu (r. 514–496 BCE). Known for leaving his kingdom to live in reclusion, Jizi was honored at several shrines.[40] Yang Xiong 揚雄 (53 BCE–18 CE)

37. Li Fang's *Taiping guangji* 319.2529 and *Taiping yulan* 883.4a have 修文朗, a Tang-dynasty title; see Charles O. Hucker, *A Dictionary of Official Titles in Imperial China* (Stanford, CA: Stanford University Press, 1985), 249a. This emendation is likely the doing of an over-zealous editor who did not recognize the underworld title. The title "Gentleman of the Imperial Gates" appears in a citation of this passage in Tao's notes (*Zhen'gao*, HY 1010, 15.7a2).

38. Li Fang's *Taiping yulan* 883.4a reads "Liang Cheng 梁成." Tao's notes in *Zhen'gao*, HY 1010, 15.4b, match the *Taiping guangji*. Jizi is also known as Jizha 季札.

39. This line is cited by Tao Hongjing in *Zhen'gao*, HY 1010, 16.11a2. He goes on to complain, "If Yang and Zhang are not higher sages, their rank should be low, not on a par with the Red Thearch. Perhaps there is a lesser Five Thearchs that are not mentioned [by Yang's informants] or perhaps the information on Yang and Zhang [given by Su Shao] is just incorrect."

40. See Tao Hongjing's notes in *Zhen'gao*, HY 1010, 15.5b8 ff. Tao mentions a Jizi temple in existence at his time. Gao Shao 高紹 (fl. 719), in his record of the restoration of the Jizi temples of the Jiangnan region, mentions that there were three related temples in

and Zhang Heng 張衡 (78–139) were both well-known literati officials of the Latter Han.[41]

One of the figures named here, Xiang Liangcheng, proves, however, to have been less prominent, and consequently more interesting. Tao Hongjing, in his note to this passage, speculates that he might be Xiang Liang, uncle of the famous Chu general Xiang Yu,[42] but goes on to complain that "such a person as this should not be given more prominence than Wu Jizi."[43] That might well be so, but whoever he may have been in life, Xiang Liangcheng interests us as one of the early figures who reported on the structure of the underworld. In this case, the terrain was that of Mount Luofeng, Yang Xi's underworld, not Mount Tai. Yang reports that Xiang Liangcheng had composed a poem of twenty thousand words on Mount Luofeng, but cites only the portion that mentions its Six Palaces, knowledge of the names of which can serve to protect against harm inflicted by the dead.[44]

Ge Hong (ca. 283–343) also knew of Xiang Liangcheng. The context in which he mentions him is significant. In Ge's *Baopuzi,* a spirited and detailed defense of the possibility of attaining transcendence, he presents his discussions with an interlocutor, who objects as follows: "Allowing that divine transcendence might be obtained through study . . . so that one could depart the world, would it not be the case that none would then carry out ritual feedings, so that the sentient ghosts of the ancestors would starve?" Ge's response addresses both aspects implied by this question, the posterity of those who depart in transcendence and their own ancestors. As to posterity, transcendents have sons and younger brothers who might continue family sacrifice and who will receive immense blessings from their illustrious forebears.[45] The transcendents' own

the region in his time (see Dong Gao, et al., comps., *Qinding quan Tang wen* [Taibei: Hui-wen shuju, 1961], 294.19a–20a).

41. For brief biographies, see David Knechtges, *Wen Xuan or Selections of Refined Literature,* vol. 2, *Rhapsodies on Sacrifices, Hunting, Travel, Sightseeing, Palaces and Halls, Rivers and Seas* (Princeton, NJ: Princeton University Press, 1982), 364–66, and vol. 1, *Rhapsodies on Metropolises and Capitals* (Princeton, NJ: Princeton University Press, 1982), 481–83, respectively.

42. Xiang Yu did inspire cultic devotion. As a brilliant, but frustrated, general, he was revered as a patron of military arts. See Mark Edward Lewis, *Sanctioned Violence in Early China* (Albany: State University of New York Press, 1990), 211–12.

43. *Zhen'gao,* HY 1010, 15.4b5–7.

44. *Zhen'gao,* HY 1010, 15.1b–4b. See also Tao Hongjing's collection of liturgical materials, the *Dengzhen yinjue,* HY 421, 2.13a8.

45. We notice the same appeal to the deeds of the "religious hero" in the case of Seng-du, considered in the introduction.

ancestors, on the other hand, will participate directly in the glorification of their descendants. Among the new powers they will enjoy will be that "in authority they might direct Luofeng [= Fengdu]; their prestige would be sufficient to rebuke Liangcheng."[46] That is to say, they may command even the lords of the underworld.

While there is no mention here of apotropaic verses, the "table turning" nature of the first part of this remark—Fengdu usually directs the dead, but these fortunates will be able to command Fengdu—suggests that Ge Hong might have known Liangcheng as a spirit whose words were sufficient to "scold" or "chastise" demons. If Liangcheng was a spirit associated with apotropaic powers, then one who could rebuke even him would be powerful indeed. Unfortunately, we have no further information on Xiang Liangcheng or the lengthy apotropaic poem that Yang Xi attributes to him.

As we shall see later in the story, Su Shao is on his way to Mount Tai, so at first it seems curious that he should be aware of Xiang Liangcheng, a key figure in the early history of the Mount Luofeng underworld complex. But, as we noted at the beginning of this chapter, our otherworldly informants seem little concerned about such specifics and tend to conflate what might seem to us distinct underworld destinations. Since we know so little of the palace complexes of Fengdu before Yang Xi came to write of them so eloquently, we must leave this observation. Instead, we follow the interests of those who came to question Su Shao. Their questions have less to do with the structure of the underworld than with the relations possible between the living and the dead.

> Jie asked how death compared to life. Shao responded, "There is no difference, except that the dead are immaterial and the living material.
>
> Jie then asked, "Why do the dead not return to their corpses?" Shao said, "Say that someone cut off your arm and threw it on the ground. When they went on to flay it would you suffer from this or not? For the dead to leave their corpses is just like this." Jie then asked, "If we provide a rich burial with a high mound, do the dead take delight in it?" Shao responded, "They are not present." "So," Jie said, "if you are not present in the tomb, why do you wish to be reburied?" Shao replied, "In truth, there is nowhere I now reside. I merely wish to express my life-time aspirations."[47]

46. Ge Hong, Baopuzi neipian jiaoshi, ed. Wang Ming (Beijing: Zhonghua shuju, 1980), 3:45–46. Partially translated in Campany, To Live as Long as Heaven and Earth, 88–89. See also Matsumura, "Shinkō ni mieru Rahōdo," 181–82.

47. This passage is translated and discussed in Nickerson, "Taoism, Death, and Bureaucracy," 345–46.

One of the younger brothers asked, "Your sons are still young and few of the elder brothers have wives. Your family undergoes hard times. Do you take thought for these things?" Shao replied, "I have no further emotions." Jie said, "Do you have longevity?" to which he replied, "All have it." So Jie asked, "As for our longevity, do you know it?" Shao replied, "I know and will tell you."

We can all comprehend fears that the person will decay with the body, but the anxieties underlying the further questions concerning the memories of the dead seem at first odd. Western traditions emphasize commemoration of the dead rather than what the dead might recall. In the cultures informed by medieval Christianity, ghosts return to ensure that they will be remembered. Anxieties projected onto the dead most often concern fears that descendants will fail to carry out the memorial services that would deliver the dead from purgatory. The Chinese ghosts we survey here seem not to have been overly oppressed by such concerns.[48] For Su Jie, and others like him, intent on making certain that their cherished dead were remembered in certain ways rather than others, the question more often addressed to the spirits of the dead was, "Do ghosts remember the living?" That is to say, Jie required confirmation of Su Shao's oath of remembrance with its concomitant promise of ancestral blessing in order to accomplish his goals. We shall thus see this question, in one form or another, expressed again in the stories Tao Hongjing collected. Given the importance of ancestral blessings and the changes that were occurring in conceptions of the dead, the answer put into the mouths of the ghosts of our stories—"We can still help you!"—must have been comforting and thus helped to ensure that the goals of the medium were accomplished.

Though we are not given details, the information Su Shao provided concerning the life spans of his family members constitutes one example

48. I do not mean to indicate by this that Chinese ghosts were never portrayed as making demands on the memories of the living. See, for instance, the mid-third-century tale translated by Gjertson, *Miraculous Retribution,* 5–6, and the poem of Ruan Yu discussed toward the end of this chapter. And even for the tales we treat here, this is a matter of em phasis, rather than of absolute difference. Jacques Le Goff, in *The Birth of Purgatory,* trans. Arthur Goldhammer (Chicago: University of Chicago Press, 1981), notes that medieval Christians believed it was "advantageous to pray for souls in Purgatory, because, once they reach Paradise, they will pray for those who have helped them out" (319). See also Stephen Greenblatt, *Hamlet in Purgatory* (Princeton, NJ: Princeton University Press, 2001), esp. 102–50. The mutual obligations of Christians and their dead are similar to those of the early medieval Chinese; however, for Christians, the fear that their dead will go off to Paradise and somehow forget them seems fairly rare. This is the anxiety our texts express over and over.

of what the dead might do for the living if the ties of mutual remembrance were maintained. On a more fundamental level, the family members stand to gain much if their ancestor's bones are allowed to rest near the imperial mausolea. But we cannot dispose of the question of commemoration by the living and the need for a corresponding "memory" on the part of the dead quite so easily. We shall return to this subject toward the end of this chapter.

> Jie asked, "This year there is a great contagion. Why?" Shao replied, "Liu Kongcai 劉孔才 was sire of Mount Tai. Wishing to rebel, he assembled a horde without authorization. The Northern Thearch then learned that he had such intentions and by now has already destroyed him."[49]
>
> Jie asked, "In my previous dream when you cut off my hair, whose procession were you leading with the armed retinue?" Shao said, "It was the Prince of Jinan 濟南.[50] You committed a capital offence and I thought to protect you. Thus I argued for the punishment you received." "Then can the dead aid the living?" Jie continued. "From time to time, the dead think to aid the living, as I helped you. If the dead had no emotions and yet the living sacrificed to them to gain blessings, there would be no benefit."[51] Jie asked, "When I dreamt of you, did I in fact meet with you?" Shao said, "When the living dream of the departed, the departed actually meet with them." Jie asked, "Are you further able to injure those against whom you had grudges when you were alive?" Shao said, "Ghosts value killing, but are not able to follow their whims."

With these paragraphs, we come to the heart of the matter. Su Shao, it becomes apparent, died in the plague years of 275–77.[52] As many in those trying times must have suspected, the rampant spread of disease and death had chthonic origins. The Lord of Mount Tai, overseer of the underworld,

---

49. Translated and discussed in Nickerson, "Taoism, Death, and Bureaucracy," 580, n. 42.

50. This was Sima Sui 司馬遂, who died in 266 (Fang, *Jinshu*, 37.1101–2). Jinan was east of present-day Licheng xian 歷城 in Shandong.

51. Here I follow the Ming text emendation given in Li, *Taiping guangji*, 319.2529.

52. Sima Guang, in his *Zizhi tongjian*, 80.2541, first reports the outbreak of the epidemic 大疫 in Luoyang in 275 with the words "those who died numbered in the tens of thousands." Whether this was related to the epidemic that had spread through the Wu kingdom in the previous three years is not noted—and would not be, given the lack of contemporary knowledge of epidemiology. Fang Xuanling (*Jinshu*, 3.65), records that the epidemic broke out in the twelfth month, which would correspond roughly to January of 276 by the Western calendar, and that "over half" of the population of Luoyang perished. Shen Yue (441–513), in his *Song shu* 宋書 (Beijing: Zhonghua shuju, 1974), 34.1009, reports the death toll at 100,000! Later in 276, the emperor himself became gravely ill and almost died. While none of these reports gives the duration of the plague, the fact that the emperor took the extraordinary step of silencing court music for three days in January of 277 because of "the numerous princes, lords, and great ministers who have died" (Fang, *Jinshu*, 20.630) seems to indicate that the epidemic was both long-lasting and widespread.

had "rebelled" against heaven and, thinking to increase his spectral hordes, had brought a plague upon the living. But now matters were about to be set right. The rebellious lord had been destroyed and a new lord appointed. While we are not explicitly told who this new lord of the underworld was to be, it is very likely to have been Sima Sui 司馬遂, the Prince of Jinan, whose ghostly procession Su attended. Sui was a member of the royal family of the Jin who died in 266, only a year after the founding of the dynasty.

Sima Sui seems not to have overly distinguished himself—his career is only briefly recorded in the histories—but he was appointed to the important task of overseeing the armies surrounding the Wei capital in 262 and so must have played a decisive role in ensuring the transfer of rule to the Sima family.[53] As a recently deceased member of the imperial family who had been enfeoffed in the region of Mount Tai, he must have seemed a natural choice to take over the lordship of the realms of the dead under this mountain. While the uncle beside whom Su Shao wished to be buried, Su Cheng, was a military man, his history of service during his lifetime is unknown. But the Su family native place is also in the region of Jinan, and Su Cheng most likely served Sima Sui in life. Thus it is fitting that Shao should find himself among the guards leading Sima Sui to his new office.

The man Sima Sui was to replace, the posthumously rebellious Liu Shao 劉劭 (byname Kongcai 劉孔才 (d. 240–49), is rather better known to history. As an official of the Wei dynasty, Liu contributed to the revision of dynastic law codes and left to posterity a book on judging men for office.[54] Liu Shao was not a general himself, but had advised the Wei dynasty on methods for quelling rebellions and maintaining the peace.[55] The irony that such a man might become a rebellious prince in the underworld would not have been lost on contemporaries. But apparently, the administration of the underworld, by this account, changed dynasty by dynasty, and so Liu's underworld rule was found as wanting as that of the earthly dynasty he had served. Thus he rose in rebellion, with the result that plague assaulted the living citizens of the new dynasty.

53. Fang, Jinshu, 37.1101–2.

54. On Liu Shao's legal contributions, see Hulsewé, Remnants of Han Law, 27. The book on human judgment, an important art of the period, is the Renwu zhi 人物志, translated by J. K. Shryock as The Study of Human Abilities, American Oriental Series, vol. 11 (New Haven, CT: American Oriental Society, 1937). Shryock translates Liu Shao's biography on pp. 20–24.

55. Chen Shou, Sanguo zhi (Beijing: Zhonghua, 1962), 21.618–19.

Notice, however, that, no matter how compelling the logic presented here for Su Shao's burial near his royal patron, there remains the need to explain why the disposition of an earthly body would matter to the dead. Since the beginning of the Wei dynasty in the early third century, when the ruling Cao family had argued strenuously for—and themselves practiced—austere burials, the question of the deceased's needs for elaborate grave furnishings was continuously debated. The second ruler of the Wei, Cao Pi 曹丕 (r. 220–26), had, for instance, included in his "living will" words that find an echo in our account: "To bury means 'to store away'; that is, one wishes people not to see [the corpse].[56] Bones have no knowledge of pain and the tomb is not a residence where the spirits rest."[57] Cao Pi goes on to demand that his burial not include the mortuary trappings thought necessary for earlier rulers. For the Cao family and many others, entertainment of the spirits of the dead at family shrines would suffice. There was no need to worry overmuch about the fate of the body.

Su Shao follows the line of argument that, by his time, had become established imperial doctrine. The body is like an arm that has been cut off, and one feels no pain no matter what more is done with it. He really resides nowhere in particular and certainly does not need an elaborate grave. He simply wants to fulfill his lifetime aspirations. Su Shao further refuses the ad hoc seat of honor, food, and drink offered to him, presumably because his body has not yet been buried and this "seat" has not been set up in the official family shrine. Although he has "no emotions" concerning the difficult straits of his descendants, he does allow that sacrifices will cause the dead to bestow blessings. The dead can harm the living, as the plague brought on by Liu Shao's underworld rebellion certainly had, but they cannot freely execute all against whom they have private vendettas.

These responses are, for modern readers, full of paradox. The seeming inconsistencies are a certain sign of changing portrayals of the afterlife. Rather than taking these as evidence of confused or unclear notions concerning the fate of the dead, we should see in them attempts to merge

56. Cao here cites a statement attributed to Guo Zigao 國子高, a Qi nobleman who was said to have requested an austere burial. See *Liji, SSJZS*, 1:1292a; and Legge, *Li Chi*, 1:155. The sentiment was also expressed by early Moists who advocated moderation in burial; see Jeffrey Riegel, "Do Not Serve the Dead as You Serve the Living: The *Lüshi chunqiu* Treatises on Moderation in Burial," *Early China* 20 (1995): 306. The logic of this definition of "burial" depends on homophony.

57. Chen, *Sanguo zhi*, 2:81.

old certainties with new exigencies. I explore some of these attempts in
the following sections of this chapter.

Finally, we do not know what became of the body of Su Shao. Jie simply provides us with a humorous and self-deprecatory exchange and then
relates his futile attempt to detain the spirit. Su Shao, upon departure,
asserts once again that he has an honored place in the bureaucracy of
the underworld, presumably under Mount Tai—a fact that seems to contradict his earlier assertion that there is nowhere that he resides:

> Jie descended from his carriage and Shao laughed loudly at his stature.
> "You are just like Zhao Linshu 趙麟舒!" Zhao Linshu, the brother of
> Shao's wife, was very short.
>   Shao then wished to depart, but Jie detained him by locking the gate.
> Shao was only detained for a moment, but then departed. Jie saw that the
> gate was still locked. In parting, Shao said, "I am now made Gentleman
> of the Imperial Gates 修門朗.[58] Because of my duties, I will not be able
> to come again." Jie grasped his hand. It was soft and weak. As he grasped
> it, Shao departed. From this time, the visions ceased.

This is, for us, a very unsatisfactory ending to the tale. We would like to
know what effect Su Shao's postmortem request for reburial had on the
imperial officials who must have heard it. Did the tale succeed in prompt-
ing Su Shao's reburial near the imperial burial grounds? We do not know.
We are fortunate that the tale survived at all. As citations in later works
intimate, it survived for two reasons. First, it restated, from the best of
all possible authorities, a shade, that the dead really did not require lavish tomb residences. Second, it provided information on the postmortem
status of several prominent figures. This second reason led Tao Hongjing
to include large portions of the story in his annotations to the *Declarations of the Perfected,* providing a paper trail that we will follow further
in chapter 3.

The reasons for which the tale was first constructed, on the other hand,
faded away over time. These motives were all too firmly tied to the occasion of Su Shao's death and his family's need for a proper commemoration for their revered ancestor, occasions that would, after a change
of dynasties, ensure continued blessings for the Su family.

---

58. Again, Li Fang's *Taiping guangji,* 319.2529, and *Taiping yulan,* 883.4b, have the
Tang-period title *Xiuwenlang.* I have corrected it based on Tao Hongjing's citation of the
title (*Zhen'gao,* HY 1010, 15.7a2). It seems that Su Shao is to join Yan Yuan 顏淵 and Bu
Shang 卜商 in this post.

MEMORY AND COMMEMORATION

Even before Buddhism began to supply the Chinese with hellishly un-
pleasant choices to add to their list of postmortem destinations, we find
frequent expressions of anxieties concerning whether or not the dead
would "remember" the living. These existed quite apart from anxieties
produced by the brutal fact of death itself. Such concerns were centered,
rather, around the ancestral cult, which required for its maintenance both
commemoration on the part of the living and memory on the part of the
dead. The former proved, of course, easier to mandate. A massive Confucian literature on ritual observance provided precedents for the ways
the living were to act toward the dead. Then, too, in a society where prestige emanated from the family, both living and dead, motives for commemoration, as we saw in the case of Cai Yong, were obvious to all. The
second requirement—that the ancestors would "remember" the living
and keep up their end of the bargain through reciprocating for the feedings they received—was unenforceable and, despite Confucius' assurances
as to the benefits of sacrificing to the ancestors "as if they were present,"
anxiety-producing.

We see this anxiety expressed already in two of the earliest and most
intriguing poems on ancestral ritual, the "Summons to the souls *[hun]*"
and "Great Summons" of the *Chuci*.[59] These poems, probably dating to
the third century BCE, were written as part of a ritual meant to call back
the spiritual constituents of a king after his death. Whether the ritual
aimed to revivify the dead king or, as is more likely, to keep the flighty
components of his person from straying after his death, its primary purpose was to keep the dead from forsaking the living. While the two poems are similar and were both likely to be at least based on hymns used
in ritual, I will here discuss only the "Summons to the *hun*."[60]

The *hun* of the dead is first warned of the dangers waiting in all directions. Even the underworld called "Murky Metropolis," precursor to
the underworlds that concern us here, proves dangerous: "[There] the
Earth God lies, nine-coiled, with dreadful horns on his forehead, and a
great humped back and bloody thumbs, pursuing men."[61] The poem then

---

59. For the "Summons to the Soul" (*Zhao hun* 招魂) and "Great Summons" (*Da zhao*
大招), see Hong Xingzu, *Chuci buzhu* (Beijing: Zhonghua shuju, 1983), 197–226.
60. For a translation of both "summons" poems, see David Hawkes, *The Songs of the
South: An Anthology of Ancient Chinese Poems by Qu Yuan and Other Poets* (Harmondsworth, UK: Penguin Books, 1985), 219–38.
61. Hawkes, *Songs of the South*, 225.

turns from threat to invitation. Enticements awaiting the *hun* (in the tomb, we suppose) are given detailed description. Fine foods and lavish diversions are promised.

The Latter Han writer Wang Chong 王充 (27–91) thought that the *hun*-summoning ritual was a supreme act of filiality, a final desperate measure to call a dead parent back to life.[62] A man of firm opinions, he also held that Confucians uniformly denied any sort of postmortem existence and provided empirical evidence in support of this assertion.[63] Nonetheless, he attests to the practices of the many during his day who sought to provide for their dead in the tomb:

> Thus those who follow the customs of the day . . . seeing that the dead appear [in visions] from their tombs before those about to die . . . say that death is like life. They commiserate with the dead who must be buried alone, their *hun* lonely and without companionship, their graves shut up, lacking supplies of grain and goods. Thus they make images to attend to the corpses' coffin and bury a great supply of food to delight the essential *hun*.[64]

While we might suspect the contemporary currency of Wang's own views, we have no cause to doubt his assertion that such ritual acts as *hun*-summoning and grave provision arose from concern over the fate of the dead. Such loving concern encompassed as well the desire that the dead might retain their ties to the family and even provide aid from whatever new station they might enjoy in the afterlife. Under such conditions, in Lothar von Falkenhausen's memorable wording, tombs "became like dollhouses or *laternae magicae* for the dead spirits to play with—and never leave."[65]

We noticed that the story of Su Shao expresses, at least in part, these old concerns regarding the efficacy of ancestral commemoration. Su Shao directly confronts the anxiety of his descendants that the dead might not remember. "From time to time, the dead think to aid the living, as I helped you," the living descendant Jie is reassured, for "if the dead had no emotions and yet the living sacrificed to them to gain blessings, there would be no benefit." But, at the same time, Jie is told that the dead have "no

62. Wang Chong, *Lunheng jiaoshi*, ed. Huang Hui (Beijing: Zhonghua shuju, 1990), 15.671; Alfred Forke, *Lun-heng*, 2 vols. (New York: Paragon Book Gallery, 1962), 2:332–33.

63. See Chou Chao-ming, "Death, Funerals, and Sacrifices in Wang Ch'ung's Philosophy," *Tamkang Review* 17, no. 2 (1986): 178–81.

64. Wang, *Lunheng jiaoshi*, 23.961; Forke, *Lun-heng*, 2:369.

65. Lothar von Falkenhausen, "Sources of Taoism: Reflections on Archaeological Indicators of Religious Chance in Eastern Zhou China," *Taoist Resources* 5, no. 2 (1994): 7.

emotions," exist nowhere in particular, and certainly have no need of the grave mounds and sumptuous burials that those of former ages so freely provided. This second, seemingly contradictory, strand of Su Shao's report from beyond the grave might only be understood in light of the change in sumptuary regulations promulgated in the late second and early third centuries.

MODERATION IN BURIAL

By at least the third century BCE, Mohists in the state of Qin had begun to propose more modest burials, denying the need for grave mounds, elaborate coffins, and sumptuous grave goods.[66] It is within this context that we find the earliest example of a "return-from-death" narrative comparable to Su Shao's. In this instance, the returnee was not a ghost, but a resurrected man. An official document excavated from a tomb at Fangmatan, Gansu province, describes the fate of a man named Dan who, having committed murder, killed himself but was sent back to the world of the living when his patron communicated to the Scribe of the Overseer of Destinies that his death had been untimely. As Donald Harper points out, this document provides very early evidence of the belief in an underworld administration staffed by those who had held office in life: the Scribe who grants Dan's release turns out to be the shade of a man who had been a ruler in the fifth century BCE.[67]

The story of Dan's resurrection parallels Su Shao's report from beyond the grave in yet another way. Dan, upon his return, provides information on the proper conduct of sacrifices for the dead. Harper's translation follows:

> Dan says: "The dead do not want many clothes. People in the market think that white woolly-grass is fortunate; when ghosts receive [offerings] in something else, they still think it is fortunate." Dan says: "Let those who offer sacrifices at tombs not dare to spit. If they spit, the ghosts depart and flee in fright. After the sacrificial food has been collected, empty [the vessels]. In this way . . . eat . . . " Dan says: "Those who offer sacrifices must sweep and purify. Do not wash the place of the sacrifice with. . . . Do not pour the boiled dish over the sacrificial food, for the ghosts will not eat it."[68]

66. See Riegel, "Do Not Serve the Dead."
67. Harper, "Resurrection," 14–16.
68. Ibid., 14.

Whatever the specific targets of all these recommendations may have been, the first two of them, at least, concern austerity in burial. As Harper notes, "a man who has been with them is quoted as saying that the dead themselves do not care for luxuries."[69]

In similar fashion, Su Shao confirms for his living descendants what had become an elite trend in mortuary custom. In 205 CE, the founder of the Wei dynasty, Cao Cao 曹操 (155–220), sent down an edict prohibiting lavish burials.[70] This austere measure had a distinct impact on the burial practice of succeeding Wei and Jin emperors, as well as those of many of the elite, as confirmed both by archeology and by the number of "last wills" recorded for those who chose modest burials.[71] Su Shao, as we noticed, echoes in his report from beyond the grave the "living will" of Cao Cao's heir, Cao Pi, that bones feel no pain and the grave is not the place where spirits reside. Likewise, Su's claim that "there is nowhere I now reside" parallels Cao Pi's assertion that "if the *hun* has numinousness, there is nowhere it cannot go."

Cao Pi composed his living will with full knowledge of the fate of the Han emperors whose sumptuous burials had, in his view, ensured that their tombs would be robbed and their remains desecrated. If buried riches entice the greedy, they will "burn [open] precious caskets and snatch [from the burial shrouds] golden threads so that the body and bones are both destroyed." He then asserts "if they were to [thus] destroy your body, would you not feel redoubled pain?" How could this be possible if, as he also argues, the dead bones feel no pain? The apparent contradiction dissolves when we notice the word "redoubled." In his living will, Cao Pi assumes an identity between the dead and the surviving descendants. While he repeats the polite ancient formula "if the dead have sentience," he believes the affirmative response should govern ritual action. Death causes pain. The severance of relations between the dead and the living would cause "redoubled pain." What this meant for Cao Pi in terms of his imagined relations with his own descendants is made clear in the threat with which he ends his living will:

> If anyone violates my present decree, wantonly changing it or adding adornments, I will become an executed corpse below the earth. One who suffered death will be murdered again; one who has died will die again! For

---

69. Ibid., 23.
70. See Zhang Jiefu, *Zhongguo sangzang shi* (Taibei: Wenjin, 1995), 126–27; and, for the rise of this trend during the Latter Han, see Poo Mu-chou, *Muzang yu shengsi—Zhongguo gudaizongjiao zhi xingsi* (Taibei: Lianjing, 1993), 254–68.
71. Zhang Jiefu (*Zhongguo sangzang shi*, 119–55) provides numerous examples.

subjects and sons to thus destroy their lord and father is neither loyal
nor filial. If the dead have sentience, I will not bring you good fortune.[72]

The vehemence of these words demonstrates clearly enough that the wish
for "meager burial" could cause vivid anxiety on the part of living descendants. Against such emotional objections, Cao argues that to go
against the wishes of an aged parent might be ritually dangerous, but
failure to honor their requests might result in even greater harm to the
interests of the family in the long run if the aggrieved dead should fail
to provide blessings for their descendants. Cao Pi, with his threat of postmortem revenge, counters what must have been a common desire to violate the living will in the interests of filially serving the interests of the
dead—and thus the family. Thus we see that the prevalence of "living
wills" was not a result of any new disbelief in the afterlife.[73] Instead, the
practice of "moderation in burial" was, as its proponents and a few modern scholars have averred, a matter of both prudence and economy.

In the case of Su Shao's appearance to his son Jie, we see the inverse
of this concern. The story expresses the desire that, even given new ideas
concerning the residence and preferences of the dead—ideas that were
advanced in support of restricting the ancient, fulsome burial practices—
the dead Su Shao might continue to serve the interests of his descendants through the construction of a tomb on Mount Mang. So, while
the story reiterates all of the pronouncements supporting modest burials, at the same time it argues for the continuation of honored, if not
lavish, burial. And the reason it gives is the old one: the dead might aid
the living.

Such concerns provide a necessary, but I believe insufficient, motive
for Su Shao's seemingly contradictory report on the potentialities of the
dead. Recall that Su Shao contradicts himself in saying that the dead have
no emotions, yet asserting that his emotions led him to save Jie from further punishment. He also contradicts himself in saying that the dead have
no control over the victims upon whom they spread disease and death,
and yet the fulfillment of his own living will—that he be buried at Mount
Mang—might aid his descendants. To comprehend the impulses behind

72. Chen, *Sanguo zhi*, 2:82. Cited in Zhu Dawei et al., *Wei Jin Nanbei chao shehui shenghuo shi* (Beijing: Zhongguo shehui kexue chubanshe, 1998), 294.

73. In his own "living will," Huangfu Mi (215–282) made the same sort of threat to ensure that his descendants would follow his wish for an austere burial, albeit one that would ensure that his corpse not be disturbed. For a discussion, see Keith Knapp, "Heaven and Death According to Huangfu Mi, a Third-Century Confucian," *Early Medieval China* 6 (2000): 15–24.

these contradictions, we need to explore yet another contemporary view regarding the power of the dead to affect the living.

O SOUL, DO NOT COME BACK!

It was not just the arrival of Buddhism, with its unwelcome news on the fates of the dead, that disrupted the old symmetries of ancestral sacrifice and ancestral blessing, commemoration and memory. Dislocation attendant on warfare, which became common in the years leading up to the fall of the Han dynasty, also separated families from their dead. The official and poet Ruan Yu 阮瑀 (d. 212) gave voice to one particular aspect of the anxiety this could cause in his poem on an old topic, "Seven Plaints." At first he expresses feelings we might all share when confronting death, but his poem soon moves into unfamiliar territory:

> Youthful years are hard to retrieve;
> Wealth and honor will not come twice.
> Good times pass in a trice,
> Then flesh and frame became ashes and dust.
> Dark are the chambers of the Nine Springs,
> Remote the towers of Endless Night.
> My body gone, my energies bound,
> My essential *hun* has no way to return.
> When fine foods are arrayed, I am not served;
> Sweet ales fill only banquet flagons and cups.
> I come forth from my funeral vault to gaze on my old home—
> But observe only mugwort and broom.[74]

Ruan quite literally imagines himself into the grave, a prisoner in the "endless night" of the subterranean "Nine Springs," who, just when he expects the ritual feeding of the ancestral sacrifice, finds that his family is gone. Now aliens, conquerors of his homeland, we suppose, feast themselves with the fine foods and sweet ale that would otherwise be his. His "old home" –how the term resonates in the Chinese poetic tradition!— has become overgrown with rank weeds. We can feel, across the centuries, sympathy for the abandoned soul, but reading the poem in the context of its times, we find in it other emotions not quite so wistful and bittersweet. Anxiety, perhaps even panic, would have been aroused among the

---

74. Ruan Yu's poem is in Ding Fubao, ed., *Quan Han Sanguo Jin Nanbeichao shi* (Taibei: Yiwen, 1960), "Quan Sanguo shi," 3.10a.

contemporary auditors of this poem with the penultimate line—"I come forth from my funeral vault to gaze on my old home."

In this time of dislocation, when even such patriots as Wang Can 王粲 (177–217) could write, "The capital is in unspeakable chaos. . . . I will leave behind the Middle Kingdom and dwell among the tribes of the Qing," Ruan Yu intuits the possible response of the extended family, the honored dead, to such abandonment.[75] The dead, he says, might emerge from their graves to find that they are alone. And what will they do then?

We know quite well, from Su Shao's tale as well as from texts that we examine more closely in the following chapters, what people of that time expected that the unfed dead might do. Starving, enraged, the dead would join the ranks of subterranean demon hordes, spread disease, and cause havoc among the living. Most terrifyingly, they would eventually come to voice their bitterness to the subterranean bureaucracy, through what were known as "plaints from the grave," or "underworld lawsuits" as I will call them, so that the family members who had abandoned them might be individually called to account.

In a series of fascinating and influential articles that inform our en-quiries at several points, Anna Seidel has analyzed funerary texts inscribed on jars and found in comparatively poorly furnished tombs. In her words,

> The function of the funerary texts is that of a passport or letter of introduc-tion by which a plenipotentiary of the highest celestial deity, the "Envoy of the Celestial Thearch," recommends the deceased to the netherworld authorities, thus assuring the newly arrived shade of a satisfactory integra-tion into the subterranean society. The real motive behind these *documents de passage* concerns, of course, the living members of his family. . . . With the loss of the body, all is lost, and the living rightly fear the boundless resentment and wrath of the deprived shade. He is placated with funerary goods, . . . he is given "sacred pharmaka" to delay the decomposition of his cadaver . . . and, above all, he is sternly ordered, with all kinds of com-mands, invocations, and threats, to go away and never come back.[76]

Seidel has shown that one motive for such documents was to relieve the deceased, and their living descendants, of any culpability that might arise

75. Citing Wang Can's own "Qi ai shi 七哀詩 #1"; see Ding, *Quan Han Sanguo*, "Quan Sanguo shi," 3.5a.

76. Anna K. Seidel, "Post-Mortem Immortality; or, the Taoist Resurrection of the Body," in *GILGUL: Essays on Transformation, Revolution and Permanence in the His-tory of Religions* (Leiden: E. J. Brill, 1987)," 228; see also her "Traces of Han Religion in Funeral Texts Found in Tombs," in *Dōkyō to shūkyō bunka* [volume in honour of Pro-fessor Akitsuki Kan'ei] (Tokyo: Hirakawa, 1987), 21–57.

from infringing the taboo against digging into the soil. Might those who constructed these graves themselves have been refugees and thus digging in unfamiliar terrain? There is not enough evidence to present even a hypothesis. Seidel shows, however, that yet another concern pervades these sometimes cruel documents. The living fear implication in any misdeeds the dead might have committed in life that will now come out before the underworld tribunals. In one case, the deceased clearly died young, and the text requests celestial officials to recheck the records to ensure that a mistake has not been made, as in the case of Dan. In others, the specific cause of the survivors' nervousness remains unspecified. We cannot even tell, from these mortuary documents, whether or not those who placed these texts in the tomb expected their dead to be available for sacrifice.

Whatever the ultimate reason for this particular approach to the dead, the repeated appeal of these texts to the bureaucracy of the underworld to release the living from any culpability emanating from the grave gives another voice to the anxieties expressed in Ruan Yu's poem. Either the dead might work out their resentments, or the imbalances they left behind might be worked out for them by the otherworld tribunals. In either case, for many in this period, the dead came to be seen not as a source of blessing, but as a potential source of disaster. The threat from the grave we noticed in the story of Su Shao was that rebellious dead might spread disease among the living. Liu Shao, apparently still working on behalf of his toppled dynasty, had sought to enlarge his ghostly hordes through slaughtering the living. To be sure, this threat was of wider concern and did not merely involve the Su family. This is why, while Su Shao might have fallen to the demon-induced plague, he yet proclaims his loyalty to the Sima family and the Jin dynasty. The presence of this disjunctive element in our story requires a closer look at one final paradox found in Su Shao's message.

SU SHAO REDUX

The contradictory messages that Su Shao was held to have brought back with him from beyond the grave mark this text as an "externalist" statement, to return to Campany's terminology. Analysis of the sorts of arguments it sets forth to distinguish its claims have led us to consider a variety of approaches to the dead that have been kept distinct in modern scholarship. Yet, in this story, which, judging by Tao Hongjing's response to it, commanded the credulity of those who wanted to know more about the structure and staffing of the underworld, these seemingly diverse concerns are merged into one representation. Su reports that the dead do not return to their bodies in the grave, and thus have no need of costly and extravagant burials. These findings accord with the Jin rulers' preference for modest burials and make Su a good candidate for burial at Mang Shan. Su then reports that the dead do, on occasion, have emotions toward their descendants and reward ancestral sacrifice just as he saved Jie's life. With this assurance, he answers the old concern over whether or not the dead think of the living at all. In the context of the tale, he thus provides his doubtful older sons with a motive for their remembrance.

Finally, Su reports that the grave is unimportant to him, since there is no permanent place where he resides, but he goes on to tell of his attendance on the new Lord of Mount Tai. He reveals the underworld etiology of the plague that has recently affected the living and announces that the appointment of a Sima Lord of Mount Tai has ended the threat. Through his revelation that the world of the dead can affect the living in this way, however, Su Shao delivers yet another ambiguous message.

One of the implicit themes of this tale is that of loyalty—loyalty within the family of the living to the dead and of the dead to the living, but also loyalty to the kingdom. Commemoration and memory, properly considered, are but functions of loyalty, the deeper commitment. Su Shao's "letter" mentions the history of Wu Qi, a story that centers on issues of loyalty and the results of its betrayal. We may view Liu Shao's underworld rebellion as arising out of his loyalty to the displaced Wei dynasty. Given the date of Su Shao's death, some ten years after the founding of the Jin, it is likely that he served the Wei in some capacity as well, but he announces loyalty to the Jin. If, Su Shao implies, his loyalty to the Sima house finds reward, as Wu Qi's loyalty did not, he might continue to faithfully serve through his new position in the underworld, as did Liu Shao. The implied alternative need not be made explicit. The Sima rulers would have understood.

Finally, we need to emphasize that this story, while recorded by Tao Hongjing in his notes to the *Declarations*, is not the product of any Daoist or Buddhist doctrine. The only references to established religion found here are to Buddhism—and these are oblique. Rather, the concerns expressed all emanate from the ancestral cult that had come to be threatened by extravagance, dislocation, and dynastic change. The Su Shao tale thus provides us with a template against which to map the changes to come.

CHAPTER 2

The Unquiet Dead
and Their Families,
Political and Agnate

We must attempt to restore what we are told of otherworldly
procedures to their real context, human society.
—Michel Strickmann

One common expression for the Chinese polity, *guojia* 國家, or "kingdom and families," well expresses the allegiances of the elite families
whose relations with their dead we are tracing. As we saw in the case of
Su Shao, the dead had not escaped from the world of the *guojia*. The
kingdom and families they seemingly left behind proved to extend into
the dark realms. Further, the voices of the dead might be mobilized to
serve both *jia* and *guo*. Su, while providing prestige for his family, explained for his kingdom the political etiology of the plague that infected
them as well as providing for the empire the news that the dead, though
given austere burial, would still remember and bless their descendants.

In this chapter, I intend to depart from the script provided by Tao
Hongjing's annotations to the *Declarations of the Perfected (Zhen'gao)*
in order to explore further the ways in which the shadow *guojia* impinged
on the sunlit world. In the documents that inform this study, we do not
hear the voices of the dead but the voices of ritualists and emperors, those
traditionally charged with regulating the commerce between the two
realms. In this case, we discover that the goal of those who wrote was
not to attend to the voices of the dead, but to silence them.

. . .

In 318, shortly after the fall of the Western Jin to marauding forces, Sima
Rui 司馬睿, the prince who had established himself south of the Yangzi
River in 307 and was soon to take the throne as first ruler of the East-

ern Jin, learned that surviving family members of certain high officials and even members of the imperial family had been conducting unorthodox rites for those who had perished with the fall of the Western Jin capital. Representative of these was one Ms. Pei 裴, who sought to bury the spiritual remains of her husband, who had died in the fall of the capital. These novel rites were given the name *zhaohun zang* 招魂葬, usually translated "soul-summoning burials." Based on one aspect of the canonical death rituals, whereby a "summoner" was to ascend to a rooftop bearing a piece of clothing belonging to the dead to call back the *hun* before burial, the soul-summoning burial was designed to accomplish the same end absent a body.

Taking time from the pressing items on his daily agenda—preparing for his accession to the throne, finding and furnishing suitable court buildings, appointing an administration, settling the masses of elite emigrants who daily poured into the region, preparing defenses against incursions from the north, and the like—Sima Rui called upon members of his court to advise him on the practice. This uncommon attention to a seemingly minor matter of ritual propriety in itself alerts us to the importance of the event.

Sima Rui's advisors uniformly condemned soul-summoning burials on the grounds that the ethereal constituents of the person, unlike the corpse, should not be confined to the tomb. In the fourth lunar month of 318, only a month after he had taken the throne, Rui issued an edict banning the practice.[1] Ms. Pei, we are told, either ignored the ban or was given an exemption and went ahead with her plans.[2]

Some of the official documents that led to Sima Rui's proscription of soul-summoning burials have survived. These give us a unique opportunity to explore one set of conflicts between familial approaches to death—particularly violent death—and the interests of the state. Doing so will lead us to reflect again on the fact that in medieval China, ancestral practice was politics continued by other means. We will be especially interested to discover what might have prompted this sudden rash of bodiless burials and what led Sima Rui, with all that must have been on his mind just then, to devote time to the question of mortuary practice.

Before beginning these inquiries, however, I briefly survey common approaches to the kinds of documents that we will examine.

---

1. Fang Xuanling et al., *Jinshu* (Beijing: Zhonghua shuju, 1974), 6.150.
2. Ibid., 59.1626.

"SOUL-SUMMONING" AND "SOULS"

The orthodox soul-summoning ritual, for which we have evidence that includes both ritual manuals and ancient hymns once used in the rite, remains the subject of scholarly controversy. Soul-summoning seems to be an archaic, shamanic survival in the ritual canons of sober Confucians. Was the rite meant as a last-ditch effort to revive the dead, or was it designed to prevent the life-force of the dead from scattering? Scholars who have studied the ritual betray intense interest in yet another question: Just what was the predominant, pre-Buddhist, Chinese notion of the soul? Traditional commentators justify the rite by reference to two sorts of entities that we might label "soul": the *hun,* yang in nature, sentient, ethereal, light, and prone to fly off in death, dream, or other moments of duress; and the *po,* yin in nature, inert, liquid, heavy, and apt to leak away in life and sink into the earth at death.[3]

Some modern commentators, myself included, have argued that the summons of the soul, along with the structure of elite graves, which were made in the image of living habitations and outfitted with foodstuffs, diversions, pottery, servants, and the like, attest to a very early and widespread belief that the dead were indeed to enjoy some sort of sentient existence in the grave. Others, basing their arguments on a wide array of textual references and grave documents, have shown that society at large maintained no clear distinction between the two sorts of "soul" in mortuary contexts.[4] Perhaps, then, the *hun/po* dualism we find in Confucian ritual texts was but a scholarly understanding based on yin-yang cosmology, and the early Chinese actually held a functional conception similar to our familiar Cartesian body/soul duality.

But was this construct even so simple as a "dual" conception of the soul? Daoist texts dating back to the third century CE give very precise

---

3. The oft-cited source in this regard is Yü, "O Soul, Come Back!" See Yü, Ying-shih. "'O Soul, Come Back!' A Study in the Changing Conceptions of the Soul and Afterlife in Pre-Buddhist China," *Harvard Journal of Asiatic Studies* 47, no. 2 (1987): 363–95.

4. See particularly K. E. Brashier, "Han Thanatology and the Division of 'Souls,'" *Early China* 21 (1996): 125–58. Brashier's evidence brings to light important data concerning the constituents of the human body and their fate at death, but I reject strenuously his conclusion that "modern scholarship should not assume the people of the Han necessarily possessed a clear idea of what death actually was" (158). In the sense that the medical definition of death is still a matter of debate, the statement is unobjectionable, but its implication that the Han Chinese did not harbor distinct notions of what happened at death is unsupportable. Textual legacies do not equal ideas. The fascinating textual evidence Brashier presents indicates, in fact, that a number of different ideas must have been in circulation.

descriptions of three *hun,* seven *po,* and a bewildering array of other spirits that inhabit and direct various parts of the human body. How old are these ideas? Since all nouns in literary Chinese are mass nouns, might it not be possible that, lacking numerical adjectives, early references to the psychospiritual constituents of the human were to be understood in the plural? And are we justified at all in searching for *the* Chinese view of the soul? In short, modern scholars have marshaled convincing evidence as to "what the Chinese believed about the soul" on all sides and, to paraphrase Mark Twain, have succeeded in casting much darkness on the subject.

The opinions presented to the throne in 318 have become embroiled in this debate in an interesting way. In 1961, Ho Wai-kam published an article in the *Bulletin of the Cleveland Museum of Art* introducing to the English-speaking world the existence of a curious sort of mortuary urn. Topped with elaborate lids decorated with pavilions, human and animal forms, and sometimes Buddha-images, substantial numbers of such urns have been recovered from tombs spanning a limited period of time, from roughly 250 to 330, and in limited geographical areas surrounding the southern capital, present-day Nanjing, and in modern Zhejiang Province. Ho gave to these mortuary jars the name *hunping,* "urns of the soul," or "soul jars." He further argues that the documents of 318 represent court reaction against soul-summoning burials that employed such urns, and that Sima Rui's proscription had the effect of leading to the total disappearance of such burials from the archeological record.[5]

On the face of it, Ho's hypothesis seems faulty. Emperors' edicts, particularly in times of dislocation and turmoil, rarely had such immediate effects. Then, too, the documents of 318 mention only northerners engaging in the practice of soul-summoning burial. Certainly, a period of one or two years would be scant time for émigrés into a new region to adopt local culture. Given the slow rate at which mortuary customs tend to change and the total lack of supporting evidence, Ho's supposition that "to many new settlers in the Wu-Yue area, a probably long-established local custom would have seemed so much more reasonable and so much more promising than to live with their guilty feelings" fails to convince.[6] Further, as Albert E. Dien has recently pointed out, one of Ho's primary pieces of evidence, that one of the 318 texts disparages those who try to

5. See Ho Wai-kam, "*Hun-p'ing:* The Urn of the Soul," *Bulletin of the Cleveland Museum of Art* 1, no. 3 (1961): 26–34.
6. Ibid., 32.

"urn" the soul in the coffin, is based on a suspiciously late textual variant.[7] More recently, Stanley K. Abe, after a rigorous examination of the evidence, has concluded that "the fact that a *hunping* was not given a special place in the tomb, particularly the absence of a close physical relationship to the coffin, mitigates against the hypothesis that *hunping* were meant to house the soul."[8] Nonetheless, the documents of 318 that we will examine here continue to be invoked in discussions of the "soul jars." These two classes of witness to the nature of Chinese death ritual—the one plastic and the other textual—have tended to discourage rather than aid closer analysis of the events of 318.

In similar fashion, I would argue, texts such as those that concern us here have been misused in our eagerness to discover just "what the Chinese believed" concerning the soul. At issue in the court presentations to Sima Rui, we need to remember, was deviant practice, not deviant belief. We might best gauge how useful the documents of 318 are for our modern preoccupations by looking at the presentation of one of the court ritualists, Fu Chun 傅純:

> The sages systematized the rites in order that our service accord with emotions.[9] We set up a grave mound and vault in order to store the body and serve it as ill-omened. We erect a shrine and ancestral hall in order to placate the spirits and to make offerings to them as propitious.[10] [In the former case] one escorts the body so that it will depart; [in the latter] one invites the essences [of the dead] so that they will return. This is the major distinction between grave and shrine; the difference between our handling of the body and of the spirits.[11] From the fact that the *fang* [offerings made

---

7. Albert E. Dien, "Developments in Funerary Practices in the Six Dynasties Period: The *Duisuguan*, or "Figured Jar," as a Case in Point," in *Between Han and Tang: Cultural and Artistic Interaction in a Transformative Period*, ed. Wu Hung (Beijing: Cultural Relics Publishing House, 2001), 541–42, n. 90.

8. Stanley K. Abe, *Ordinary Images* (Chicago: University of Chicago Press, 2002), 92. For the arguments over whether or not these vessels were meant as soul-containers, see Kominami Ichirō, "Shinteiko to Tōgo no bunka," *Tōhōgakuhō* 65 (1993): 225–74; Li Gang, "Han Jin Huyong fawei," *Dongnan wenhua* 3, no. 4 (1991): 73–81; and the nuanced discussion in Dien, "Developments in Funerary Practices."

9. Fu Chun here paraphrases the *Liji*, "*Fangji* 坊記," *SSJZS*, 2:1618b: "Ritual is based on human emotions and makes regulations for them on this basis 禮者因人之情而為之節文." (see also James Legge, *Li Chi: Book of Rites, An Encyclopedia of Ancient Ceremonial Usages, Religious Creeds, and Social Institutions*, 2 vols. (New York: University Books, 1967), 2:284.

10. This characterization of the rites at the grave as "ill-omened" and those at the temple as "propitious" derives from the *Zhouli* (*SSJZS*). See Wu Hung, *Monumentality in Early Chinese Art and Architecture* (Stanford, CA: Stanford University Press, 1995), 88.

11. For another translation of this passage and a discussion of the precedents for regarding the rituals of the tomb as ill-omened and those of the ancestral shrine as propitious, see Brashier, "Han Thanatology," 156, n. 117.

at the door to] the chambers of the ancestral temple and the *ji* offerings at the hall of repose [in the rear of the] ancestral hall are not conducted in the same place,[12] we see that even the precedents for conducting a wide search for the spirits [of the deceased] include not a single provision for sacrifice at the grave. From this it is clear that the grave is not the place where spirits reside. Now, no transgression of the established meaning of ritual could be greater than confusing the distinction between body and spirits or erring in what is proper for shrine and tomb.[13]

This constitutes a fair summary of the positions of the court erudites and high officials whose opinions were collected by Du You 杜佑 (735–812), the scholar whose collection of governmental writings contains our evidence for the debate. It might appear to modern eyes to be about belief—"the grave is not the place where spirits survive"—but the way that this conclusion is reached points in different direction. Fu's "evidence," a pastiche of ritual descriptions, contains not a single ontological remark concerning the soul or the makeup of the human body. Ritual precedent forms the sole basis for his conclusions, and ritual practice constitutes the extent of his concern. Even questions as to why the rituals he describes would be efficacious fall outside the bounds of polite inquiry. "One escorts the body," and it departs; "one invites the essences [of the dead]," and they return to be feasted in the ancestral temple. The distinction between the body and its spiritual components, which the memorialists of 318 call variously "spirits" 神, "souls" 魂, "numina" 靈, "essence" 精, or various combinations of these terms, was proven for them by the mechanistic laws of this ritual dance as enshrined in the Confucian classics. As usual with the Confucian handling of such matters, much that we would like to see explained—the existence or nonexistence of these entities, their nature, their numbers, their mode of residence in the body and even their possible postmortem destinations—proves unimportant compared to the sanctity of ritual precedent, which alone constituted all one could know or needed to know. Since this was so, the memorialists felt no need to cite outside sources of knowledge or even to be precise about their terms. This is bad news for modern scholars, but ample excuse for us to direct our attention elsewhere.

Scholars have long complained of the "unclear," "confused," or "contra-

---

12. Fu cites the *Liji,* "Liqi 禮器," *SSJZS,* 2:1441c: "The *ji* offerings were set in the hall and the *fang* offerings were presented without." This passage emphasizes that the sacrifices were carried out in different locations because the participants did not know where the spirits of the dead could be located. See Legge, *Li Chi,* 1:412.

13. Fu Chun, quoted in Fang, *Jinshu,* 59.1626.

dictory" notions that Chinese of this period held concerning the after-life. The evidence available to us from graves does seem to contradict what ritualists had to say, and ritualists' Confucian counsels of agnos-ticism are further belied by the widespread interest in spirits and an-cestral ghosts at all levels of society. To make matters worse, no one, before the advent of Daoism, showed much interest in normalizing views of the afterlife. Our self-appointed task of reconciling these bodies of evidence is thus doomed at the outset, but we should not allow our un-derstandable resentment at this state of affairs to obscure what we can know.

We shall have no more to say in this chapter concerning either "souls" or "jars." Given that the nature of contemporary belief concerning the *hun*, singular or plural, widespread or not, still remains uncertain to us, we shall call the rites banned in 318 "*hun*-summoning burials" rather than "soul-summoning burials." Two fundamental and well-attested, but to us logically incommensurate, Chinese conceptions of the "soul" furnish enough data for us to pursue our inquiries into the events of 318. First, the spiritual components of the body were, for many Chinese, plural and could forsake the person piecemeal at moments of illness, stress, or dis-traction, as they did totally at death.[14] Second, the spiritual components of personhood, whether singular or plural (and again reconstituted), could become what we call "ghosts" to haunt the living.[15] Armed with this basic structure, we can make sense of the attempts of some to sum-mon and properly bury the spiritual aspects of the person, the *hun*, with-out concerning ourselves much about how well this concept accords with our own idea of the soul.

THE DISEMBODIED

Once we have disassociated the *hun*-summoning burials of the first days of the Eastern Jin from those curious mortuary jars, from the conviction that this was a southern practice adopted helter-skelter by some guilt-ridden northern émigrés, and from our desire to learn more about pre-Buddhist, Chinese conceptions of the soul, we are free to consider the

14. See Brashier, "Han Thanatology."
15. See Robert F. Campany, "Return-from-Death Narratives in Early Medieval China," *Journal of Chinese Religions* 18 (1990): 91–125; and Poo Mu-chou, "The Concept of Ghost in Ancient Chinese Religion," in *Religion and Chinese Society: Ancient and Medieval China*, ed. John Lagerwey (Hong Kong: Chinese University of Hong Kong Press and École française d'Extrême-Orient, 2004), 1:173–92.

practice within a wider historical context. Doing so, we find that the year 318 was not the only time that *hun*-summoning burials came to the attention of official historians. Two Tang Empresses and a high-born second wife of a Tang emperor are also recorded as having received *hun*-summoning burials. Again, the time was one of violent death, if on a lesser scale, and of threat to the legitimate succession.

In 690, Wu Zhao 武曌, known to history as Wu Zetian 則天, who had been *de facto* ruler of the Tang dynasty since at least 660, compelled her puppet monarch, Li Dan 李旦 (Tang Ruizong, r. 684–90; 710–12), to abdicate in her favor and established herself as emperor of the new Zhou dynasty. She thus became the only woman to ever rule in China as "child of heaven" in her own right. The murderous machinations through which she accomplished this feat are carefully, if with certain malicious bias, recounted in the standard histories of the period.[16] Among Wu Zhao's many victims were two empresses, Empress Liu 劉, wife of Li Dan, and Empress Zhao 趙, wife of Li Zhe 李哲 (Tang Zhongzong, r. 684, 705–10), and a third woman, surnamed Dou 竇 and known posthumously as Empress Dou, who at the time of her death was a secondary wife of Li Dan.

Empress Zhao was the first of the three to perish at the hands of Wu Zhao. Daughter of Zhao Gui 趙瓌 (d. 688?) and the Changle princess, who was the daughter of the founder of the Tang, Empress Zhao was stripped of her title when her parents were implicated in the 688 Princes' Rebellion against Wu Zhao.[17] She died under unknown circumstances in the compounds of the Palace Domestic Service. Her grave was never located.[18] She was given a *hun*-summoning burial when her husband, Li Zhe, died in 710, and her *hun* was interred with him in his mausoleum.[19]

Empresses Liu and Dou met their fate together. Sequestered in the palace with their deposed husband, they were accused by Wu Zhao in

16. Richard Guisso, "The Reigns of Empress Wu, Chung-Tsung and Jui-tsung (684–721)," in *The Cambridge History of China*, vol. 3, *Sui and T'ang China, 589–906* (London: Cambridge University Press, 1979), 290–332; and Charles D. Benn, *The Cavern-Mystery Transmission: A Taoist Ordination Rite of A.D. 711* (Honolulu: University of Hawaii Press, 1991), 5–9.

17. Ou-yang Xiu, Song Qi, et. al., *Xin Tangshu* (Beijing: Zhonghua shuju, 1975), 4.87, 83.3644. For the uprising of Li Zhen, prince of Yue, see Guisso, "The Reigns," 303–4; for Zhao Gui's death, see *Xin Tangshu*, 83.3644–45.

18. See Liu Xu et al., *Jiu Tangshu* (Beijing: Zhonghua shuju, 1975), 51.2171. The *Xin Tangshu* (76.3485) adds the grisly detail that guards found her body rotted away after noticing that no cooking smoke emerged from her cell "for a number of days," but says nothing about her place of temporary interment being lost.

19. Liu et al., *Jiu Tangshu*, 51.2171.

693 of having attempted to bring about her death by spell-magic. As with Empress Zhao, their bodies were never recovered. Both were given *hun*-summoning burials and "interred" in separate tumuli when Li Dan was restored briefly to the throne at the death of Li Zhe. When Li Dan died in 716, both empresses were given posthumous titles and buried with their husband.[20]

But what was it, precisely, that was buried and then reinterred in these cases, since the physical remains of the three women were never recovered? Fortunately, historians have preserved one memorial concerning the ritual that was followed in the case of Empress Zhao. Presumably the burials of the other two women were conducted in the same fashion.

There was no dispute over *hun*-summoning burials in this instance, but once again the ritualist stance, as represented by the Erudite of the Chamberlain for Ceremonials Peng Jingzhi 彭景直, was that the practice was uncanonical. He is quoted as writing the following:

> Anciently, there was no ritual for *hun*-summoning burial. It is [thus] not appropriate to provide inner and outer coffins or to construct a hearse. According to the precedent of the burial of the Yellow Thearch's cloak and cap in Qiaoshan that is to be found in the *Treatise on Sacrifices* of the *Hanshu*,[21] it is fitting to use the Empress' ritual tunic[22] to summon her *hun* at the Inner Hall of the burial mound.[23] Then place the garment in the *hun* conveyance,[24] announce sacrifice using the grand-pen animals, and convey the garments into the Inner Hall, arraying them to the right of the imperial

20. Ibid., 51,2176.

21. Ban Gu et al., *Hanshu* (Beijing: Zhonghua shuju, 1962), 25A.1233. Liu Che, the Martial Thearch of the Han, visited and made sacrifices at the Yellow Thearch's tomb. On this occasion, he asked why there was a tomb at all, since he had heard that the Yellow Thearch had transcended. The response was that the tumulus enclosed only the cap and cloak of the Thearch. Given the critical tone of this chapter of the Han history, one suspects that Peng Jingzhi may have intended to dissuade the emperor from performing the *hun*-summoning burial. If so, he was frustrated. His implied criticism was not acknowledged.

22. The "ritual tunic" (*huiyi* 褘衣) was a tunic decorated with a multicolored pattern of soaring pheasants and worn by empresses when sacrificing to the imperial ancestors; see the *Zhouli*, "Nei sifu 內司服," *SSJZS*, 1:691a–c.

23. The *qin gong* 寢宮, or "inner hall," might also be translated as "retiring hall." A replica of the inner chamber of a house in the sunlit world, it was outfitted in the tomb with eating and drinking vessels, foodstuffs, toiletry items, images of servants and musicians—everything the deceased would need for "life" in the tomb. See Wu Hung, "Art in a Ritual Context: Rethinking Mawangdui," *Early China* 17 [1992]: 111–44. Through the procedures described here, the empress will be moved to this space to serve the emperor in the tomb.

24. The *hun yu* 魂輿, or "*hun* conveyance," also known as the "*hun* cart" 魂車, is mentioned in a very similar context in the third of Lu Ji's (261–303) "coffin-puller songs 挽歌" (see Xiao Tong (501–31), comp., *Wen xuan* 文選 [Hong Kong: Shangwu yinshu guan, 1974], 28.626): "The *hun*-conveyance is lonely and silent, One only sees the cap and belt [of the deceased]." Apparently, this vehicle, which figures in the "auspicious" part of the

resting place [in the tomb]. Cover them with a burial shroud. In this way, accomplish the twin burial [of the Empress with the Emperor].[25]

As in the rituals criticized by Sima Rui's erudites in 318, the *hun*-summoning procedure described by Peng Jingzhi takes place entirely at the "gravesite." But, at least in the cases of Empresses Liu and Dou, we know that *hun* tablets were also established for them in the ancestral temple.[26] This was likely done for Empress Zhao as well, since she also received a temple-name. For the Tang-period ritualists, then, there seems to have been no concern that the *hun*-summoning burial would somehow confine the *hun* in the grave, for they could still be feasted in the ancestral hall.

Most important, though, the brief description given by Peng of the ritual—the only account that we possess—reveals that it was the *hun*-summoning garment itself that was covered with a shroud and buried in place of the body. Clothing worn in life, and particularly that worn on ritual occasions when the wearer had cleansed body and mind to come into contact with the spirits, was also used in the canonical *hun*-summoning ritual employed when the corpse was present. This garment, forgotten by modern scholars in their scurry to find evidence of Chinese beliefs concerning the soul, gave the *hun* something to which they could "attach." What was done with the garment next is significant.

According to the *Yili* account of the *hun*-summoning ritual, the summoner, having ascended to the roof to call out three times for the *hun*, handed the garment down to a helper, who placed it in a bamboo casket. The garment was then briefly laid over the corpse, "as if 若 the *hun* had been obtained" according to the commentator Zheng Xuan.[27] We should be cautious in the presence of "as if" phrases used by ritualists

---

funeral ceremony that did not deal with the corpse and death, was to bear the clothing items that had been used in the *hun*-summoning ceremony in other cases as well. According to Zheng Xuan (*Yili, SSJZS*, 1:1147c), the vehicle was to be like that used in life.

25. Liu et al., *Jiu Tangshu* 51.2171.

26. Sacrifices for Empresses Liu and Dou were first carried out at the Yikun miao 儀坤廟 and only later moved to the imperial ancestral temple (Liu et al., *Jiu Tangshu* 51.2176).

27. *Yili, SSJZS*, 1:1129a. Wu Hung, arguing that the famous Mawangdui banner was not used in *hun*-summoning ritual, notes that the *Records of Rites (Liji)* specifies that the garment used to call the *hun* should not be used to dress the corpse or as a burial shroud ("Art in a Ritual Context," 115). But Zheng Xuan's note to the passage Wu cites (*Liji, SSJZS*, 2:1572b) refers to the *Yili* passage (*SSJZS*, 1:1129a) which states that the corpse should be covered with the garment, using the same term, *yi* 衣 "to clothe." Zheng Xuan then adds, "[The *hun*-summoning garment] should be removed when [the corpse is] washed 浴而去之." Wu's argument concerning the Mawangdui banner may thus be correct, but he goes beyond the evidence in concluding that "this garment symbolized the person's living existence and functioned as a 'healing' instrument to attract the soul back. Death, on

when they are describing death. Perhaps out of reverence in the presence of the dead or perhaps in deference to Confucius's injunction that one sacrifice to the dead "as if" they were present, ritual accounts never speak with certainty on the subject of "souls." Yet, this intimate and spiritually charged garment, treated "as if" it could at least briefly act as a physical medium for the evanescent *hun*, reveals what many who conducted the rite must have thought they were accomplishing thereby. The use, both in the classical *hun*-summoning rites and in *hun*-summoning burials, of garments as simulacra for the body—body-doubles, as it were—opens a vast new line of inquiry, one that we can only sketch here in broad outline.

Early Daoists, alchemists, and ritual technicians of every stripe knew quite a few methods for replacing the body with various simulacra, including clothing. The method known as *shijie*, "deliverance by means of a [substitute] corpse," has received the most scholarly attention.[28] This practice, which took a variety of different forms, replaced the body with some personal object—for example, a sword, a staff, sandals, hat and robe—allowing the owner to escape death altogether. Take, for example, the alchemical formula found among the recipes section of the *Scripture of the Arrayed Five Talismans* of *Lingbao* and dating to perhaps the third century CE.

The adept is advised first to slaughter an ox during the third month of the year and boil one and a half *jin* of its fat. This is to be mixed with one and a half *jin* each of mercury and tin. Then, at a "secret location in

---

the other hand, meant that such an effort had failed, so the garment should be discarded" (Wu, "Art in a Ritual Context," 115). Other garments and shrouds were indeed used in the grave to cover the corpse, but the *hun*-summoning garment was brought into contact with the corpse in a way that suggests that at least some people thought that the *hun* could be transferred back to the body—not to restore life but to restore the integrity of the deceased before burial. Further, while these texts do not say what was to be done with the *hun*-summoning garment, the Tang dynasty proposal of Peng Jingzhi indicates that the garment was not simply "discarded." This may have been especially true when the body was not present. In the case of Empress Zhao, at least, the *hun*-summoning robe was interred. I suspect this was the regular practice, though I agree with Wu that the Mawangdui banner was unlikely to have been used in such a fashion. All *hun*-summoning descriptions of which I am aware in fact specify that the garment used is to be something the deceased wore in life.

28. See Ursula-Angelika Cedzich, "Corpse Deliverance, Substitute Bodies, Name Change, and Feigned Death: Aspects of Metamorphosis and Immortality in Early Medieval China," *Journal of Chinese Religions* 29 (2001): 1–68; and Robert Ford Campany, *To Live as Long as Heaven and Earth: A Translation and Study of Ge Hong's "Traditions of Divine Transcendents"* (Berkeley and Los Angeles: University of California Press, 2000), 52–60.

the mountains," the tin is to be melted in a bronze pot, with the mercury and fat added in order. The resultant mixture is to be made into eighty-one "bean-sized" pellets, three of which are to be eaten thrice daily for nine days. The ingestion of this much mercury (more than three-quarters of a pound) would likely result in death, but a death that was held to be apparent rather than real, as the following directions make clear:

> Once the number of days is up, write the [prescribed] talisman in red on white silk and place it on your breast. On a *maosi* day lie down with your head to the west and visualize yourself as dead. After a long while, take off your clothing and leave it where you were lying. Then proceed directly into the mountains. You should go to a distant region, change your name, and never return to your old home. Once you leave, people will at first see only the corpse of a dead person at the spot where you lay, but after awhile the corpse will suddenly disappear.[29]

This procedure at first seems intended to effect precisely the opposite result promised by the *hun*-summoning ritual. Rather than providing lodging for the spiritual components of the person, methods of release from the corpse allow the adept to escape, bodily, with all faculties intact. As those who have studied such rites point out, however, methods of corpse release do share with *hun*-summoning rituals the notion that physical objects can represent an absent corpse.

Another Daoist ritual, recorded in a manual of petitions assembled in the ninth century, though it may be a later revision of an earlier rite, employs items of clothing or jewelry to substitute for the dead in the absence of a body in a manner more reminiscent of the *hun*-summoning ritual.[30] In the scenario for which this petitioning ritual was designed, as in the cases I explore in chapter 5, living family members are experiencing illness that they believe to be caused by the fact that their dead relative is now in the Three Offices of the underworld, undergoing punishment for past transgressions. Clothing or personal jewelry of the deceased is offered to "redeem the *hun*," possibly by allowing the *hun* to attach to the garment when it is presented in the netherworld by spirit-gener-

---

29. HY 388, 2.25a–26a. I have reversed the order in which the instructions are given in favor of the order in which they are to be performed. See also Campany, *To Live as Long as Heaven and Earth*, 54–57, for another treatment of these instructions.

30. HY 615, 6.12b–14b. The procedure is called "Petition for Delivering Clothing or Items of the Deceased to Achieve Transfer [into the heavens] through Acquittal from Indictment." For a discussion of this petition in the context of the book as a whole, see Franciscus Verellen, "The Heavenly Master Liturgical Agenda According to Chisong zi's Petition Almanac," *Cahiers d'Extrême-Asie* 14 (2004): 335–36.

als invoked in the rite. In this case, unfortunately, we do not know what was done with the articles after they were "presented."

In addition to wooden tablets used in Confucian ritual as a site for the *hun* to rest, the use of which I explore in the next section, a number of excavated grave documents tell of human figurines made of wood, metal, and even ginseng that were meant both to serve the dead and to replace them if any underworld service were required.[31] Such figurines, complements of the ceramic human figures that originally replaced human sacrifice and were employed in Chinese graves thereafter, clearly serve as body-substitutes.

There were, in short, numerous methods for using physical objects as simulacra of the human body in mortuary contexts. In none of these cases, except perhaps for the interred figurines that housed the souls of servants, were the spiritual components of the person said to be trapped permanently in this body substitute. But that was precisely the argument that the ritualists forwarded to Sima Rui in 318. It is to that event that we now turn.

BANNING "*HUN*-SUMMONING BURIALS"

We have two sources of written evidence on the 318 discussions of soul-summoning burials. The incident that brought these burials to the imperial attention, the request of the wife of Sima Yue 司馬越, a woman surnamed Pei 裴, to perform such a burial for her husband, is mentioned several times in the *Jinshu*, the "official" history of the Jin dynasty compiled by Fang Xuanling 房玄齡 (578–648) and his staff under the Tang dynasty. The biography of Sima Yue gives a few details of this event, together with an extract from the opinion submitted by the Erudite Fu Chun 傅純, translated above. In the biography of the Secretarial Censor Yuan Gui 袁瓌 we find another brief account of the affair.[32]

Our second source is the *Tongdian*, compiled by Du You 杜佑 (735–812) in 805. Du collected the opinions of twelve of Sima Rui's advisors and one proponent of the rite, though the opinions of several others are cited by the opponents.[33] When we read through these memorials, several

31. See Anna K. Seidel, "Traces of Han Religion in Funeral Texts Found in Tombs," in *Dōkyō to shūkyō bunka* [Volume in honor of Professor Akitsuki Kan'ei] (Tokyo: Hirakawa, 1987), 43; and Ikeda On, "*Chūgoku rekidai boken ryakkō*," *Tōyō-bunka kenkyūjo kiyō* 86 (1981): 273, 275–276, for a few examples.

32. Fang, *Jinshu* 83.2166–67.

33. Du You, *Tongdian* (Shanghai: Shangwu, 1935), 103.547–48. I am extremely grateful to Albert E. Dien for sharing with me his unpublished, preliminary translation of this passage. My work is indebted to his prior research, but any errors are my own.

things arouse our attention. First, not one of the memorials concerns itself with the soul-summoning burial of Sima Yue, though the event is mentioned. Instead, we find that the discussion centers on rites that were conducted for other figures: three officials and two further members of the imperial family.

Second, while the emperor's advisors are, as we would expect, men of some prominence and for the most part easily identifiable, not one of the *proponents* of the rite is known to history beyond the records collected by Du.[34] The official memorials cite and refute arguments presented by Zhou Sheng 周生 (perhaps a student?) and Li Wei 李瑋. There appears as well a longer extract from a memorial by one Gongsha Xin 公沙歆, of Beihai.[35] Additional proponents of soul-summoning burials are cited only by the locution "someone said." Who were these other men? Were they perhaps the ritualists who proposed to undertake soul-summoning burials? One passage in the memorials of Kong Yan 孔衍 (d. 320), the twenty-second-generation descendant of Confucius and a critic of *hun*-summoning burials, seems to indicate that the proponents were, at any rate, under the influence of unorthodox ritualists of some description. After characterizing *hun*-burial as "a rite of the back lanes,[36] emanating from the hearts of the ignorant and base," he ends his memorial with this pronouncement: "[They] falsely construct the rituals of a Master and thereby wreak havoc on the canons of the sage [Confucius]."[37] The "Master" is unknown to us.

34. Those listed as presenting arguments against the rite include Yuan Gui 袁瓌, the secretarial censor who, according to Du You, began the debates by bringing to the attention of the throne the rites conducted for Cao Fu (for his biography, see Fang, *Jinshu*, 83.2166–67); Erudite Ruan Fang 阮放, of the National University (biography: *Jinshu*, 49.1367); Erudite Fu Chun 傅純 (no biography, but cited for his positions on ritual at *Jinshu*, 19.604 and 59.1626); Xun Zu 荀組 (257–322), who held the preeminent position of Grand Guardian and concurrently served as Chief Secretary for the Emperor (biography: *Jinshu*, 39.1159–60); Zu's son Xun Yi 荀奕 (d. 332), who at that time served as Palace Cadet in the service of the Heir Apparent; Kong Yan 孔衍 (267–320), the reputed twenty-second-generation descendant of Confucius, who at that time served as Adjutant to the Eastern Pacification Army (biography: *Jinshu*, 61.2359); Gan Bao 干寶 (d. 336?), court diviner, historian, and interpreter of portents (biography: *Jinshu*, 82.2149–51); He Xun 賀循 (259–319), who, of advanced age, served as Chancellor and Military Advisor at this time (biography: *Jinshu*, 68.1824–31); and Zhang Ping 張憑, known for his skill as a moralist and conversationalist (biography: *Jinshu*, 75.1992). Among those who opposed *hun*-summoning burials, I was unable to locate further information on only two: Zhang Liang 張亮 and Jiang Yuan 江淵.

35. Beihai was a commandery located east of modern Yidu County 益都縣, Shandong Province.

36. This phrase is drawn from the *Liji*, "*Tangong* 檀弓," *SSJZS*, 1:1282a.

37. Du, *Tongdian*, 103.547b.

We shall perhaps never know just who developed and promulgated *hun*-summoning burials, but we do well to note the uneven status of the two sides in what some have described as a court "debate."[38] Given the proponents' lack of court status and the scant space given their opinions, the documents we have seem more concerned to marshal evidence than to present a disinterested collection of differing opinions.

Two scenarios are thus possible: either the emperor was truly perplexed concerning the ritual, and our evidence simply favors the winning position, or Sima Rui's call for discussion was merely an exercise in consensus-building concerning a matter he had already decided. We should not discard this latter possibility out of hand, for such an act is something we might expect from a prince about to take the throne.

Despite the uneven nature of the evidence, a close reading of all the documents can tease out some information concerning the motives of those who undertook *hun*-summoning burials. Those who favor *hun*-summoning burials (who are not always named in our source) forward two sorts of arguments: (1) precedent and (2) evidence from the ritual classics. We begin with the former.

ARGUMENTS FROM PRECEDENT

As we have seen, *hun*-summoning burials did not end with Sima Rui's proscription in 318. Nor did they begin with the events that led up to the proscription. As did Peng Jingzhi in the early eighth century, Zhou Sheng and "someone" else cited the legend of the Yellow Thearch, whose crown and cloak were said to have been buried in a tumulus after he physically ascended to heaven on a dragon. The ritualist response was that people of the time simply buried what remained to them in commemoration of the great ruler. Gan Bao 干寶 (d. 336?) even cites Confucius to prove that "the Yellow Thearch also died, and to speak of his transcendence is absurd." Because *hun*-summoning burials were conducted for the dead, not for those believed to have somehow bypassed

---

38. Wu Hung, in "Buddhist Elements in Early Chinese Art (Second and Third Centuries A.D.)," *Artibus Asiae* 47 (1986): 263–376, describes the discrepancy as follows: "The debate seems to have been sustained on uneven levels. Those Confucianists who were rigidly orthodox insisted that the rightful place for commemorating the departed was not the tomb but the ancestral temple. . . . Their opponents, on the other hand, simply hoped to find a solution to the puzzling situation as to how people who had lost their parents' bodies could practice filiality. They borrowed the idea of 'burial of the summoned soul' from sources other than Confucianism" (287–88). I argue below that more was involved in the proponents' project than the practice of filiality.

death, this assertion would seem beside the point. Surely, whether the Yellow Thearch had died or not has little bearing on the issue of what was gained by storing his clothing in a grave. Had we more information on the cult of the Yellow Thearch at his tumulus, visited for instance by the Han emperor Liu Che 劉徹 (r. 140–87 BCE), we would doubtless find that this "commemoration" also involved claims on the part of shamans to be able to communicate with him there. Some such claim—that one might communicate through relics—is probably what Gan Bao and the rest object to when they argue that the interment of the Yellow Thearch's crown and cloak "was not the burial of his spirit." We have seen in the Tang period memorial of Peng Jingzhi that the case of the Yellow Thearch continued to be cited in support of *hun*-summoning burials and that clothing, as body substitute, was used in the preferred procedure for conducting the rite. Such procedures did indeed constitute for some a means of restoring orderly communications with the spirits of the ancestors in the ancestral hall.

The other precedents cited are less well documented. "Someone" cited the case of Liu Yuan 劉元, princess of Xinye and sister of the founder of the Latter Han, Liu Xiu 劉秀 (r. 25–57). Murdered by the forces of Wang Mang before the restoration, a *hun*-summoning burial was conducted for her in 49 CE, on the death of her husband, so that the two could rest side by side. "Someone" also cited the instance of Guo Xun 郭循, better known as Guo Xiu 脩, of the Wei kingdom, who was taken prisoner by the Shu kingdom and killed after he attempted to assassinate the Shu emperor and succeeded in slaying their commander-in-chief. In Guo's case, the historians mention no *hun*-summoning ritual, nor do they specify in either instance what happened to the bodies of these two unfortunates, though we can assume that they were not recovered. In fact, Guo Xun is likely to have been dismembered for his crimes.

A more questionable precedent is cited by Li Wei. This is the story of Bo Ji 伯姬, wife of Duke Gong of the pre-Han Song state (r. 588–75 BCE), who perished in a house fire rather than violate the rules of propriety that prohibited women from leaving the house unaccompanied by a matron or governess.[39] Li implies that the burial given Bo Ji was a *hun*-summoning burial. Since historical sources do not specify what remained of her corpse or how the burial was conducted, this claim is easily countered by Kong

---

39. See Albert Richard O'Hara, *The Position of Women in Early China According to the Lieh nü chuan, "The Biographies of Eminent Chinese Women"* (Washington, DC: Catholic University of America Press, 1945), 103–6; *Zuo zhuan, SSJZS*, 2:2012b–c.

Yan with the words "her ashes were real [remains], so why would they have discarded the real [option] of burying the ashes, to bury the *hun?*"

From these three precedents, a pattern begins to emerge. In all of these cases, including those of the Tang dynasty and those of 318 that we will examine more closely in a moment, *hun*-summoning burials were undertaken not just for those whose bodies were unavailable, but for those who met with a violent end. The Yellow Thearch's ascension into heaven, unlike the other three precedents, was violent only in its unexpected suddenness.

Further precedents cited by those who supported *hun*-summoning burials deal not with the rite itself but with the contention that the spiritual components of the person might inhabit the tomb. Li Wei, for instance, refers to the story in which Duke Cheng of the pre-Han Wei kingdom 衛成公 dreamt that offerings made to his forebear were being seized by the spirit of a prince of the Xia dynasty to whom sacrifices had been discontinued.[40] We need not examine these in detail to apprehend the point that those who favored *hun*-summoning burials were trying to establish: *hun* were in fact traditionally thought by some to exist in the grave, at least at times.

ARGUMENTS FROM THE CLASSICS

Those who supported *hun*-burials also attempted to engage the court ritualists on their own ground, through recourse to the Confucian ritual classics. The following lengthy passage from the memorial of Gongsha Xin 公沙歆, a person from Beihai about whom nothing further is known, demonstrates how proponents of *hun*-summoning burials marshaled evidence from revered sources in support of their position.

> When the spirits are not in motion, they reside in the body; when they exit [the body] they attach themselves to the ancestral tablet. [Thus] the meaning expressed by the seat 座 in the tomb and the tablet in the temple is proximate. If, in all cases, we return the body to the earth and the spirits to the heavens, then indeed the rites of high antiquity are correct, and *hun*-summoning is incorrect.[41] If [funerary matters] are strictly divided into the propitious and unpropitious, so that we never provide a chamber several

---

40. *Zuo zhuan, SSJZS,* 2:1832a.
41. This appeal to the simple burial rites of "high antiquity" 上古 emanates from the Mohist position criticized by Xunzi 荀子. Xunzi characterizes the position as follows: "Those who construct persuasions concerning the customs of the age say that in Grand Antiquity 太古 there were frugal burials. Coffins were three inches thick, three layers of

tens of feet in depth,[42] never raise a mound and plant trees on the tomb, then the regulations of middle antiquity win out, and *hun*-summoning should be abandoned.[43] But, if the five types of mourning clothing are to be used and we doubly unfurl dragon-pennants; if we have rites for interment and rankings [for funerals] of one hundred different degrees; then [funerals] are a matter of the living putting the deceased at a distance, and the rites should be arranged according to the emotions [of the surviving]. This being so, the calculations of the present age are close [to the heart of the matter], and the rationales for *hun*-summoning are justified. And as to why, in summoning the *hun*, one must also bury it, this is just a matter of the filial son doing his best to carry mourning to the utmost.[44]

In supporting his argument as he did, Gongsha Xin followed the lead of such Confucian works as the *Lunyu, Mengzi,* and *Xunzi* that advocated "serving the dead as one serves the living," complemented by references to the prescribed funeral practices of the *Yili* and *Liji.* Notice, however, that he begins not by arguing for *hun*-summoning burial, but for the classical *hun*-summoning rite. Proponents of *hun*-burial saw no difference between the two procedures.

Against the accepted Confucian classics, Gongsha places the prospect of returning to the austere burial practices of high antiquity or middle antiquity, as had the early Mohists.[45] Through this strategy, he implies that only by adopting non-Confucian practice could one find the *hun*-summoning rites incorrect. Finally, he justifies the bodiless "burial" with the common Confucian dictum that the filial son will "carry mourning to the utmost."

---

burial shroud [cloaked the body], and the burial ground did not encroach on cultivated fields." See Jeffrey Riegel, "Do Not Serve the Dead as You Serve the Living: The *Lüshi chunqiu* Treatises on Moderation in Burial," *Early China* 20 (1995): 310–30," for a full discussion of the issues.

42. The translation of this phrase is conjectural. Gongsha may in fact here be referring to the *zhong* assemblage and the regulation by size of the "name banners" that covered it.

43. In the chapter entitled "*Tan Gong*" of the *Liji* (*SSJZS,* 1:1275a), Confucius, when burying his parents, is recorded as having said, "I have heard that, in ancient times, burials were without tumuli, but I am one who travels to the four directions and cannot follow this, since I would then not be able to recognize [the spot.]" (Legge, *Li Chi,* 1:123). On the division of funerary procedures into the unpropitious (from death through the deposit of the body in the grave) and the propitious (all later services and sacrifice), see Brashier, "Han Thanatology," 156, n. 117. The dividing line between the two was the *yu* 虞 ritual (Zhang Jiefu, *Zhongguo sangzang shi* (Taibei: Wenjin, 1995), 44–45). Gongsha's point here is that the piling of earth to make a tumulus and the planting of trees, both common features of contemporary burial ritual, occurred after this supposed divide.

44. Du, *Tongdian,* 103.547c.

45. See Riegel, "Do Not Serve the Dead," 316–30.

Information concerning the beliefs of those who performed *hun*-burials might be derived from Gongsha Xin's opening statement. For Gongsha, and the other defenders of the practice, the spiritual components of the person, though they were free to move about, as they did when they entered the tablet in ancestral rites, typically lingered in the grave with the body. The support he and his fellows find in the Confucian classics for this assertion is the *zhong* 重 assemblage, which they refer to as a "seat" or "numinous seat" 靈座 of the *hun*. A wooden structure hung with balls of rice and covered with the name pennon of the deceased, the *zhong* served as a resting place and site of food offerings for the *hun* during handling of the corpse and interment.[46] Accordingly, both the seat provided in the tomb and the tablet provided in the temple serve as resting places for the *hun*. As Gongsha Xin puts it, "The meanings expressed by the seat in the tomb and the tablet in the temple are proximate."

The court ritual advisors uniformly deny this interpretation of the "seat." They hold that items placed in the tomb are not evidence that the spiritual components of the person exist there. For them, to summon the *hun* and bury these elements is to "nail" them down, "lock" them away, to "bury" them, even to "consign [them] to the [underworld realms], the Nine Springs." This is clearly not the intention of those who support *hun*-summoning burial. Like Gongsha Xin, they portray the spiritual components of the body as capable of moving in and out of the tomb, not as free to roam *everywhere but the tomb*, as the court ritualists contend. Li Wei 李瑋 cites both ancestral and imperial ritual in support of this point:

> The ancestral temple is the normal site for the *zheng* and *chang* offerings [of foodstuffs to the ancestors], but it is not that the transcendent numina always stay in the ancestral temple, just as the Round Mound is the normal place for suburban sacrifices, but that does not mean that the celestial spirits always reside on this mound. The *Book of Odes* states, "The [imperial] progenitors come to the service,"[47] so we know that they come from elsewhere. And it also says, "The divine protectors tranquilly return."[48] That is, they "return" to the stygian darkness.

---

46. See Zhang, *Zhongguo sangzang shi*, 40; John Steele, *The I-li, or Book of Etiquette and Ceremonial* (Taibei: Chengwen, 1966), 54–55; and the *Yili*, *SSJZS*, 1:1135a. Legge (*Li Chi*, 1:168) calls the *zhong* "the first tablet for the spirit"; see also *Liji*, "*Tan gong xia* 檀弓下," *SSJZS*, 1:1301b.

47. Li here cites the *Shangshu* ("*Yiji* 益稷," *SSJZS*, 1:144a), not the *Shijing*. Kong Yan repeats the error in his refutation.

48. Li cites Ode 209, *Shijing*, *SSJZS*, 1:469c. See Bernhard Karlgren, *The Book of Odes* (Stockholm: Museum of Far Eastern Antiquities, 1974), 163. For a study of the ancestral

The response of Kong Yan to these assertions seems weak: "As for the Thearch's mound and the 'come to the service' and 'tranquilly return' of the *Book of Odes*, these simply clarify that the *hun* all comply 無不從, and that is all." Like the other court ritualists, he returns repeatedly to the claim that proponents of *hun*-summoning burials wish to "bury" the spiritual components of the person in the tomb. It is as if the court ritualists cannot see past the name of the rite to comprehend what its supporters are actually proposing.

The lengthiest exposition of the imperial sentiment comes from Gan Bao, who at about this time was made Director of Court Historians. Bao writes in direct contradiction to Gongsha Xin's contention that spiritual components might exist in the grave: "I hold it to be the case that when a person dies, the spirits, rising, return to heaven, and the body, sinking, returns to earth. Therefore we construct ancestral shrines to provide "guest" rituals for the spirits and use shrouds to enwrap the body."[49] This strong claim seems strange, coming from Gan Bao, author of the well-known collection *Records of an Inquest into the Spirit-Realms,* a work that contains a fair number of stories concerning spirits residing in graves.[50] In fact, according to an anecdote recorded in the *History of the Jin,* Bao himself early in life encountered evidence that sentience might remain in the grave. It seems that Bao's father was fond of a maid, who, at the death of the father, was secretly forced into the grave with him by Bao's mother. Some ten years later, when Bao's mother died and the family opened the tumulus to inter her with the father, the maid was discovered, quite alive. The poor woman, once she had regained her strength, "said that their father often obtained food and drink to give to her, with the same gracious concern he had shown while alive."[51] The food and drink could hardly be other than the family offerings presented in ancestral ritual, which the "father" then shared with his lover in the tomb. How could this event have convinced Bao that the spiritual components of the person knew nothing of the grave?

We should note at this point that the *History of the Jin,* notorious for drawing extensively on the tale-literature of the period, may well be cit-

---

ritual expressed in this ode, see Martin Kern, "*Shi jing* Songs as Performance Texts: A Case Study of 'Chu ci'(Thorny Caltrop)," *Early China* 25 (2000): 49–111.

49. Du, *Tongdian,* 103.547b.

50. On the surviving recensions of this work, and for analysis of its contents, see Robert Ford Campany, *Strange Writing: Anomaly Accounts in Early Medieval China* (Albany: State University of New York Press, 1996), 55–62.

51. Fang, *Jinshu* 82.2150.

ing a lost work meant to criticize Gan Bao for his paradoxical stance on this occasion. Yet even if this is the case, because Bao's work on the supernatural has survived largely intact, we cannot but notice the discrepancy between the stance he takes in that work and the public pronouncement he makes here.

THE OPPONENTS RECONSIDERED

While we today cannot properly revisit the arguments presented to Sima Rui to decide who should have won, it is difficult to escape the impression that the court ritualist position, as presented in the documents we have, does indeed contradict some elements of established burial practice. Quite aside from the overwhelming evidence provided by modern archeology, the ritual items—particularly the *zhong* (or seat) and the clothing interred with the dead—do seem to indicate, as Gongsha Xin and the rest argue, that *hun* somehow linger in the tomb. None of the arguments presented by the court ritualists quite succeed at debunking this claim. *Hun*-summoning burials were indeed practiced both prior to and after 318. The best the court ritualists can proffer in refutation is the explanation that these provisions for the dead "accorded with the sentiments" of the living. But, as they quickly add, such sentiments mislead those among the living who seek to conduct this particular rite. As Gan Bao haughtily remarks, "even the name *hun* burial comes close to being rebellious!"

In their haste to disparage the *hun*-summoning burials, the ritualists clearly set up an easily refutable straw man when they persist in regarding the rite as nothing more than an attempt to "lock away" the *hun*. As Kong Yan writes in response to Li Wei's observation that one sacrifices *in the tomb* on the third day after death at the numinous seat: "In sacrificing one always must set up an altar; this is not to say that the spirits *must be* in the tomb. If the spirits *must* be in the tomb, then the [imperial ancestral] temples at Chengzhou and Luoyi were both established for nothing."[52] Such proofs beg the question. As Gongsha Xin states clearly, *hun* prove fully capable of being in both ancestral temples and in the tomb. In short, we are left with two contrary interpretations of the same facts, but only one side even attempts to fully engage the arguments of the other.

52. Du, *Tongdian*, 103.547c. Chengzhou and Luoyi are both names that refer to the capital of the Eastern Zhou dynasty, which was located near present-day Loyang, Henan Province.

For those who wish to conduct *hun*-summoning burials, the spiritual components of the person are able to go anywhere, but they may be summoned to a substitute body and otherwise ritually manipulated. For those who support the imperial position, the spiritual components of the body are, following proper burial of the body, barred from the grave and thenceforth to be feasted only at the ancestral shrine. They further hold that those who think to ritually inter the bodiless dead only want to lock them away in some fashion. Given this refrain from the court ritualists, it is no surprise to find the same chord sounded in Sima Rui's proclamation banning *hun*-summoning ritual: "The grave is for the purpose of storing away the body; the ancestral temple for settling the spirits. The *hun*-summoning burials of the present age aim to bury spirits. They are hereby banned."[53] Contrary to what the emperor and his ritualists claim, they are actually the ones who wish to restrict the movements of the *hun*. The spiritual components of the body must be "settled" or "fixed" 定 in the ancestral tablets, and the body must be "stored away" 藏 in the tomb.

The tenor of the arguments presented to the throne in 318 thus leave us with the uneasy feeling that the ritual crisis was really about something other than the ontological question of where the *hun* might reside. Perhaps the real concern lay elsewhere. We need then ask, who were the men whose unorthodox funeral rites caused such imperial consternation, and who stood to gain thereby?

THE SUMMONED

The documents collected by Du You mention six *hun*-summoning burials, three for members of the imperial family and three for military men. When we look at what was at stake in the performance of rites for these particular dead men, we see the quibbles over precedent and ritual protocol in a different light. While the grisly stories that follow help us to clarify Sima Rui's goals, the reader should be aware that the following paragraphs are riddled with unfamiliar names and references to historical events of great significance to those so named, but little remembered today on this side of the Pacific Ocean. In each instance I provide clarifying phrases, but cannot promise the smooth sail to distant shores and

---

53. See Yan Kejun, comp., "Quan Jin wen," in *Quan shanggu Sandai Qin Han Sanguo Liuchao wen* (Taibei: Hongye, 1975), 2:1507a; Li Fang, *Taiping yulan* (Beijing: Zhonghua, 1960), 555.2510a and 886.3935b (both citing the now-lost *Jin zhongxing shu* 晉中興書). The *Jinshu* states only that the emperor "for the first time" banned *hun*-summoning burials and does not give the text of his proclamation (Fang, *Jinshu* [6.150]).

times that I would like to provide. Those impatient with historical detail might skip to the closing paragraphs of this section.

1. The Prince of Donghai

The most notorious of the group was the prince of Donghai 東海王, Sima Yue 司馬越. Yue had emerged victorious in the internecine struggle for supremacy of the years 299–306 known to history as the Rebellion of the Eight Princes. As *de facto* ruler in the Jin court when it began to fall to the non-Han invaders, he sought to use the invasion as a pretext for establishing himself as emperor. Denounced to the reigning emperor, he led his troops in flight eastward from the eastern capital of Loyang on the eve of the attack. Yue died in 311 of what historians describe as "panic." His followers kept his death a secret and thought to take his body back to Donghai for burial, but the invading general Shi Le 石勒 caught up with the procession, slaughtered his followers, and burned Yue's coffin, saying, "This person has brought disorder to all under heaven and, on their behalf, I take revenge. I now burn his bones to announce the fact to heaven and earth."[54]

Shi Le then killed Yue's son, Pi 毗, and sold his wife, Pei. Pei was later able to make it south of the Yangzi, where she pressed for the *hun*-burial of her husband. Since Sima Rui's earlier move to the south had been at Pei's suggestion, the emperor was, we are told, well disposed toward Pei and often visited her residence. This is perhaps why she was able to ignore the proscription against *hun*-summoning burials. Further, Sima Rui made his own third son Chong 沖 heir to Pi 毗, who continued to be listed as "missing" (*Jinshu*, 59.1626). Pei's *hun*-summoning burial thus had the effect of preserving for her the title Grand Consort, with an official residence and grain-producing districts to support her. Only at her death were funeral services finally held for Pi, so that Sima Chong, the emperor's chosen heir, could receive the full title of prince (64.1726).

2. The Prince of Xincai

The prince of Xincai, Sima Teng 司馬騰, Yue's younger brother, ruled the city of Ye (west of modern Linzhang in Henan Province). Though he

---

54. Fang, *Jinshu*, 59.1625 (in the rest of these numbered vignettes, the *Jinshu* is cited parenthetically in the text by the appropriate reference numbers); Sima Guang, *Zizhi tongjian* (Beijing: Guji, 1957), 87.2759–61.

prided himself on having held this northern stronghold against "barbarian" incursions for some seven years, his forces were insufficient against those of a renegade Jin general, and chaos ensued. He and his four sons were slaughtered. Since it was the middle of summer, their bodies were unrecognizable by the time Ye was retaken by loyal Jin forces. Their bones were never recovered. Teng was succeeded by Sima Que 司馬確, his son from a secondary wife, but Que was subsequently killed by Shi Le. Since Que died childless, Sima Tao 滔, from a collateral line of the family, was then named his heir. Tao also disappeared when the Western Jin fell (37.1096–97).

South of the Yangzi River, Sima Rui in 317 appointed as Teng's heir Sima Bi 弼, son of You 祐, a member of the imperial family who had come south to join Rui in 312 (6.149).Tao then showed up in the south, quite alive, to reclaim his inheritance. Fortunately for his claim, Sima Bi died childless less than a year after receiving the fief (37.1097; 6.151). This did not solve matters for the beleaguered Tao, however, for he did not get along well with Teng's wife, who still survived and held the title Grand Consort of Xincai 新蔡太妃 and had been living on the support provided thereby. Sima Tao thus submitted a memorial requesting that he be made heir of his elder brother, to be enfeoffed with Zhangwu 章武, though his elder brother was still only reported missing. Sima Rui granted his request in 319 (37.1087–88).

We have no record of who held the *hun*-summoning burial for Sima Teng, but it is unlikely to have been either Sima Bi or Sima Tao, since neither was related to him directly. Most likely, as in the case of Sima Yue, the rite was commissioned by Teng's widow, known to history only as the Grand Consort of Xincai. Beyond the fact that she feuded with Sima Tao to the extent that an imperial decision was needed, we know nothing more about her. Since she was not personally beloved of the emperor, the edict of 318 probably deprived her of any hope of passing the title of prince of Xincai, with its emoluments, to any of her closer relatives.

3. The Prince of Wuling

The prince of Wuling 武陵王, Sima Zhan 司馬澹 served as general for the most infamous of the eight rebellious princes, Sima Lun. But he apparently changed sides. Both he and his son and heir were killed by Shi Le as they accompanied Sima Yue's body for burial (5.122).[55] We have

---

55. See also Sima, *Zizhi tongjian*, 87.2760–61.

no further information on the fate of his wife, a daughter of the powerful Guo clan (38.1122–23).

In this case as well, we have no report on who sought to provide a
hun-summoning burial; we know only that they sought to follow the
precedent provided by Ms. Pei. Interestingly, Sima Rui appointed his own
son by a secondary wife, Sima Xi 司馬晞, as prince of Wuling only two
months after banning *hun*-summoning burials (6.150).

4. Cao Fu

Cao Fu 曹馥 , the Vice Director of the Imperial Secretariat, to give him
his highest rank, was given a *hun*-summoning burial by his grandson,
Yun 允, who is otherwise unknown.[56] Cao Fu served as a military commander under Sima Yue when the latter took control of the court in 305
and perished in 312 when Loyang fell to Shi Le (59.1623; 5.123).

5. Wang Long

Wang Long 王隆, an Army Supervisor, is little known to us.[57] By the time
of Yuan's memorial in 318, he had already been given a *hun*-summon-
ing burial.

6. Liu Xia

Liu Xia 劉洽, Commander on the Staff of the Grand Mentor, also had
been given a *hun*-summoning burial by the time Yuan Gui submitted his
memorial. The Grand Mentor he served was Sima Yue. He was, in fact,
the one who persuaded Sima Yue to seize control of the court and had
been recommended to take the position of Military Commander in 311,

---

56. Yan, "Quan Jin wen" (*Quan shanggu*, 2:1781) has 胤, rather than 允. If this variant is accepted, we might read "his grandson and legitimate heir."

57. Du, (*Tongdian*, 103.547a) gives the name 王崇, but Wang Wenjin, in *Tongdian jiaodian ben* (Beijing: Zhonghua, 1988), 3:2708, n. 25, points out that Du You avoided using
the second character of the Tang emperor Li Longji's given name. If this suggestion has
merit, Wang Long may be the only one given a *hun*-summoning burial who was not a member of Sima Yue's faction. We have only a single sentence in the histories concerning Wang
Long, saying that he abandoned his troops in the face of Shi Le's armies and tried to take
refuge with Zhou Fu 周馥 (biography: Fang, *Jinshu*, 61.1663–1665), a bitter enemy of
Sima Yue (see *Jinshu*, 5.120). It is difficult to establish a theory based on this single sentence. Is "Zhou Fu" a mistake for "Cao Fu"? Was Wang Long murdered by Zhou Fu and
thus considered a postmortem enemy? Or is Wang Long indeed an exception? We cannot
know.

just before Yue's death (59.1623; 61.1667). It is thus likely that he was among those killed by Shi Le as followers tried to escort Yue's body back to Donghai.

•   •   •

Our foray into the historical background of the men given *hun*-summoning burials supports the suspicion that the real reasons for Sima Rui's proscription had less to do with metaphysics than with politics; that the emperor cared less for what might be placed inside of graves than for what occurred outside of them. Rather than being widespread events, as a simple listing of names might indicate, *hun*-summoning burials occurred among a rather restricted group. All of those for whom complete records are available were closely associated with Sima Yue, the *de facto* ruler in the closing years of the Western Jin and a man who once had just as strong a claim to the imperial throne as did Sima Rui. Of course, others may have been conducting the rite, but those who incited imperial consternation all belonged to Sima Yue's faction.

Further, while records for this chaotic period are sparse, and the number of heritance disputes that arose during this period must have been very great, issues of legitimate succession important enough to be noted in the histories followed upon the deaths of all three of the imperial family members (1–3 above) involved. That Cao Fu (4 above) was given a *hun*-summoning burial by his grandson also suggests that the latter wished thereby to claim the status of rightful heir, even though his father was listed as "missing." A few of the cases suggest that Sima Rui wished to replace imperial descendants associated with Sima Yue with his own close relatives.

All of this suggests that, our interest in *hun* notwithstanding, we should direct our attention to more quotidian concerns.

ON THE GROUND IN 318

In several recent works, the art historian Wu Hong has described the development of the "twin centers of ancestral cult"—temple and tomb—that figure so prominently in the arguments of the ritualists we have examined. To greatly simplify a complex argument, Wu describes the development of ancestral temples during the putative Xia and the Shang dynasties, the Zhou deployment of ancestral temples within palace compounds as spiritual and administrative centers, and the Qin and Han shift of ancestral practice to the gravesite. Wu's description of the final stage of this shift will concern us here.

Liu Xiu, the Guangwu Emperor of the Latter Han (r. 25–57) was not
the legitimate successor to the emperors of the Former Han; he was from
a distant branch of the Liu clan and actually two generations senior to
the last legitimate Han emperor. He thus, insofar as possible, conducted
his major rituals not in the ancestral temple, where his generational position would have forced upon him a ritual status unbefitting an emperor,
but in the imperial mausolea. His son, Liu Zhuang 劉莊, the Ming Emperor (r. 57–75), following a dream vision of his dead father, transferred
all imperial ancestral sacrifice to the graveside. All Latter Han rulers followed suit. As Wu writes,

> Thus, during the next 160 years, the royal temple became nominal. Instead,
> the graveyard became the focus of ancestral worship. The royal example
> was in turn imitated by people throughout the country. . . . The graveyard
> was no longer the silent world of the deceased; it became a center of social
> activities. There yearly, monthly, and daily sacrifices were offered, and large
> social gatherings were conducted. The royal mausoleums became the
> political and religious headquarters of the court, and family graveyards
> provided the common people with a proper place for banquets, musical
> performances, and art displays.[58]

If this were still the situation in 318, it would be easy to see why Sima
Rui would not want graves constructed for the likes of Sima Yue and his
cronies. But, as Wu notes succinctly, "this golden age ended as abruptly
as it had begun." The rulers of the Wei dynasty ordered that all above-
ground funerary structures be destroyed and otherwise took measures
to ensure that elite families would practice austerity in the matter of ancestral ritual, especially with regard to the construction and furnishing
of tombs.

As other scholars have detailed, the preference for "austere burials"
was continued during the Jin. The modern scholar Zhang Jiefu notes
that all five Western Jin rulers ordered that Halls of Repose (*qin gong*
寢宮) not be erected at their tumuli and that the two tombs that have
been identified so far are the most modest imperial tombs in Chinese
history. He also cites the "last wills" of a number of important figures
who followed suit by enjoining their survivors to provide them with austere burials.[59]

Gan Bao, in his memorial of 318, suggested an alternative course of action for the grieving survivors. They might "go to the place where the [deceased] met with calamity and there undertake rituals for receiving the spirits; using the ancestral temple as a place to give them ease."[60] Quite apart from the unfeasibility of this solution during wartime, Gan's suggestion does raise the question of why those who wished to conduct *hun*-summonings were so intent on constructing a grave. Given the changes in imperial and elite mortuary practice, would the construction of ancestral temples not have sufficed, as Gan Bao says, to "bring rest" to resentful spirits?

Yet we know that those who sought to provide *hun*-summoning burials did insist on graves, and the insistent charge of the court ritualists that they sought to "bury" the *hun* of their ancestors also focuses our attention on the grave. The question becomes, then, if the grave was not a center of social and political activity as it had been during the Han, what occurred at Jin gravesites to make *hun*-summoning burial desirable for survivors and anathema for the emperor?

To answer this question, we must return again to the basic distinction between grave and temple. As Rubie S. Watson points out, graves were the site of two distinct sorts of ritual performance, the funeral, "concerned with converting [a] volatile spirit into an ancestor," and grave rites, conducted only for the "remembered dead."[61] Our evidence suggests that proponents of the *hun*-summoning ritual wished the dead to be remembered and sought to "convert volatile spirits" into ancestors to facilitate this.

During the Jin, the grave was still public space, as it had been even during the Han. The ancestral temple, on the other hand, was private. Despite its location in public space, the grave was also individual, in that each Jin tomb generally contained only a single man and his wife, while the ancestral temple was dedicated to a lineage. Finally, as Watson aptly notes, "Hall rites emphasize power arrangements as they currently stand, whereas grave rites constitute one of the battlegrounds for disputing those arrangements."[62]

During the Jin, the grave remained the site for the public performance

---

60. Du, *Tongdian*, 103.547b.
61. Rubie S. Watson, "Remembering the Dead: Graves and Politics in Southeastern China," in *Death Ritual in Late Imperial and Modern China*, ed. James L. Watson and Evelyn S. Rawski (Berkeley and Los Angeles: University of California Press, 1988), 204–10.
62. Ibid., 204.

of certain sorts of commemoration for a dead ancestor, who was, by that act, converted into an especially powerful sort of divine benefactor for the clan. In other words, the rituals conducted at the grave that constituted public remembrance were, as in the cases Watson studied, part of the process by which new status and power arrangements were asserted by living descendants.

While our sources do not indicate how widespread graveside observances might have been, the histories do record continuations of Latter Han practice. During the Jin, filial sons continued to express their virtue as Cai Yong had, by setting up huts by the graves of their parents and carrying out daily sacrifice, even beyond prescribed time limits for mourning.[63] Special sacrifices and announcements to the spirits of the dead were also conducted at the gravesite.[64] Another public form of filial display involved the erection of stelae in front of graves to announce the accomplishments of the tomb occupant.[65] Finally, as the Tang-period example given above indicates, *hun*-summoning burials also involved funeral processions to escort the clothing of the deceased to the grave. The order of mourners in such processions and during burial ceremonies would indicate clearly to everyone the status of the descendants. Thus, even though the ancestral tablet was at this time the preferred object of veneration, graves still provided venues for the rehearsal of power and status.

It is likely that those who sought to conduct *hun*-summoning burials were contemplating displays such as these, both to resuscitate the sullied names of Sima Yue and his supporters and to solidify their own positions as rightful heirs.[66] They might, and this is what Sima Rui likely feared most, have come to contemplate contestations of a more violent

---

63. For examples of those known for such acts, see Fang, *Jinshu,* 51.1434–5; 74.1941; 75.1959; 77.2044; 88.2277; and 88.2279.

64. One famous example is the oath made by Wang Xizhi 王羲之 (309–ca. 365) at the grave of his parents (Fang, *Jinshu,* 80.2101). For sacrifices at the gravesite, see *Jinshu,* 67.1790 and 69.1845.

65. For examples, see Fang, *Jinshu,* 51.1434 and 54.1485; Shi Zhicun, *Shuijing zhu bei lu, Shuijing zhu bei lu* (Tianjin: Guji, 1987), 87, 133, 321, and 238. There are stories behind all of the events referenced in this and the preceding two footnotes, but I defer the telling for another book.

66. One of Gongsha Xin's remarks, in comparing the burials of the current age with those of ages past, indicates that the proponents of *hun*-summoning burials were likely planning to stage funerary processions such as those carried out in the Tang. "If," he writes, "we follow regulations regarding the five types of mourning garb, [employ] dragon pennons with redoubled tassels, so that the rite consists of sending off the departed; if the hundred food offerings are arrayed in order, so that the living draw near to push away the departed, and we conduct ritual in accord with emotions; then we are close to the planned procedures of the present age, and the logic of *hun*-summoning is established"; see Du, *Tongdian* 103.547c.

sort.[67] Certainly, the precarious state of Sima Rui's regime invited challenge. This possibility casts a new and interesting light on the claims of the court ritualists that such persons intended to "bury" the *hun* of the dead, for it is now brilliantly clear that it was in fact Sima Rui who would have preferred the emanations of these particular dead generals to be buried and "stored away" 藏 once and for all. The prospect of their storage south of the Yangzi, however, was a different matter.

In this regard, Wu Hong's analysis of Liu Xiu's ritual crisis alerts us to the similar problems faced by Sima Rui. As Albert Dien has noted, Sima Rui "faced the dilemma that the mausolea of the previous Jin rulers were unavailable and so offerings at an ancestral temple were inevitable."[68] Sima Rui set up ancestral temples in Jiankang in 317 as part of his preparation for assuming the throne, but there remained a problem, which he articulated in a proclamation of 320:

> Though I continue the line of the founder, yet I faced north and declared myself vassal to the two emperors Huai [r. 306–11] and Min [r. 313–16]. Now, in the sacrifices at the Imperial Temple, I do not personally hold the goblet to offer it, but order officiants to carry out this rite. This makes me uneasy with regard to the ritual. The ritual precedents should be reconsidered.[69]

The issue that the emperor faced was that he could not personally hold the offerings goblet because he was not the descendant of the two emperors he claimed as predecessors. In this instance, in part through reference to Liu Xiu's solution, the matter was settled without effecting any kingdom-wide change in mortuary ritual. Temple sacrifice was not an ideal solution for Sima Rui, but neither did he possess the status to perform *hun*-summoning burials for his two immediate predecessors, both buried in the north. The unavailability of Sima imperial tombs in the north was to remain a ritual problem throughout the remainder of the dynasty.

Since he could not employ *hun*-summoning to his advantage, Sima Rui opposed the practice. In so doing, he solved at the same time a number of succession disputes within the imperial family, installing his own chosen descendants in each case, and blocked any claimants to the throne arising from among the heirs of Sima Yue.

---

67. Gan Bao's statement that "even the name *hun* burial comes close to being rebellious 幾於逆" seems to indicate that this was indeed on the mind of the ritualists.

68. Albert Dien, Unpublished ms.

69. Fang, *Jinshu*, 19.603–604; Shen Yue, *Songshu* (Beijing: Zhonghua shuju, 1974), 16.449–450.

SPIRITS RECONSIDERED

The ritualist debate we have traced involves intimately the spirit world. As Gan Bao's proposed solution—that those concerned might "go to the place where the [deceased] met with calamity and there undertake rituals for receiving the spirits"—implies, both sides of the debate agreed that the spirits of these violently murdered men needed to be settled. We should not let our confusion over what the medieval Chinese understood *hun* to mean deter us from considering what they clearly thought *hun* might do. In the fratricide and internecine struggles of the Eight Princes' Rebellion and through the fall of the Western Jin, we notice an increase in expressed concern over "wronged *hun*" 冤魂, the unquiet dead. Those who suffered a violent death, burial insufficient to their station, or no burial at all, were capable of taking their grievances to a higher court, the offices of the underworld. Settling their grievances in an appropriate manner could lead to disaster and disease wrought on the living—particularly on the descendants of the wronged spirits, but also on those held responsible for wrongful death and burial.

The unfortunate case of Sima Yu 司馬遹 (d. 300) will here stand for the many who certainly haunted the dreams of both Sima Rui and those others who sought to provide a suitable, if uncanonical, burial for their forebears. Son of the Hui emperor by a concubine and favorite of his imperial grandfather, Sima Yen 司馬炎 (r. 265–90), Yu was designated crown prince in 290. His murder by associates of Empress Jia 賈, consort of the imbecile Sima Zhong 衷, the Hui emperor (r. 291–306), and *de facto* ruler of the Jin until her death in 300, precipitated the Rebellion of the Eight Princes. After the empress's death, the future emperor, Sima Chi 熾 (Huai, r. 306–311), issued a patent of enfeoffment restoring the deceased Sima Yu to his former position as crown prince. This document included the following words:

> How might we repair the brutal pain wrought by the poisoning of this wronged *hun*? I can only act upon the distress and mournful regret that shakes my internal organs. Now I restore [to Sima Yu the title of] imperial Crown Prince posthumously through funerary ritual, returning [his body] for burial in the capital, offering grand pen animals. If his *hun* be numinous, I understand his feelings.[70]

On the day of the reburial, however, there were signs that the "wronged *hun*" had not yet rested. The proceedings were greeted with a massive

70. Fang, *Jinshu*, 53.1462–63.

thunderstorm. This prompted the emperor to issue a further document of mourning, which, in addressing the "wronged *hun*," included these words:

> Your demotion was in fact due to my lack of perspicacity. . . . At your departure, who can restore your bodily form? Of old, Shen Sheng held in the wrong done him and did not lodge a plaint.[71] Now, [the grievances] you bear might be taken as a grudge to the east.[72] Though, distant and departed, you have cognizance, do not cry out in your grief! [73]

That Sima Yu's "wronged *hun*" manifested itself in a rain squall accorded with contemporary belief that, according to the five phases, water was associated with winter and the dead. Thus floods and violent rainstorms were frequently interpreted as signs that ritual service toward the dead had been neglected, resulting in an overflow of resentment among the shades.[74] The perception that certain of the dead were restless, shown by such signs, was almost always conditioned by the manner of their death and by the subsequent treatment of their physical remains. As in the case of Sima Yue, the ritual "solution" to such perceived crises often demanded reburial.

As we shall see in the following chapters, because those who stood to gain or lose by the condition of *hun* in the otherworld were primarily the family members of the deceased, the immediate descendants of Sima Yue and his cronies were intimately concerned that their own "wronged *hun*" be laid to rest. As Gongsha Xin puts it in his description of contemporary mortuary practice, "[Funerals] are a matter of the living putting the deceased at a distance."[75] While it might seem counterintuitive

---

71. The story of Shen Sheng 申生, recounted in both the *Zuo zhuan* (*SSJZS*) and the *Guo yu* (in the *Sibu beiyao*) tells of a crown prince betrayed by a secondary wife of his father who commits suicide rather than act against the perceived wishes of his father. Burton Watson, who recounts the story in his *Early Chinese Literature* (New York: Columbia University Press, 1962), 69–73, calls him a "figure tragically paralyzed by the ideal of filial piety." But, while the story was clearly a monitory one—warning against the common tendency of fathers to favor the sons of living wives and concubines over the elder offspring of deceased wives—Shen Sheng was traditionally regarded as an ideal son. Here Sima Chi urges Sima Yu's shade to take Shen Sheng as a model and still his resentment.

72. As we saw in chapter 1, the administrative seat of the dead was traditionally held to be Mount Tai, in the east. The implication of this line is that Sima Yu could certainly carry his resentment to the courts of the underworld, but that he should refrain from doing so.

73. Fang, *Jinshu* 53.1463.

74. The "Treatise on the Five Phases" of the *Jinshu* (Fang, *Jinshu*, 27.811) explains in detail how failures in imperial sacrifices to the dead, associated with water and the north, abode of the dead, led to rain squalls and floods.

75. Du, *Tongdian*, 103.547c.

that *hun*-summoning could serve as anodyne to restless and dangerous family spirits, in this respect, the court ritualists were quite correct in their assessment: those who sought to perform *hun*-summoning burials, whatever else they hoped to achieve, wished to avoid the dangers caused by missing tombs and thus properly "bury" their dead. Such burials could restore family harmony, repair broken lines of descent, and convert dangerous spirits into ancestors who might aid the claims of their descendants in the halls of power. The proponents of *hun*-summoning rituals thus had much to gain, both in terms of their own livelihood and in terms of their psychological and physical well being, by conducting such burials. Sima Rui, who was also distantly related to some of the dead at issue, would gain more, in both social and psychic terms, by keeping the same dead at a distance.

CONCLUSION

There is little question that the memorials of 318 are externalist arguments. They are marked by genre and occasion as documents meant to position the ritual views of the respective parties with regard to a perceived "tradition." We have seen, however, that arguments like these often place into contestation more than would be indicated by a surface reading. Their most vital concerns are often disguised, repositioned, and forwarded in ingenious ways.

Attending to the precedents cited by the proponents of *hun*-summoning burials, we have learned that the practice was not really novel. We also found that the rite continued in later times to provide suitable burial for those who died violent deaths and whose bodies could not be recovered. Turning then to the cases cited, whose burial in the southern capital of Jiankang was challenged by the emperor through these proceedings, we found that these involved a limited circle of men: Sima Yue and his supporters. Sima Yue and his heirs had a legitimate claim to the throne, so the exclusion of this faction from commemoration in or near the new capital makes certain political sense. That the imperial argument for keeping these particular dead at a distance should be conducted as a ritual debate not only fit the situation, but also protected the emperor from charges of favoritism when he renamed his closer relatives as appropriate successors to Sima Yue and his partisans.

Finally, however, I have suggested that both parties in this debate, though their views on location and manner differed, had an interest in "settling" these potentially dangerous dead. Evidence for this assertion does not arise directly from the documents presented by the debaters. While the memorials and statements collected in 318 do make frequent reference to "settling" 安 the spiritual constituents of the person, this is common in discussions of mortuary ritual. In fact, we would not expect to find mention of "wronged *hun*" in formal discussions of mortuary rites, though the concern can often be detected hovering behind certain ritual procedures and prescriptions. Those proposing *hun*-summoning burial clearly wished to handle their dead in the south, and this could easily lead to the sorts of manipulation—hauntings, apparitions, and possessions—by which ghosts came to work real effects in the world. Those opposing *hun*-summoning burial appear concerned to avoid such unpleasantness. Still, my suggestion that the emperor reacted to the possibility that Sima Yue might come to lead ghostly hordes spreading disease (as did Liu Shao in the Su Shao story) or punish the living with climactic disaster (as his own relative Sima Yu had done) must remain conjecture. Nonetheless, one further bit of circumstantial evidence lends credence to the claim.

Remember that Ms. Pei either ignored the emperor's ban on *hun*-summoning burial or was given an exemption, depending on which source we believe. She buried the *hun* of her husband at Guangling 廣陵, just northeast of the Jin capital in Jiankang [modern Nanjing]. This might not have been coincidental. Guangling was the prior fiefdom of Sima Yu, our "wronged *hun*." Yu had been installed there by his father, the reigning emperor, upon the advice of a fortune-teller who pronounced that the place had the "atmosphere of a Son of Heaven [i.e., emperor]."[76] Guangling would thus have been a highly propitious and politically powerful burial site. Further, all of this happened within living memory of most who participated in the debates of 318. It should not surprise us, then, that within two years Sima Yue's grave at Guangling was destroyed by persons unreported and his "remains" moved to a new grave at a less auspicious site.[77] While we cannot know whether or not the emperor had anything to do with ordering the destruction of Sima Yue's grave, the deed remains testimony to the fact that the dead—and this shade in particular—still mattered.

While I want to avoid making claims concerning what the emperor Sima Rui or those who sought to conduct imperially unauthorized buri-

76. Fang, *Jinshu*, 53.1457.
77. Fang, *Jinshu*, 59.1626. The new grave was at Dantu 丹徒, in present-day Jiangsu Province.

als might *personally* have believed, it seems to me undeniable that, as men of their time and place, they were perfectly capable of maintaining both a sense of awe toward their dead and a desire to manipulate them. While we might today regard these attitudes as incommensurate, we find this same combination of attitudes expressed in the texts and scriptures that are the subjects of the following chapters. Thus it seems to me undeniable that Sima Rui feared the political opportunities that would be available to possible enemies if Sima Yue and the rest were provided with tombs near the capital *and* that part of this fear involved the ways that Sima Yue's heritors might turn their forebear into a powerful, and dangerous, shade in service to their goals.

CHAPTER 3

Questionable Shapes

How the Living Interrogated Their Dead

The worship of the ancestors not only validated status;
it gave access to power.
　—David N. Keightley, "The Making of the Ancestors"

Benedict Anderson has introduced the concept of "imagined communities" to explore the ways in which religions, kingdoms, and nations invent themselves and imagine connectivity across boundaries of space and time.[1] The imagined community we have been exploring is even more nebulous than any human grouping, but the strategies of collectivity prove the same. The medieval Chinese recognized their dead to be insubstantial yet rarely wraithlike (though we know little of the precise imaginings of ancestral practice).[2] They were separated from the solid human realm—when they drank or ate, the sustenance remained; when they wrote, the writing was unrecognizable. And yet the dead belonged to the same kingdoms and families as did the living. Their actions impinged on the human world in definite, uncontrollable, and sometimes catastrophic ways. We have explored the blessings they might bring in the case of Cai Yong. But we have also seen how their rebellions might result in plagues among the living, as reported by Su Shao, and how the dangerous dead might threaten the foundations of the realm in the case of Sima Yue. In

---

1. Benedict Anderson, *Imagined Communities: Reflections on the Origin and Spread of Nationalism* (London: Verso, 1991).
2. Poo Mu-Chou has explored some of the ways in which ghosts were imagined. There were doubtless many more. See his "The Concept of Ghost in Ancient Chinese Religion," in *Religion and Chinese Society: Ancient and Medieval China,* ed. John Lagerwey (Hong Kong: Chinese University of Hong Kong Press and École française d'Extrême-Orient, 2004), 1:173–92.

all of these instances, the voices ascribed to the dead had, at least potentially, actual results among the living and were to be heeded. But that
does not mean that they were never contested.

As we move even more deeply into this imagined community, we shall
attend more closely to the intertextual nature of reports from the afterlife. That is to say, as frightening revelations from the underworld increased in intensity, if not in number, during the fourth century, they
tended more and more to enter into dialogue with one another. Claims
made in one account are explicitly denied in another. With startling rapidity, shades are said to be promoted or demoted, so that reputations
are made and lost in the courts of the dead quite as quickly as in the halls
of the quick. Power struggles among the living sometimes find resolu-
tion beyond the grave, only to be reignited in later accounts. There are,
of course, political and familial stakes involved in this conversation. The
second set of revelations that Tao Hongjing compared with those he found
in the Yang/Xu fragments—the story of Guo Fan 郭翻—allows us to trace
one set of interlocking stories, demonstrating quite nicely how political
instability and interfamilial rivalries might shape tales of the dead and,
in a more speculative vein, how tales of the dead might be deployed to
achieve results in the world of the living.

Guo Fan was in life a recluse whose services were sought out by the
powerful governor Yu Liang 庾亮 (289–340), whom he refused. When
he reappears as a shade to his youngest son, however, he reports that he
now serves in the otherworld under Yu. Like Su Shao, Guo Fan returns
with a series of "where are they now?" reports on the dead, though in
Guo's case the departed are almost entirely men of recent memory.
Through tracing these, we shall see how the bitter rivalry between Yu
Liang and the General Tao Kan 陶侃 (259–334) continued beyond the
grave. Further, thanks to the scholarly thoroughness of Tao Hongjing,
we can compare several tales that served to counter Guo Fan's, evidently
circulated by partisans of Tao Kan or members of his family. Though we
lack precise information on the status or motives of those who channeled
these particular dead men, their stories provide enough detail that we
can form hypotheses, because Guo Fan's revelations portray favorable
postmortem rank for partisans of the Yu clan and unfavorable positions
for partisans of the Huan 桓 and Xie 謝 clans, who were just coming to
power in the 350s when this account was written.

We will want to know more of the sort of person who could with such
ease enter into the counsels of the departed. This leads us to consider another segment of society, religious practitioners, who came to play a role

in such subterranean family dramas. Yang Xi, about whom our records are most complete, will here represent the independent medium, a class of citizen about whom we have only fragmentary information in the received historical record.[3] In the next chapter, I probe aspects of his ministry to the family of his primary patron, Xu Mi. In this chapter, as an introduction to his strategies of engagement, I review the bits of divine revelation that Yang Xi directed toward a friend and political ally of Xu Mi, Chi Yin 郗愔 (313–84). The status of Chi Yin's dead father had been revealed by Guo Fan, but Yang Xi has even more information. In addition to telling Chi Yin of imminent danger emanating from the family grave, Yang has more enticing information to reveal.

Finally, I examine Tao Hongjing's own, very different, strategies and motives in collecting tales of the eminent dead. Writing some one hundred and thirty years after the latest of the revelations upon which he comments, Tao was not involved in the intense family claims that provided their original occasion. The placement of this or that individual in the subterranean bureaucracy seems to have been of no particular moment to him. Instead, Tao is most intent on discerning the regularities of promotion and demotion in the underworld. His primary concern was with the bureaucracy itself rather than with the fates of specific officeholders. I thus trace how Tao attempts to coordinate disparate information on the world of the dead derived from Su Shao, Guo Fan, Yang Xi, and another, more mysterious, rapporteur, Xin Xuanzi 辛玄子. The latter figure, Tao believed, communicated directly with Yang Xi, and yet his reports contradict in almost every detail the information provided by Yang Xi's primary informant on the otherworld, Marquis Xun. Thus we can observe Tao's reactions to these contradictions in his sources. Finally, Tao's scholarly methods are tempered by his credulity with regard to the veracity of all these sources. His struggle to find logic in this disparate mass of data on the underworld is thus invaluable in assessing the new meanings such reports began to take on for Daoists.

---

3. In Yang Xi's case, though, we also know something of his training. Unlike the younger sons of Su Shao and Guo Fan, Yang was a Celestial Master Daoist. See, in particular, Michel Strickmann, *Le Taoïsme du Mao chan: Chronique d'une révélation* (Paris: Collège du France, Institut des Hautes Études Chinoises, 1981); Isabelle Robinet, *La révélation du Shangqing dans l'histoire du taoïsme*, 2 vols., Publications de l'École française d'Extrême-Orient, no. 137 (Paris: École française d'Extrême-Orient, 1984); and Stephen R. Bokenkamp, *Early Daoist Scriptures*, (Berkeley and Los Angeles: University of California Press, 1997), 275–372. Still, Yang Xi's reports on the underworld, as Tao Hongjing shows, are most readily comparable with those of other mediums such as Su Shao and Guo Fan.

GUO FAN

The second story Tao Hongjing compared with the autograph texts he collected in his *Zhen'gao* emanated from the shade Guo Fan 郭翻, byname Changxiang 長翔, whose family home was in Wuchang 武昌.⁴ According to the official Jin history, his father, Cha 察, was the governor of Ancheng 安城⁵ and his uncle, Na 訥, reached the office of regional inspector of Guangzhou. Despite these promising connections, Fan went to some lengths to avoid official service, making a home for himself farther to the south in Linchuan 臨川.⁶ There he lived by hunting and fishing, distinguishing himself by acts of selflessness such as giving up his chariot to a sick person he met by chance when hunting a considerable distance from home.⁷

We know these details of Guo's life because someone, likely a member of the Guo family, composed an "independent tradition," a form of unofficial biography, of Guo Fan, entitled the *Guo Fan biezhuan* 郭翻別傳.⁸ Elements of this work, which seems to have dealt with marvels and further acts of distinctive self-abasement performed by Fan, found their way into encyclopediae and the standard histories. The work seems to have included the story of Guo's ghostly reappearance. It was also the likely source of the only dated incidents in the life of the recluse.⁹

---

4. Wuchang is in modern Echeng 鄂城 County of Hubei Province.

5. The county seat was southeast of present-day Runan 汝南 County in Henan.

6. Linchuan was roughly in the area of modern Linchuan County 臨川縣, Jiangxi Province.

7. Fang Xuanling et al., *Jinshu* (Beijing: Zhonghua shuju, 1974), 94.2446; see also Li Yanshou, *Nanshi* (Beijing: Zhonghua shuju, 1975), 75.1868.

8. This work is cited in Li Fang, *Taiping yulan* (Beijing: Zhonghua, 1960), 555.2513a and 424.1957a. The cited passages match passages found in the biographies of Guo Fan in the *Jinshu* and *Nanshi* (see note 7 above), demonstrating that this biography was the source used by the compilers of the standard histories. I suspect that all of what we know of Guo Fan comes from this source.

9. As in the case of the Su Shao story, I use Li Fang, *Taiping guangji* (Beijing: Zhonghua, 1961), 321.2542–43, as base text. The *Taiping guangji* editors give no source for this account, and I suspect it may have been rearranged. It is a matter of conjecture whether or not the *Guo Fan biezhuan* is the source of this story, but the conjecture seems more likely when we note that Guo lacked the prestige that would have prompted a later author to reconstruct such an account. Further, while he does not use the title *Guo Fan biezhuan*, Tao Hongjing's citations of the tale attest to its antiquity. Tao, using Guo's byname, cites what he calls the "Guo Changxiang *lingyu* 郭長翔靈語," or "Spirit Pronouncements of Guo Changxiang," which may have been a section of the *Guo Fan biezhuan*. In line with his concerns, Tao cites only those sections of the text that recount the postmortem careers of famous individuals. Variants found in the *Zhen'gao* (HY 1010) are given in footnotes to the story. See also Yoshikawa Tadao and Mugitani Kuniō, *Shinkō kenkyū: Yakuchū hen* (Kyoto: Kyōto daigaku jinbun kagaku kenkyūjō, 2000), 578 and 590.

In 335, Guo Fan was called to office, together with another distinguished hermit, Zhai Tang 翟湯, by Yu Liang 庾亮, then one of the most powerful men in the capital. Guo did not respond to the summons. On another occasion, sometime around 340, we are told, Guo was graced with a visit by Liang's younger brother, Yi 翼 (d. 345), with yet another summons to the Yu court. This time, too, Guo refused to serve.

Whatever the truth of these records—and we shall see that the first summons figures prominently in Guo Fan's posthumous reports—they make a certain sort of historical sense. The Yu brothers dominated the political life of the Jin dynasty between 328 and 345 because of their strategic control and military prowess in Wuchang.[10] As a worthy of local renown, Guo Fan was the sort of figure whom they would have wanted to grace their courts. Be that as it may, Guo Fan's posthumous reputation briefly matched that of his living years.

The precise date of Guo Fan's supposed revelations to his youngest son is impossible to pin down. The latest figure Guo mentions is Xie Shang 謝尚, who died in 357.[11] But Guo reports that Xie was deemed unfit for one underworld position and consequently nominated for another, rather than portraying him as having already taken a posthumous office. This could mean that, at the time of these revelations, Xie was still among the living, having scarcely missed being summoned to a netherworld post. Indeed, Shang's fatal illness began in 356, so that we might provisionally accept that year as a possible date for the Guo Fan revelations.

After briefly introducing Guo Fan, the surviving fragments of the *Guo Fan biezhuan* relate his first post-mortem appearance as follows:

> Several days after [Fan] died, his youngest son suddenly was as if he had had a stroke 中惡狀 and no longer recognized those around him. He began to speak in a spirit voice that sounded like the voice of his father. [The possessed youth] knew much of the affairs of the dark world[12] and would respond to whatever questions were addressed to him.

As presented in the *Taiping guangji,* this introduction is followed immediately by responses to questions of the "where are they now?" sort

---

10. Wuchang is on the upper Yangzi River, not far from modern Wuhan. For a fine summary of the Yu brothers' careers, see Richard B. Mather, *Shih-shuo Hsin-yü: A New Account of Tales of the World* (Minneapolis: University of Minnesota Press, 1976), 607–8. See also Charles Holcombe, *In the Shadow of the Han: Literati Thought and Society at the Beginning of the Southern Dynasties* (Honolulu: University of Hawaii Press, 1994), 29–31.

11. See Mather, *Shih-shuo,* 528.

12. Literally, the text reads "generations of the dark" 陰世; that is to say, he knew who occupied the realms of the dead and their successive promotions and demotions.

addressed to Guo Fan through his son. Before dealing with these, however, we should note the more ornamental elements of the account. Like
that of Su Shao, this series of communications contains general responses
to the sorts of questions that were on people's minds because of the perceived changes in the preferences of the dead and the actual social changes
in burial practice. Guo Fan himself, as we know from his unofficial biography, asked for and received an austere burial of the sort that, as we
saw in chapter 1, caused some concern for living descendants.[13] Thus
Guo's testimony on the question of whether or not the dead remember
the living was invaluable.

> Many people asked, "After one dies, does one think of one's descendants?"
> Guo said, "When one has been dead for a long time, one no longer thinks
> of the living. But for those who have just died, like me, personal concerns
> have not yet come to an end. I still think [of my descendants]."

By this account, as with the report of Su Shao, the living could rest assured that even those provided with austere burials, though they had no
lavish tomb residence from which their spirit might easily ascend to the
ancestral temple, did not just float away, but continued to remember—
and to respond to the needs of—their descendants. And, like the Su Shao
revelations, Guo Fan's reports were also delivered to spectators who both
witnessed these events and asked questions of their own. We note several further similarities between the two stories. Both shades speak
through their youngest sons. Both, as ghosts, write horizontally, though
the Guo Fan tale has no shaving of pates and only one further reference
to Buddhist practice or cosmology.

> The youth who was speaking in spirit language asked for paper and a
> brush, since [Fan] wished to write letters to his relatives and old acquain-
> tances. Fan held the brush and ordered the youth to write. The writing
> was horizontal, like that of the Eastern foreigners. When he had completely
> filled a page, he said, "This is ghost writing. No [living] person can read
> it." So he ordered people to hold the paper and orally transmitted his
> letters. When he had finished, the people all said, "Su Xiaoxian (Su Shao)
> composed many things like this."

The editor of the *Taiping guangji* supplies several graphs at the end of
this passage from some other edition of the text, and the syntax remains

---

13. See Li, *Taiping yulan*, 555.7b, citing the *Guo Fan biezhuan*. The passage goes on
to relate that Guo's living will provided that he be buried with only the two-scroll text of
the *Laozi*, "to show that he preserved the Way and its Virtues."

in some disorder. Still, the written transmissions of Guo Fan clearly prompted contemporaries to compare them with those of Su Shao.

Guo Fan did go beyond Su Shao, however, in leaving behind verses from the other world. Though the verses appear to be even more garbled than the final sentences of his account, they bear repetition here in that they respond in at least some fashion to the comparison made above with Su Shao. Fan further bestowed two poems, which read as follows:

> When one's spirits scatter, ascending into autumnal grey 旻蒼,
> One's body, then, suddenly perishes . . .

> I think back on my former aspirations,
> While essence and *hun* [souls] still roam freely.
> I try to calm my heart, but cannot command it;
> There is no avoiding the exigencies of time.
> Tell these inadequate words to all my kin;
> Though I fear they will say my words are demonic.
> There is no consciousness or residence in great oblivion . . .
> Of old, there was Su Shao . . .

> At this his voice faded away and he departed.

These verses are garbled and seem incomplete. It remains here only to point out that, as in the story of Su Shao, there is logical inconsistency. The shade of Guo Fan echoes tropes derived from Buddhism and the contemporary philosophic discourse it informed in describing death as "great oblivion" 大沒 where the dead have neither consciousness 識 nor place of residence 在. But he goes on to describe himself as an underworld official privy to the station and fortunes of his fellows. Again, we should not rush to conclude that Chinese notions of the otherworld were confused. This single reference seems a clear sign that Buddhist metaphor is being employed in what Erik Zürcher has described as an "ornamental" way.[14]

For those who witnessed the event, the heart of Guo Fan's revelations clearly resides not in his poetry but in his reports on the officials of the underworld. These are also portrayed as responses 應 to unnamed interlocutors. We might assume that those who posed questions concerning the fate of specific deceased individuals, if not asking about their own relatives, had some interest in their fates.[15] But the story does not name those who asked questions of Guo Fan.

---

14. Erik Zürcher, "Buddhist Influence on Taoist Scripture," *T'oung-pao* 66 (1980): 86 and 142.

15. This is suggested by the case of Yang Xi, where we do find family members asking about their dead. See the sections on Yang at the conclusion of this chapter.

Because the underworld officers whose stations Guo relates were, at the time of telling, all among the recently deceased, in analyzing them we will spend even more time considering their worldly careers than we did in the case of the Su Shao accounts in an effort to determine the relevance of this information to the living.

We go back, then, to the beginning of the tale, which relates something of Guo Fan's earthly career:

> Formerly, Yu Liang [289–340] had wished to take [Fan] as his Principal
> Territorial Aide 上佐, but Guo Fan would not serve. His family members
> then asked him, "In life, you were renowned for virtue and now, in death,
> you are a spirit. How is it that you now accept an official position?"
> "Originally, I had no ambition for official promotion," Fan responded.
> "When I was summoned by Lord Yu, I was unwilling and thus able to
> escape service. But now [in death] I am shackled, and cannot follow my
> original ambitions. I am intensely grieved at this."
>   Then they asked him what rank Yu had achieved. Fan said, "He has
> been employed by heaven as Supreme General of the Pacification Army
> 撫軍大將軍. At present, he resides east of the Eastern Seas, where he
> commands 100,000[16] spirit soldiers. He has chosen me as his Adjutant
> 司馬.[17]

This exchange gives us ample data for a hypothesis as to why these revelations might have occurred in the first place. In life, Guo Fan had not served his family well. Through his single-minded reclusion and his failure to respond to the summons of Yu Liang, then at the height of his influence, Fan had not opened avenues of advancement for his progeny. In death, we might well imagine, he will be made to do better. This might seem a severely skeptical reading of the evidence, for there could be many factors behind the reappearance of a dead relative. But, as we shall see, the information Guo vouchsafes his son does tend to flatter, through good news about their forebears, certain powerful families over others. These families were all aligned with the Yu clan against others, particularly the Huan 桓 and Xie 謝 clans, who were in the 350s and 360s beginning to usurp the Yu clan's place in the centers of power.[18]

By Guo Fan's account, Yu Liang's posthumous position is an extremely powerful one. "East of the Eastern Seas" refers to the isles of transcen-

---

16. This number appears in *Zhen'gao*, HY 1010, 16.2a4.

17. Tao Hongjing (*Zhen'gao*, HY 1010, 16.2a2–5) abbreviates the initial paragraphs of the story, but relates the words of this paragraph precisely as recorded in Li, *Taiping guangji*, 321.2542, adding only the number of spirit soldiers.

18. See Holcombe, *Shadow of the Han*, 30–33; and Erik Zürcher, *Buddhist Conquest of China*, 2 vols. (Leiden: E. J. Brill, 1959), 1:110–11.

dence, which were believed to float freely in the ocean, frustrating the attempts of the living to discover them by boat. While the number of troops he commands does not seem large, these are immensely power-ful "spirit soldiers." The former recluse, Guo Fan, thus seems to have finally ascended to a position of influence and prominence. To see how the recently deceased members of families allied to and opposing Yu Liang fare in the otherworld, we cite the remaining fragments of Guo's reve-lations in one piece.

Originally, [Yu] wished to have Xie Renzu 謝仁祖 (Shang 尚, 308–57) for an aide, but the Selection Officer 選官 felt that [Xie's] qualifications and prospects were insufficient.[19] Moreover, Supreme Marquis Jiang 蔣大侯 had already selected him to be his commander. Thus, [Yu's] hands were tied. He took Wang Changyu 長豫 (Yue 悅, d. prior to 339) to be his aide.[20] He entrusted Wang with military affairs. Wang thus has an eminent reputation.[21]

Then they asked him the rank of Defender-in-Chief Tao [Kan] 陶侃 (259–334). He responded, "Tao's sufferings are unspeakable. He is just now awaiting banishment for his transgressions. He has not yet received an appointment."[22]

Again, they asked, "What rank is Counselor in Chief Wang [Dao] 王導 (276–339)?" Fan responded, "Lord Wang is now Director of the Imperial Secretariat.[23] This is a fine appointment. He has now much influence and decides thousands of important matters.[24]

19. The *Taiping guangji* is garbled at this point, reading, 本欲取謝仁為祖之選官 (321.2542). I follow *Zhen'gao*, HY 1010, 16.2a4.

20. Tao (*Zhen'gao*, HY 1010, 16.2a6) reports that Wang Yue was Wang Dao's eldest son, who died in his youth. Mather (*Shih-shuo*, 598) relates that Wang Yue 王悅, died be-fore 339, that is, before his father. Prior to his death, Wang Yue held only the rank of Clerk in the Central Secretariat. The *Taiping guangji*, 321.2542, reads as follows: 是以不能 ("Thus he was unable [to make the appointment]"). I have followed *Zhen'gao*, HY 1010, 16.2a5, 是以拘逼 ("Thus he was compelled [to make a different appointment]").

21. The latter three sentences appear in Tao's notes, *Zhen'gao*, HY 1010, 16.2a4–5, and are elided from the *Taiping guangji*.

22. For the latter two sentences, I follow Tao's notes at *Zhen'gao*, HY 1010, 16.2b9. The *Taiping guangji*, 321.2542, emends the final phrase 未得敘用 ("He has not yet re-ceived an appointment") to 過此大得敘用 ("After this, he will be given a great appoint-ment"). The editors note that they have added the two graphs 過此 from another source, and the graph 大 in their source was clearly a mistake for the very similar graph 未.

23. I follow *Zhen'gao*, HY 1010, 16.2a5 for Wang Dao's title. In this case, the under-world title matches that of the sunlit world. On the rank of Director of the Imperial Secre-tariat 尚書令, see Charles O. Hucker, *A Dictionary of Official Titles in Imperial China* (Stanford, CA: Stanford University Press, 1985), 412a. The *Taiping guangji* gives the lesser title 尚書郎, Secretarial Court Gentleman (321.2542), for Wang's postmortem appoint-ment, but, given Guo Fan's remark on the appropriateness of the appointment, the *Zhen'gao* witness is to be preferred.

24. The *Taiping guangji* leaves out the account of Chi Jian, but retains the graph 屈 ("humiliation") from that notice (321.2542). Some redactor has seemingly pasted over the

Fan said, "Lord Chi [Jian] 郗鑑 (269–339) was greatly humiliated with appointment as Managing Clerk of the Gates of Heaven. Formerly, [in life] he was selected to be Regional Inspector and General to Subdue the Four Quarters, at 2,000 bushels [salary]. He was never appointed among the Three Dukes."[25]

According to these revelations, the most favored in the otherworld are Wang Dao, cohort of Yu Liang during his life, and Wang's favorite son, Wang Yue. Those with poor appointments are Xie Shang, Tao Kan, and Chi Jian. We begin our analysis with these latter three.

The most severe judgment reported by Guo Fan is pronounced on Tao Kan, of whom the surviving histories and anecdotal collections uniformly have good things to say. Tao Kan is portrayed in such works as a straightforward warrior and a trustworthy supporter of the royal family who worked his way up from poverty and was, according to many legends about him, favored of the gods.[26]

If we assume the position of a partisan of Yu Liang, however, there is no mystery as to which "transgressions" led to his banishment. Tao strenuously opposed the regency, which was to continue until the heir-apparent reached the age of majority, that Sima Shao 司馬紹 (the Mingdi Emperor, r. 322–25), on his deathbed, granted to Yu Liang. Not only was Tao unhappy with Yu's assumption of power, he even went so far as to spread the rumor that Yu had misrepresented the emperor's wishes. The resulting uncertain situation led, at least indirectly, to the rebellion of Su Jun 蘇峻 (d. 328) in 327. When Su occupied the capital, captured the young emperor, and set himself up as regent in Yu Liang's place, Yu had no re-

---

rift by adding an editorial remark on Wang Dao, creating thereby a somewhat contradictory message: 大屈事, 更萬機. 位雖不及生時而貴勢無異也 ("This is a great humiliation. He now has even more duties. Although his rank does not equal that he held in life, his nobility and power are no different than before"). I follow Tao Hongjing's transcription at *Zhen'gao*, HY 1010, 16.2a5 and 16.9a5–6.

25. Not included in the *Taiping guangji*, this paragraph appears in Tao's notes (*Zhen'gao*, HY 1010, 16.9a5–6). The titles Chi held in life seem to have been greatly abbreviated in Fan's account.

26. See Fang, *Jinshu*, 66.1768–79; Mather, *Shih-shuo*, 575. As an example of the miraculous legends that circulated concerning Tao Kan, see Liu Jingshu 劉敬叔 (fl. early fifth century CE), *Yiyuan* 異苑, in *Shuoku*, ed. Wang Wenru (Taibei: Xinxing shuju, 1963), 5.4a (for his encounter with the transcendent Wang Zijin 王子晉) and 7.2b (for his dream of growing wings and flying to heaven). There also circulated books by the name of *Tao Kan gushi* 陶侃故事 (Old tales of Tao Kan) and *Tao Kan biezhuan* 陶侃別傳 (An unofficial biography of Tao Kan) that tell of wondrous possessions and gifts possessed by Tao. See Li, *Taiping yulan*, 341.1566b; 357.1641a; 708.3157a; 759.3371a; and 760.3375b. On the *Yiyuan*, see Robert Ford Campany, *Strange Writing: Anomaly Accounts in Early Medieval China* (Albany: State University of New York Press, 1996), 78–80.

course but to ask Tao Kan for military aid. Overhearing Tao's remark that "the blame for Su Jun's having started a revolt can be traced to the Yu family. If the Yu brothers were all executed, it still would not be an adequate apology to make to the realm!"[27] Yu almost decided not to make his request, but was pressed by another general to plead for assistance even in the face of this insult.

Two separate accounts of the fateful meeting between Yu Liang and Tao Kan survive in the *Shishuo xinyu,* a book of anecdotes that is our earliest surviving source on the history of the period. In the chapter "Appearance and Behavior," we read that "Yu's manner and bearing had the aspect of a god, and the moment Tao saw him he reversed his viewpoint, and they talked and laughed the whole day. Love and respect had come on him all at once."[28] But in the chapter "Guile and Chicanery" we read that Yu first prostrated himself before his adversary, leading Tao to remark "For what reason is Yu Yuangui [= Liang] prostrating himself before Tao Shiheng [= Kan]?" Then, "when Yu had finished, he made his way down to the lowest seat. Again Tao himself demanded that Yu come up and sit with him. After he was seated, Yu finally confessed his faults and blamed himself and made his profound apologies. Quite unconsciously Tao found himself becoming generous and forgiving."[29]

The modern scholar, Qian Nanxiu, emphasizes this latter portrayal to prove that the Yu Liang of the former account was a fraud as well. But while later historians, in their pursuit of historical "facts," have tended to conflate the two, these are clearly incompatible accounts of what happened that day. One could not, in those days or in our own, emanate a "manner and bearing [that] had the aspect of a god" by prostrating oneself and then taking the lowest seat in the hall. Rather than presenting a unified view, the two accounts seem more likely to demonstrate contemporaries' conflicting views of the characters of the two men. Yu Liang was the scion of a northern émigré family whose daughters were considered suitable mates for the emperor. He was well-bred, highly literate, and adept at the currently popular mode of philosophical repartee based on the *Zhuangzi* and the *Laozi.*[30] His "god-like bearing" emanated from this mastery of current modes of refined discourse and bearing. Tao Kan was a southerner of poor family background and a mil-

27. Mather, *Shih-shuo,* 313.
28. Ibid., 313.
29. Ibid., 444.
30. See Fang, *Jinshu,* 73.1915–24; and Xu Song, *Jiankang shilu,* ed. Zhang Chenshi (Beijing: Zhonghua, 1986), 194.

itary man. Decisive and direct, he discouraged his subordinates from meaningless chatter concerning the mysteries of existence, precisely the sort of discourse in which Yu Liang excelled.[31]

Opposition between these two character-types, as Richard Mather points out, dominates the accounts of the *Shishuo xinyu* and hence our view of this period. Thus the first account of their confrontation gives the effortless and wordless victory to the northern aristocrat Yu Liang, member of the faction of "naturalness," whose members were "inclined toward Daoism in their philosophy, unconventionality in their morals, and non-engagement in their politics." The second account, with its graphic description of how the lofty Yu was made to approach his opponent with the deference of the ritually punctilious, gives the pyrrhic victory to Tao, the southern partisan of "Confucian tradition[s] . . . conventionality in morals, and a definite commitment to public life."[32]

But does the same opposition inform Guo Fan's revelations as well? Apparently not. First, Yu Liang takes a role after death, that of general, that he was less than successful at fulfilling during his life. In short, the Guo Fan revelations imagine a different, more martial and politically engaged, Yu Liang than we find in the first *Shishuo* anecdote. (Of course, like Guo Fan, Yu may have found that the living persona he had created was denied him in the afterlife.) Second, and perhaps most tellingly, two other figures whose postmortem destinies are reported to have been less than ideal—Chi Jian and Xie Shang—were both of northern stock and, particularly in Xie's case, involved to some extent in the effete pursuits of high culture. They are, on the other hand, representatives of families that were becoming especially prominent just when Guo Fan appeared to his youngest son. Third, though less decisive, in that by the second half of the fourth century this could not be a clear indicator of which social style he preferred, Guo Fan was himself a southerner.

It seems clear, then, that what we have here is not a replay of the Yu Liang-Tao Kan confrontation as contemporary literati authors portrayed it, but—and this is much more valuable—an expression of realpolitik. Put differently, the descendant who animated the ghost of Guo Fan seems concerned not with defending or destroying a literati ideal but with real-life power arrangements (and possibly interesting a patron?). Whether the actual confrontation between Yu Liang and Tao Kan was a refined encounter decided almost wordlessly, as would occur in the lit-

31. See Fang, *Jinshu*, 66.1774 and Xu, *Jiankang shilu*, 185.
32. Mather, *Shih-shuo*, xvii.

erary salons of the day, or a ritualized encounter between a man of morals and a pretender, Tao's transgressions—his slander of Yu Liang and opposition to Yu's regency—were not thereby erased. In fact, the result of their meeting was not even in life a permanent rapprochement. Tao went on to support Yu's resumption of power, but Yu continued to distrust the man who had aided him, even to the extent of executing one of Tao's sons after Tao's death.[33]

While we have no evidence on how early it circulated, there was another tale indicating that the enmity between the two continued after Tao Kan's death. Tao Hongjing ends his brief biographical notice of Yu Liang with the remark that "[w]hen [Yu Liang] had not yet become ill, he saw Tao Kan [who had died earlier] riding a chariot. Others did not see Tao. [Tao] drew near and cursed at him. At this, [Yu] became ill and died."[34]

Whether he was aware of the tale or not, Guo Fan's youngest son tells of a different fate for Tao Kan. While he may be used in an underworld office later, he now suffers unspeakable torment and is about to be banished. Chi Jian, who was "greatly humiliated" with his post in the underworld, had been a comrade-in-arms of Tao in quelling the rebellion of Su Jun.

We cannot, by reference to events surrounding the Su Jun rebellion, account for the similarly low ranking of Xie Shang, whom the underworld Selection Officer passed over. Indeed, Xie won the favor of Wang Dao through his musical talents and thus at one time would have belonged to the Yu Liang faction. Perhaps this is the reason Yu Liang was depicted as having tried to appoint Xie.

Significantly, though, toward the end of his life, Xie Shang held a prominent military position as General for the Pacification of the West and was stationed in Wuchang, Guo Fan's family home. At the time Guo's revelations were recorded, Huan Wen dominated court politics.[35] Huan also rose to power in Wuchang, where he replaced Yu Liang's brother, Yu Yi 庾翼 (d. 345), in the same post as General for the Pacification of the West.[36] Both the Chi and the Xie families were active and well-rewarded

33. Fang, *Jinshu*, 66.1780–81.

34. *Zhen'gao*, HY 1010, 16.2a2.

35. See Miyakawa Hisayuki, *Rikuchō shi kenkyū: Seiji, shakai hen* (Tokyo: Nihon Gakujutsu Shinkōkai, 1956), 110–19; Zhou Yiliang, *Wei Jin Nanbei chao shi zhaji* (Beijing: Zhonghua, 1985), 100–107; Holcombe, *Shadow of the Han*, 30–32; and Mather, *Shih-shuo*, 536–37.

36. On Yu Yi, see Fang, *Jinshu* 43.1931–35; Xu, *Jiankang shilu*, 212; and Mather, *Shih-shuo*, 607–8.

members of the Huan faction. Given that (1) the height of Huan's re-gency occurred just as the Guo Fan revelations were taking place, (2) his power-base was Wuchang, and (3) such disappointing underworld posi-tions go to members of prominent families that supported Huan, it is tempting to conclude that these current events also played a decisive role in shaping the narrative. Since we have no further information on the precise political affiliations of the Guo family itself, we must leave this conclusion, like much else in my reconstruction of Guo Fan's account, as conjecture.

Those listed in the Guo Fan revelations as holding lofty positions in the otherworld, on the other hand, were in life all comrades of Yu Liang. Wang Dao played a key role in establishing Jin rule in Jiangnan and was espe-cially noted for including likely members of the southern gentry in gov-ernment. He was also given joint power with Yu Liang by the Emperor Sima Shao from his deathbed.[37] While Wang Yue never attained a posi-tion of prominence in administration, he was Dao's eldest and most fa-vored son.[38] Guo Fan's news concerning Wang Yue may, in fact, have been constructed to counter another legend concerning Yue's death. This leg-end also features the appearance of Supreme Marquis Jiang, Jiang Ziwen 蔣子文, the one Han-period figure to appear in the revelations of Guo Fan.

> When [Wang Yue] became seriously ill, [his father Wang] Dao, out of concern for him, came to where he was. He was sitting on the northern side of the bed platform and had not eaten for many days, when suddenly he saw a man, who appeared very vigorous, dressed in armor and carrying a sword. When Wang asked him who he was, he replied, "I am Marquis Jiang. Your son is not well and I have come to beg for his life. Do not concern yourself further." Wang's face moved in joy and he immediately requested food. He consumed several *sheng,* but none of his attendants knew why. After [Wang and Jiang] had eaten, Wang's face again became grief-stricken. [This occurred because Marquis Jiang had] said to Wang, "The Vice Director's life-span has come to an end. I was unable to save him!" Once [Jiang] had finished speaking, he could no longer be seen.[39]

If this story, as seems likely, was in circulation when Guo Fan appeared to his son, then Guo Fan provided not only confirmation of Jiang Zi-

---

37. See Fang, *Jinshu,* 65.1745-54; Xu, *Jiankang shilu,* 190; and Mather, *Shih-shuo,* 595.

38. Fang, *Jinshu,* 65.1754-55; and Mather, *Shih-shuo,* 598.

39. This story appears in the *Youming lu* 幽明籙 (Records of the hidden and the vis-ible worlds), attributed to Liu Yiqing 劉義慶 (403-444; see Campany, *Strange Writing,* 75-77). It is cited in the *Taiping guangji,* 293.2330, and in Daoshi, *Fayuan zhulin,* T 2122, 53:989a.

wen's attempted intervention in the life of the Wang family, but also a measure of consolation for them as well. While Wang Yue was not Yu Liang's first choice for the office he now holds, he is doing very well. In death he serves not the local deity who once tried to intervene for him, but Yu Liang, whose administrative seat is on the eastern isles of the blessed.

The role played by Jiang Ziwen in Guo Fan's revelations thus proves to be an interesting one. He is portrayed as an underworld lord of status. In the tale of Wang Yue's death we have just examined, Jiang Ziwen is shown to have power, although not ultimate authority, in matters of divine summons.

Jiang Ziwen was, in fact, a prominent spirit who was held to reside within Mount Zhong 鍾山 (also known after him as Mount Jiang 蔣山), some five kilometers to the east of the Jin capital, Jiankang. Gan Bao, in his *Soushen ji*, records that Jiang was originally a district commander during the Latter Han who was murdered by bandits he had pursued to Mount Zhong.[40] As often was the case in China, violent death led to his becoming a god. His cult began, Gan Bao writes, early in the Wu period (222–80), when he prevailed upon the emperor to build a shrine for him by afflicting the region with a series of plagues. The emperor granted Jiang the title of Marquis, which remained in effect until the Liu-Song dynasty (420–79) during which, after an initial attempt to stamp out the cult failed, Jiang received a series of increasingly exalted titles.[41] Jiang's highest rank came during the Chen dynasty (557–89), when he was given the title of Thearch" 帝, Supreme Lord of Heaven. All of these dynasties were southern and had Jiankang, hard by Mount Zhong, as their capital.[42]

Nothing, I think, better exemplifies the traditional porousness of boundaries between the spirit and human worlds than this fairly commonplace story of a god who threatens and cajoles humans to do homage to him and of humans who confidently reward him by granting him ever higher celestial positions. But the fact that gods could be manipulated just like ancestors meant that they, too, were fully politicized. When the Jin dynasty first came south in 317, the god Jiang Ziwen was under the control of southern shamans who had to be persuaded to accept the new rulers and who, since persuasion came in the form of patronage, easily

40. Gan Bao, *Soushen ji* (Beijing: Zhonghua shuju, 1979), 57–58.
41. Shen Yue, *Songshu* (Beijing: Zhonghua shuju, 1974), 17.488.
42. On the history of the cult of Jiang Ziwen, see Lin Fu-shih, "The Cult of Jiang Ziwen in Medieval China," *Cahiers d'Extrême-Asie* 10 (1998): 357–75.

fell under the sway of political factionalism. We find this process still underway at the time of Su Jun's rebellion in 327–28. According to an early Jin history,

> When Su Jun set up camp in front of Mount Zhong [prior to attacking the capital], he entreated the god of the mountain, who permitted [himself to appear] and be painted with red sidelocks, purple-footed steeds, a cyan canopy, and a chariot with vermilion streamers.[43] Later, when Chi Jian came to defend [the capital], he also stopped to entreat the god, who said to him, "Both humans and gods are enraged that Su Jun has rebelled. It is appropriate that you should join with me, Jiang Ziwen, in eradicating him. Though Su Jun has also entreated me, how could I help him to do evil? Now I will give you the written memorial [that he presented to me]. Once you have captured him, show this memorial to him."[44]

Both Su Jun and Chi Jian, the man later "greatly humiliated" by his postmortem appointment as Managing Clerk of the Gates of Heaven, were northerners, yet both sought the aid of the god Jiang Ziwen in preparation for battle.

Given the status of Jiang Ziwen's cult among both southerners and northerners, the fact that Guo Fan reports Xie Shang to have been chosen as his commander leads to no firm conclusion beyond the obvious: a local god, however influential, could not match the influence of one whose home was situated in the eastern seas, where Yu Liang now found himself. That Yu's Selection Officer had found Xie wanting even before news came of his alternate appointment also indicates that Xie's prospects in the underworld were not good, even before he found himself bound in fealty to a southern regional deity.

The Guo Fan tale shows us how worldly conflicts were relocated and continued beyond the grave. With Tao Kan's postmortem "banishment," one of the most controversial confrontations of the age leads to what looks very much like the underworld lawsuit that played such a prominent role in the revelations of Yang Xi that we examine in the succeeding sections of this chapter. But supporters of Yu Liang, as we have seen, were not the only ones to carry their well-known dispute to the courts of the afterlife. The anecdote Tao Hongjing cites that tells of Tao arriving in a chariot to bring about Yu's death was clearly the report of someone who supported Tao Kan's faction and wished to present him as a

---

43. The text has *zhu luoche* 朱絡車, "vermilion silk-spinning machine," which cannot be correct. Obviously, some sort of chariot is meant.

44. Xu, *Jiankang shilu*, 174, citing the lost *Jinshu ji* 晉書紀.

powerful shade. Yet another tale, drawn from an "independent record" detailing the life of Tao Kan, mentions an underworld lawsuit directly:

> Shortly after Lord Tao [Kan] 陶公 died, he sent someone who had formerly died in combat to pass on his instructions 遣先奮死傳教 to his son. His instructions said, "The lord entrusts you to discuss the following matter directly with Lord Yu [Liang]. The matters of heaven are just now beginning to be adjudicated. I wanted you to know of this." At this time, Yu Liang was still alive. Three or four years after this incident, he died.[45]

This report, granted Tao's son, implies that Tao Kan has prevailed upon the underworld authorities to bring charges in the underworld against Yu Liang. The implication is that, after the charges were verified—a matter that took three or four years—Yu Liang was brought into the underworld to answer to them. Guo Fan's report provides a counter-revelation: according to him, the otherworldly adjudication indeed occurred, but in Yu Liang's favor.

We might see a number of stories as participating in the bitter factional disputes of this period, but our reconstruction of their messages and of what was at stake must remain conjectural. No medieval Chinese historian would forthrightly record the results achieved by such reports from beyond the grave, for to do so would endorse a highly unstable and easily contested strategy. We turn now to revelations for which we have, at least in part, evidence that we have so far lacked of the direct social results of intercourse with the dead.

PROFESSIONAL INTERVENTION: YANG XI AS MEDIUM

So far, we have considered only one array of motives for producing revelations concerning the fates of those in the underworld—familial concerns. Su Shao's request for reburial would have raised the status of his living descendants and allied his family, in this world and the next, with the Jin ruling house. While the goals of Guo Fan's son are less clear, it seems highly likely that, in bearing good news for some families and bad news for others, he sought to ally himself with the Yu family and against those surrounding the powerful regent Huan Wen. Both revelations contain, besides news of postmortem promotions and demotions, reassuring statements for the immediate family that their powerful dead will "remember" them and continue to work on their behalf from their new stations

---

45. *Zhen'gao,* HY 1010, 16.2b10; Yoshikawa and Mugitani, *Shinkō,* 574.

in the otherworld. In the case of the emperor Sima Rui, we saw the inverse of this concern—an attempt to keep the dangerous family dead at a distance so that descendants could not manipulate their prestige in these ways.

Along the way, we have begun to gauge the extent to which ancestors were now portrayed as sources of calamity, death, or illness as frequently as they were regarded as sources of familial blessing. The Guo Fan revelation alerts us to the fact that, beyond promotions and demotions in the underworld or enlistment in the rebellious hordes of disease-bringers, the dead might also be subject to otherworldly lawsuits brought by wronged shades against the deceased for deeds committed in the realm of sunlight. What could family members do about this threat, which, by the laws of corporate family responsibility, threatened equally the living? They might rely upon the mediumistic gifts of family members to interrogate their dead, but as we saw in the reports on Yu Liang and Tao Kan, different mediums might present different findings. Beyond that, ritual remedies available to the family itself seem to have been slight. Some buried documents with their dead, absolving the family of all entanglements arising from the grave. Others, like the relatives of the murdered Crown Prince Sima Yu that we examined briefly in chapter 2, might conduct reburial, renaming, and renewed offerings to placate spirits known to be threatening.

The mediums we have encountered so far are sons of the deceased, so it is no wonder that the conversations with the dead have been so unidirectional. With Yang Xi we need to consider the role of the professional medium. For the Daoist with ritual services to offer, the news that an ancestor had failed to attain a rank in the underworld or was somehow involved in messy litigation might be turned into a source of income through offers of ritual remedy. Yang Xi, whose revelations form the primary materials of the *Declarations of the Perfected (Zhen'gao)*, served the Xu family in just such a way. Yang was not simply gifted with the ability to interrogate the dead. He could also intervene in their world through techniques that higher deities had made available to him. This was how he earned his living.

I am not suggesting that Yang was the first Celestial Master adherent to undertake communication with the dead. His intervention into the family affairs of his patrons remains, however, the most fully documented.[46]

---

46. Following a suggestion originally made by Hu Shi, I have speculated (*Early Daoist Scriptures*, 150–51) that the "Commands and Admonitions for Families of the Great Dao,"

We make full use of some of this documentation in chapter 4. The remarkable insight we are able to gain into Yang's practice is due to the scholarly efforts of Tao Hongjing, whose own understanding of the revelations we have been tracing we examine below. First, we must briefly survey the means by which a medium from outside of the family could intervene in what were normally tightly guarded family affairs.

Nothing is known concerning Yang Xi beyond the documents collected by Tao Hongjing. He was born in 330, and the date of his death is unknown. He was a Celestial Master Daoist and began receiving scriptures at the age of eighteen. He seems to have been of obscure lineage or at least did not regard his family background as worth recording.[47] This makes his first appearance on the historical stage all the more remarkable. In 361, Sima Yu 司馬昱, the future Jianwen emperor (r. 371–72), consulted Yang on the matter of his lack of an heir. Bringing the question to the Perfected, the divine beings who spoke through him, Yang predicted, correctly, that Sima Yu would father two sons and provided him with simple ritual instructions for obtaining this end.[48] The communications that Yang received and passed on to Sima Yu on that occasion survive in the *Declarations of the Perfected*, but the text does not relate how Yang came to Sima Yu's attention or what he gained thereby.

Fuller documentation on Yang Xi's activities begins one or two years after this incident, when we find Yang employed by Xu Mi 許謐 (303–73), a member of a southern family and a minor official in the Jin court.[49] We explore what was likely to have been Yang's earliest involvement with the Xu family in chapter 4. To learn something of his methods, though, we can look briefly at the revelations he directed Xu Mi to pass to another, even more powerful, official of the Jin court, Chi Yin 郗愔 (313–84).

Chi Yin was the scion of a northern, elite family that had emigrated south with the remnants of the Jin aristocracy in 318. His influential father, Chi Jian, we have already met as the "greatly humiliated" Manag-

a Celestial Master circular dated 255 CE, was written by a medium in the voice of the third Celestial Master, Zhang Lu. For another indication of Celestial Master channeling of the dead, see Terry F. Kleeman, *Great Perfection: Religion and Ethnicity in a Chinese Millennial Kingdom* (Honolulu: University of Hawaii Press, 1998), 78, n. 65.

47. For what can be known, see Tao Hongjing's brief biography of Yang Xi in the *Zhen'gao* (HY 1010, 20.11a10–12a8); and Strickmann, *Le Taoïsme du Mao Chan*, 85–87.

48. See Zhong Laiyin, *Changsheng busi de tanqiu: Daojing Zhen'gao zhi mi* (Shanghai: Wenhui, 1992), 51–56; see also *Zhen'gao*, HY 1010, 8.9b6–10a10.

49. See Strickmann, *Le Taoïsme du Mao chan*; and "The Mao-shan Revelations: Taoism and the Aristocracy," *T'oung-pao* 63 (1977): 1–63.

ing Clerk of the Gates of Heaven in Guo Fan's revelations. An initiate
into Celestial Master Daoism, Yin spent periods in reclusion, but also
managed to achieve high office. During the year 365, while Yang Xi was
passing information to him concerning his own fate and that of his ancestors, Yin was disengaged from worldly affairs, though he held the tit-
ular office of governor of Linhai 臨海 Prefecture (in the southwestern
portion of modern Zhejiang Province). The cause of Yin's lack of interest in governmental affairs during this period, we are told, was the recent disgrace and subsequent death of his younger brother, who had dis-
astrously failed in a military campaign due to illness.[50] Chi Yin is
reported to have mourned excessively at the death of his brother, as indeed he had at the death of his father.

Whatever Chi Yin's mental state when he first encountered Yang Xi,
Yang's approach to him was, as we shall see, the same as the one he employed with Xu Mi: he first reported on the postmortem fate of Chi Yin's
father, Chi Jian 郗鑑 (269–339). Yang's own spirit informant on the affairs of Fengdu, Marquis Xun 荀候, improved on Guo Fan's news that
Chi Jian had received a low postmortem posting. Guo Fan had reported
that "Lord Chi [Jian] has been greatly humiliated with appointment as
Managing Clerk of the Gates of Heaven. Formerly, [in life] he was selected
to be Regional Inspector and General to Subdue the Four Quarters, at
2,000 bushels." But Marquis Xun reported that Chi Jian had been demoted from even that post and that "Zhou Fu 周撫 (d. 365) has been employed as Neighborhood Chief of the Southern Gate to replace Chi Jian."[51]

We have no account of how this information on his father was first
passed on to Chi Yin, but it was undoubtedly Xu Mi who did so. Our
evidence is that in the eighth month of 363, one of the Perfected who
regularly appeared to Yang presented the following message in answer
to a question asked by Xu Mi with the instruction that Chi Yin be informed of it:

50. Mather, *Shih-shuo,* 510; Fang, *Jinshu* 67.1802.
51. *Zhen'gao,* HY 1010, 15.6b9; Yoshikawa and Mugitani, *Shinkō,* 547. The Japanese
translation team follows a variant in the Yu Anqi   安期 edition of the *Daozang* stating
that Fu was the son of Zhou Fang 周魴 (byname Ziyu 子魚) of the Three Kingdoms period (see Yoshikawa and Mugitani, *Shinkō,* 549, n. 32). Instead, the Ming edition of the
canon has the correct name. Zhou Fu's father was Zhou Fang 周訪 (byname Shida 士達;
260–320); see Fang, *Jinshu,* 58.1582. The date given for Fu's death in this history accords
with that given by Tao. Zhou Fu ended his days as governor of Yi Province (western Sichuan
Province) after helping Huan Wen in the campaign that ended the Cheng-Han dynasty. See
Kleeman, *Great Perfection,* 106–7; 201ff. Given that this information was revealed while
Zhou Fu was still alive, it is likely that the news was meant for Fu or his family members.

Chi Yin's[52] father killed several hundreds of innocent persons, seizing their property and treasures. The investigations turned up very serious [charges]. The aggrieved came endlessly to bring their complaints. The celestial officers 天曹 long ago announced punishment. According to the law, Yin's family should all be eradicated. Since Yin's cultivation of virtue has been estimable, he alone has been allowed to escape. But how can his children and grandchildren remain healthy? Yin should be able to maintain the years allotted him by heaven, but he is still far from the way of transcendence.[53]

Here we see that Chi Jian's "great humiliation" occurred because aggrieved shades had successfully brought postmortem lawsuits against him for crimes he had committed during life. By laws of familial implication that operated in the world of the living as well, all members of the family should suffer death as recompense for these deeds. And, to make matters terrifyingly immediate, Marquis Xun goes on to report the names of some of the "aggrieved" and their particular charges.[54]

The juridical mechanism for handling such matters was the Three Offices of Heaven, Earth, and Water that had played a role in Celestial Master Daoism as the bureaus that kept records of the deeds of all humans. By the second half of the fourth century, we see the same record-keepers rendering decisions and meting out punishment in a fashion identical to that of earthly magistrates. The "earth prisons" became a place much like the "prisons" of the world, where district magistrates might confine, torture, and interrogate wrongdoers. When this happened, the distraught dead might barter the fate of their living descendants in exchange for their own.

As the evidence presented in chapter 4 makes clear, the danger of this sort of bartering with the underworld lords might become particularly acute when women found themselves implicated in the misdeeds of their conjugal families. Such a threat seems to have fallen on Chi Yin as well,

---

52. The Perfected use an abbreviation of Chi Yin's byname, Fanghui 方回. Such intimacy, as we will see in the next chapter, is typical of these spirit communications.

53. *Zhen'gao*, HY 1010, 8.5b–6a; see also Yoshikawa and Mugitani, *Shinkō*, 281. Strickmann was of the opinion that this message was never delivered to Chi Yin; see his *Chinese Magical Medicine* (Stanford, CA: Stanford University Press, 2002), 18–19. While they are all marked as "given in answer to questions from Senior Officer Xu [Mi]," subsequent communications on the subject of Chi Jian and the Chi ancestors make it nearly certain that Chi Yin was told of the dangers to his family posed by his father's subterranean trials. Had Chi Yin not expressed interest, the Perfected would hardly have spent so much time discussing Chi Yin's family and the advantages he might gain by following Yang Xi's proffered Way.

54. *Zhen'gao*, HY 1010, 8.8a2–4; Yoshikawa and Mugitani, *Shinkō*, 286.

since Yang Xi later reported in a letter that Chi Yin's mother "has not yet been assigned and seeks members of the family to stand in for her."[55]

Yang Xi's knowledge of underworld affairs is thus precise and immediate. He is able to "overhear" the conversations of spirits regarding the fate of his client's father and seems to know in detail the progress of the case. His apparent knowledge of Chi Yin's own deeds and family background is equally impressive. He relates specific misdeeds that Yin has committed and lists ancestors whose past deeds might either help or harm his client's fate.[56] As Strickmann writes of these blandishments, "From all these cases we can see that communication with the Daoist hierarchy in time of crisis inevitably meant learning about things in one's family background that one might well prefer not to know. To ask a Daoist priest to diagnose and treat an illness was to invite a general exhumation of all skeletons in the family closet."[57]

As Strickmann goes on to relate, however, the inducements to prospective clients offered by Daoists such as Yang Xi were not limited to diagnosis, but included promised cures as well. We have already seen in the first passage explicitly addressed that Chi Yin's "cultivation of virtue has been estimable, and he alone has been allowed to escape [implication in his father's crimes]." Further enticements were soon forthcoming. The Perfected passed on an alluring verse, urging Chi Yin to maintain equanimity in the face of the various threats and to undertake meditation practice. They assess his chances for obtaining a celestial posting, thus at death bypassing Fengdu altogether. Even more important, they direct that one of the biographies of the Perfected, a work replete with detailed accounts of various Shangqing practices, be given to Chi Yin and promise him his own celestial mate to oversee his practice if he will but undertake it.[58] In this final instance, Chi Yin is referred to as Xu Mi's "fellow student."

55. *Zhen'gao*, HY 1010, 8.8a6–8; Yoshikawa and Mugitani, *Shinkō*, 286.
56. *Zhen'gao*, HY 1010, 8.7a6–7b10; Yoshikawa and Mugitani, *Shinkō*, 286. While the names of these ancestors are unknown to history, they must have meant something to Chi Yin.
57. Strickmann, *Chinese Magical Medicine*, 20.
58. For the Perfected's suggestion that the *Biography of Lord Pei* be shown to Chi Yin, see *Zhen'gao*, HY 1010, 2.18b. Tao Hongjing, in his note to this passage, suggests that the reason the Perfected believed the *Biography* suitable for Yin was that "it contains [methods of] repentance for transgressions and [accounts of] masters who passed through the seven [trials]." Tao refers here obliquely to the troubles involving Chi Yin's ancestors that we have outlined. The extant copy of this biography is collected in HY 1026, chap. 105. For an analysis of the text, see Robinet, *La révélation*, 2:375–83. For the mention of a celestial mate in a fragment of a revelation to be shared with Chi Yin, see *Zhen'gao*, HY 1010, 3.6b.

The response the Perfected expect from Chi Yin is that he should "keep his emotions free of further worries."[59] Daoist equanimity in the face of familial illness and sepulchral threat might be extremely hard to come by, but what Yin stands to gain is immense. This message was presented poetically by the goddess Wei Huacun 魏華存 on the very day that Yin was told of his grandfather's fate:

> Calm and focused, with bodily form serene,
> One deeply communicates with the wondrous numina.
> One's spirits reaching the doubly remote
> Resting in perfection and managing one's life-forces.
> Grand Mystery establishes tablets,[60]
> Grand Simplicity registers your name.[61]
> The Golden Court glows within,
> Jade Flower glistens without.[62]
> In a vermilion chaise you gallop to the four quarters,
> Whistling of your lifespan, amassing your essences.
> Driving your dragons toward the Mystic Continent,
> Flying amongst clouds, floating with the obscure.
>
> In this way you will certainly befriend the Dukes of the Idle Towers[63]
>   above and inspect Grand Clarity below.[64]

We today risk missing the exotic allure of such verses. I have glossed some of the more obvious terms from Yang Xi's occult lexicon in the notes, but to Chi Yin, they would have seemed as incomprehensible as they likely do in translation to the modern reader unfamiliar with the poetic language of Daoism. The awe-inspiring prospect of projecting the protective spirits of his body to a rich "Golden Court," while a "Jade Flower,"

---

59. *Zhen'gao*, HY 1010, 8.7a5–6.

60. "Grand Mystery" refers to the "Mystic Metropolis 玄都," sometimes imagined to be atop Mount Kunlun in the far western reaches of the world, but at any rate a celestial capital where registers of life and death are maintained; see Bokenkamp, *Early Daoist Scriptures*, 215, 426.

61. The term "Grand Simplicity" here likely refers to the "Three Ladies of Simplicity 三素元君," mothers of three male deities residing in the palaces of the dead who are responsible for communicating with the gods of heaven and maintaining the registers of life. See Isabelle Robinet, *Taoist Meditation: The Mao-Shan Tradition of Great Purity*, trans. Julian F. Pas and Norman J. Girardot (Albany: State University of New York Press, 1993), 128–29, 143–47.

62. "Golden Court" and "Jade Flower" seem to be the names of structures in the Shangqing heavens, but none of Yang's poems that mention these landmarks are precise as to their nature or location. Such mysteries, of course, constitute a good part of the attraction of Yang's writing.

63. This seems to be the only time this term appears in the *Zhen'gao*. It is likely a generic reference to those Perfected who live beyond Grand Clarity in the heaven of Upper Clarity.

64. *Zhen'gao*, HY 1010, 8.6a1–6; Yoshikawa and Mugitani, *Shinkō*, 284.

at once delicate and durable, protects them, and all the while roaming freely beyond the clouds to the ends of space to commune with impossibly august celestial beings, must have seemed to Chi vastly preferable to the familial tangles in which he had newly discovered himself.

Viewed from the standpoint of traditional Chinese ancestral practice, Yang Xi's proposed response to Chi Yin's ancestral threat represents a radical break. Here we find no trace of memory or commemoration; no anxiety as to whether or not the dead will remember the living. Instead, Yang reports in dizzying detail the family entanglements that have brought illness and death to the Chi family. The escape he offers Chi Yin is precisely that—an escape from the family into the remote realms of the highest heavens, where he will consort with beings untroubled by human concerns.

There is, as I have said, sufficient evidence to indicate that Yang was not the first to propose such a radical solution, which, in Celestial Master and Shangqing circles, had no relation to Buddhist calls to "leave the family" as a monk or a nun. What is striking in Yang's practice, though, is the specificity of the postmortem threats that he was able to discern surrounding Chi Yin. We are here far from the more formulaic prognoses of Daoist ritual manuals, such as the one studied by Peter Nickerson.[65] The manuals' formulas, meant as templates to be applied in particular cases, list several possible causes for supplicants' maladies, cast in the form "perhaps it is A, . . . perhaps it is B." Yang Xi claimed, as other Daoists who employed these manuals in particular cases undoubtedly did, to know precisely the hidden causes underlying the troubles facing Chi Yin. In this respect alone, his revelations are comparable to those of Su Shao and Guo Fan. And we know that the records of all three were compared by Tao Hongjing. We turn now to an analysis of Tao Hongjing's reception of these diverse revelations.

THE "MYSTERIOUS MASTER" AND TAO HONGJING'S ROLE

Tao Hongjing (456–536), whose editorial trail we have been following, was one of the foremost Daoists and scholars of his age. Born of a prominent family whose forebears had emigrated south of the Yangzi river at the end of the Han (220 CE), his writings included works of poetry and treatises on medicine and pharmacology as well as on Daoism. Accord-

---

65. Peter S. Nickerson, "The Great Petition for Sepulchral Plaints," in Bokenkamp, *Early Daoist Scriptures*, 261–62.

ing to his own accounts, he first encountered the autograph manuscripts of Yang and the Xus in 484, while he still served in the Qi (479–502) court, but his editorial work on them began in earnest in 492, when he retired to Mount Mao, where Yang Xi had worked.[66] His annotated collection of the materials, the *Zhen'gao,* or *Declarations of the Perfected,* was completed in 499 and included a supplement detailing all he could learn of the history of the manuscripts, as well as his editorial procedures. For instance, since it was the distinctive handwriting of Yang and the Xus that allowed him to identify the surviving fragments of their communications, Tao is careful to note who wrote each section of text. When he could obtain only a later copy, he marked these, according to style, as written by "hand A," "hand B," and so on.[67] Tao's scrupulous documentation secured Yang Xi's place in the history of Daoism and gives us an unparalleled opportunity to view the procedures of one medieval Daoist's practice.

Since none of the autograph records upon which he based his work survive, it is somewhat foolhardy to second-guess Tao Hongjing's scholarship. Nonetheless, I believe that in one case involving revelations from the underworld received by Yang, Tao's own concerns may have led him to mistake the source of one of the documents that he had before him—the revelations of one Xin Xuanzi 辛玄子. Tracing this possible discrepancy allows us to gauge to some extent how Tao approached such revelations. As a well-trained scholar, his concerns differ in some respects from those of his contemporaries; in other ways, they are the same.

The records of two underworld informants are collected in book 5 of the *Declarations,* "Expounding on the Dark and Tenuous."[68] One informant is known only by his Daoist name, Xin Xuanzi, "Master of the Mysterious Xin." The other, Palace Marquis Xun 荀中侯, is known by his title and station in the underworld. Since Xun appears regularly among Yang Xi's celestial informants, we shall begin with the mysterious Xin, whose true identity puzzled Tao Hongjing as well.

Tao Hongjing notes at the conclusion of the Xin Xuanzi revelations

---

66. See Edward H. Schafer, *Mao Shan in T'ang Times,* 2nd ed., Society for the Study of Chinese Religions Monograph, no. 1 (Boulder, CO: Society for the Study of Chinese Religions, 1989), esp. 1–9, for the spiritual geography of this mountain.

67. Strickmann, *Le Taoïsme du Mao chan,* 11–14.

68. Book 5 now takes up chapters 15 and 16 of the *Zhen'gao.* For an outline of the work, see Strickmann, *Le Taoïsme du Mao chan,* 12; Peter S. Nickerson, "Taoism, Death, and Bureaucracy in Early Medieval China" (PhD diss., University of California, Berkeley, 1996), 542–46; Xiao Dengfu, *Han, Wei, Liuchao Fo Dao liangjiao zhi tiantang diyu shuo* (Taibei: Taiwan xuesheng, 1989), 410–13.

that his only copy of the text was in Xu Hui's hand and not in that of
Yang Xi, though Yang's comments are interspersed throughout.[69] These
Tao would have originally copied out in a different color of ink, so we
have no way now to recover what Yang's comments might have been or
how Tao identified them. Although Tao merely states that the manuscript
had "Yang's words interspersed" 雜有楊君之辭, the Xu Hui copy that
Tao saw may have contained marginalia in Yang Xi's hand. Further, Tao's
manuscript was torn at the end and so might have continued. A continuation would likely have included Yang Xi's judgment, or that of his celestial informants, on the Xin Xuanzi revelations. We can postulate this
because the Xu Hui autograph copy of Xin's revelations that Tao possessed concluded with these words: "To the right are the words of Xin
Xuanzi. He also had much more to say on the affairs of the dark world,
but I have only made a rough copy of their general outline and will not
go into detail."[70] That is to say, any continuation of the document would
not have contained more of Xin Xuanzi's otherworld revelations, but
some other material.

We can only accept Tao's implied judgment that the copy he had in
Xu Hui's hand was based on an original by Yang Xi. Tao generally assumes that anything commented upon by Yang and not marked as from
some other source originated with Yang's celestial informants. As we have
seen, however, similar "revelations" circulated in manuscript form and
were sometimes copied into family histories. Still, no matter how this
material fell into Xu Mi's hands, it is undoubtedly *not* a revelation that
Yang received from the celestial beings directly (though Tao believed it
was). If it had been, Yang would not likely have dared to abbreviate it.
The "much more" Xin had to say would have been recorded.[71] In addition, the details of the Xin Xuanzi revelation differ in important respects
from those that we know Yang Xi *did* receive from celestial beings.

Since the Xin Xuanzi fragments have come down to us entirely
stripped of their context, so that we cannot know when they were revealed or to whom, they are not readily comparable with the revelations
of Su Shao and Guo Fan. Tao Hongjing, however, did attempt such a
comparison. Tao's annotations offer us a valuable record of one scholar's
understanding of such revelatory material.

69. *Zhen'gao*, HY 1010, 16.9b9–10; Yoshikawa and Mugitani, *Shinkō*, 590–91.
70. *Zhen'gao*, HY 1010, 16.9b8–9; Yoshikawa and Mugitani, *Shinkō*, 590.
71. The deities sometimes summarize or abbreviate lists in their communications with
Yang, as Lord Xun does for instance at *Zhen'gao*, HY 1010, 15.4b4 and 15.9a2, but I
have not found an instance where Yang feels free to summarize their words.

Tao Hongjing, himself a Daoist, thought that he, too, might be destined for a position in the otherworldly bureaucracy.[72] Nonetheless, the sorts of questions and doubts that he brought to this material differed little from the scholarly concerns of his contemporaries among the elite, whatever their religious affiliations. The "proofs" Tao sought were those that his social position and training taught him to seek.

First and foremost, Tao looked for confirmation of the revelations in the histories and privately circulated biographies such as those we have read above. For each figure that appears in both the Xin and the Xun revelations, Tao provides a brief biography, including information from the histories available to him and from other accounts relating the individual's postmortem career. Here Tao acts as scholar and historian, carefully noting discrepancies as well as outside confirmations of the material he finds in the revelations.

The Xin Xuanzi fragments begin with Xin's autobiography. Xin first details, as was the practice with biographical entries, his home district and parentage. A person of Dinggu 定谷 in Longxi 隴西, Xin presents himself as the "son of Xin Yin 辛隱, the Grand Master of Remonstrance and Governor of the three commanderies of Shangluo, Yunzhong, and Zhaoguo during the reign of the Luminous Emperor of the Han [r. 57–75]."[73] Such assertions are easily checked by the historical scholar. Tao notes that he can find no reference to a Xin Yin, nor to such a position as he is here said to have held in "outside"—that is, nonrevealed—writings.

Again relying on the histories, Tao goes on to note that the Xins are a prominent clan of the Guanlong region; he gives the names of several eminent members of the family. Among these is Xin Pi 辛毗 (d. 234), whom Xin Xuanzi claims as his "seventh-generation descendant."[74] This degree of relation would, according to Daoist doctrine, make their fates intimately conjoined. After noting, with apparent approval, that the brief

72. See Stephen R. Bokenkamp, "Answering a Summons," in *Religions of China in Practice,* ed. Donald S. Lopez Jr. (Princeton, NJ: Princeton University Press, 1996), 188–202.

73. *Zhen'gao,* HY 1010, 16.6a; see also Yoshikawa and Mugitani, *Shinkō,* 587. Longxi Commandery occupied the southeastern portion of present-day Gansu Province. The name Dinggu is unknown to me.

74. For this claim, see *Zhen'gao,* HY 1010, 16.8a9–8b2, where Xuanzi gives a brief biography of Xin Pi. Tao here notes with approval that this notice "accords with the *Weishu* 魏書." Tao here refers to the "Weishu" chapters of Chen Shou's *Sanguo zhi* (Beijing: Zhonghua, 1962), which do indeed contain the same information (25.695–700). On Xin Pi, see also Mather, *Shih-shuo,* 529–30.

biographical notice Xuanzi gives of Xin Pi accords with the histories at
his disposal, Tao, applying the sort of logic that we associate with modern historians, points out that "if Xin Pi is the seventh-generation descendant [of Xuanzi], then he is the eighth generation from [Xuanzi's
claimed father] Xin Yin. To have eight generations in the space of 140
or 150 years seems too rushed."[75]

The most important technique that Tao Hongjing employs to test the
reliability of the Xin Xuanzi revelations, however, remains the test of internal consistency, not just within the Yang/Xu manuscript remains themselves, but among all of the testimonies concerning the otherworld that
were known to him. Here we see Tao in his role as seeker, gleaning all
possible information concerning the organization, regulations, and inhabitants of the unseen world. It is to this impulse that we owe Tao's
lengthy citations from the Su Shao and Guo Fan revelations, as well as
his references to other ominous events and spectral apparitions that I have
cited in this chapter.

But Tao does more than cite these as parallel bits of evidence on the
underworld. He attempts to arrange them in a logical order. Where different ranks are reported for the same individual, he postulates unreported promotions. Where promotions seem to occur too quickly, according to the schedules given by Yang Xi's informants, he notes the fact.
For Tao, the revelations granted Yang Xi carry the most evidentiary
weight, yet even when these are contradicted, he rarely concludes that
any report from the otherworld is in error. Quite the opposite. Tao in
fact takes as his starting assumption that each of these informants from
the beyond is substantially correct and has something valuable to contribute.

With regard to Xin Xuanzi's revelations, Tao finds that every entry
contains discrepancies from the account that Yang Xi had received from
Marquis Xun. Nonetheless, he believes that they were granted to Yang
Xi by Xin himself. His logic is worth following in detail.

First, in his autobiographical notice, Xin relates his dedication to reclusion and desire to study the Dao. This impulse, he says, was frustrated
by the sins of his ancestors, which resulted in a shortened span of life
that prevented him from completing his Daoist practice. As a result of
these unnamed transgressions on the part of his forebears, Xin died a
most unpropitious death by drowning. After he died, two deities, the

75. *Zhen'gao*, HY 1010, 16.6b1–2d; Yoshikawa and Mugitani, *Shinkō*, 587.

Queen Mother of the West and the Northern Thearch of Fengdu, realm of the dead, took pity on him due to his arduous pursuit of Daoist practice, and rescued him from the Three Offices. They transferred him to the Southern Palace, where individuals' spirits and bodies were smelted to perfection for residence in the heavens. Here he was to await an appointment among the celestial transcendents. Just recently, he reports "the Great Thearch [of the North] has ordered me to replace Yu [Liang] as Marquis commanding the Eastern Seas. Moreover, I have been selected to fill the position of Leader of Court Gentlemen within the Palace Enclosure, to serve as Overseer of the Ghosts and Spirits of Wu and Yue 吳越鬼神之司. Service to the king allows no leisure. This is really quite laborious!"[76]

The final plaint echoes that of Guo Fan, another recluse who refused earthly office only to find himself an official in the afterlife, but Tao is more interested in the offices that Xin claims for himself than in such sad ironies. After the introduction to the three poems that Xin reveals, Tao notes that Yang Xi himself was promised the celestial rank "Overseer of Destinies of Wu and Yue, with charge of all ghosts and spirits 吳越司命, 董統鬼神." Given his extremely similar title, Xin Xuanzi must, Tao reasons, have been destined to be Yang's subordinate. "Thus, he first approached [Yang] to express his sentiments," a sort of courtesy call to his future boss. Further, reasons Tao, since the writing of ghosts differs from that of humans, it could not be the case that Xin wielded the brush himself. Instead, he must have recited them for Yang to transcribe, in the same manner as Yang's other revelations were received.[77]

This is a neat bit of reasoning, but there is only scant and inconclusive evidence that Xin Xuanzi ever appeared in Yang Xi's midnight visions.[78] Contrary to his usual habits, Tao also does not provide evidence that an Overseer of Destinies 司命 should have as underlings "Overseers 司."

---

76. *Zhen'gao*, HY 1010, 16.7a2–5; Yoshikawa and Mugitani, *Shinkō*, 588. As the Japanese team notes, Xin Xuanzi here cites *Shijing* Ode 162, "Si mu 四牡." The relevant lines are "Do I not long to go home? But service to the king allows no leisure 豈不懷歸, 王事靡盬" (*SSJZS*, 1:406b); see also Bernhard Karlgren, *The Book of Odes* (Stockholm: Museum of Far Eastern Antiquities, 1974), 105.

77. *Zhen'gao*, HY 1010, 16.7b6–7.

78. The only further citation from Xin Xuanzi in the *Declarations* concerns the fact that tombs are not the final resting place for those who practice benevolence and the techniques of personal transcendence (*Zhen'gao*, HY 1010, 10.16a6–10). This fragment was copied out in Yang's hand. While this information is said to have been "spoken" 言 by Xin, Yang may well have copied the information from another written source that recorded Xin's words. He may have copied it, in fact, from the "missing pages" at the end of Xu Hui's copy of the Xin revelations.

Second, Tao takes discrepancies between several of the underworld ranks as reported by Xin Xuanzi on one hand and Central Marquis Xun on the other as indicative of the respective dates of the revelations. The first of these concerns the man Xin will replace, Yu Liang, whose other-worldly office was also reported by Guo Fan. Xin reveals that

> The Northern Thearch 北帝 formerly employed [Yu Liang] as General for Pacifying the East 撫東將軍 and later as Marquis of the Eastern Seas 東海侯. Now he has been transferred to serve as Imperial Supervisor of the Right, Attendant to the Thearch's Levee within the Terraces of Feng [du] 酆臺侍帝晨右禁監 . . . He has recently taken Feng Huai 馮懷 as his Adjutant. "Imperial Supervisor of the Right" is similar to the earthly rank of General of the Right Guards, only more exalted.[79]

Tao has several problems with these assertions. Marquis Xun had reported that Fengdu contained eight "Attendants to the Thearch's Levee," a rank similar to the earthly title of Palace Attendant, a personally chosen advisor to the emperor. Xin Xuanzi was not among the eight.[80] Nor did these Attendants have "Adjutants" attached to them. As Tao states at the beginning of his annotation, Xin Xuanzi's information on Yu Liang proves to be "very much different" than what Xun had revealed. He concludes that Marquis Xun's revelations must have preceded those of Xin Xuanzi.[81]

At this point, it is worth reviewing the various records that Tao is here attempting to harmonize. As we saw above, Guo Fan had said that Yu Liang was appointed "Supreme General of the Pacification Army 撫軍-大將軍 residing "east of the Eastern Seas, where he commands 100,000 spirit soldiers." Guo further asserted that Yu had chosen him as his Adjutant. The information provided by Marquis Xun does not greatly contradict this. According to Marquis Xun, Guo Fan is still among Yu Liang's personal assistants, and Yu is still a general, though of Fengdu rather than of the isles of transcendence in the east:

> Yu Yuangui (= Liang) is the Supreme General of the Central Guard of the Great [Northern] Thearch 太帝中衛大將軍. He has taken Guo Changxiang (= Fan) as his Senior Officer and Hua Xin 華歆 (d. 231) as his Adjutant. These are called "Military Dukes." They [each?] lead several thousand ghost troops.[82]

---

79. *Zhen'gao*, HY 1010, 16.8b3–6; Yoshikawa and Mugitani, *Shinkō*, 589.
80. *Zhen'gao*, HY 1010, 15.11b8–9; Yoshikawa and Mugitani, *Shinkō*, 569.
81. *Zhen'gao*, HY 1010, 16.9b1; Yoshikawa and Mugitani, *Shinkō*, 590.
82. *Zhen'gao*, HY 1010, 16.1b8; Yoshikawa and Mugitani, *Shinkō*, 577.

Following Tao's arrangement of the revelations, Yu was transferred from the rank Guo Fan had given him, first to "Central Guard of the Great Thearch," reported by Marquis Xun. Finally, Tao Hongjing, noting that the title Xin Xuanzi gives for Yu Liang is more exalted that that given by Marquis Xun, concludes that the Xin Xuanzi revelations seem to be later.[83] Given what we have seen of contestation regarding otherworldly promotions, this string of uncontested promotions is not an entirely safe hypothesis. Nor do the other bits of evidence that Tao cites prove convincing in this regard.

Third, Tao finds a discrepancy, albeit a minor one, in Xin Xuanzi's report that He Chong 何充 (242–346) had recently received documentation as a transcendent, left the Southern Palace, where he had been undergoing refinement of his physical form, and traveled to the Southern Marchmount.[84] Xin has very good things to say of He, who, when alive, "achieved much merit through his acts of generosity and thus was able to return to his body early."[85] The Buddhist flavor of the phrase "return to his body" bothered Tao, who here and at one other point in the Xin Xuanzi revelations takes care to note that what is meant by such phrases is a transcendent and not an earthly body. In fact, He Chong *was* a patron of the Buddhist way, renowned for his contributions to temples.[86] Both Xin Xuanzi and Marquis Xun attribute his postmortem rank to his "generosity," using the same term used in Buddhist texts to translate *dāna* (Sanskrit: "meritorious acts of giving"), a fact not mentioned by Tao. It

83. Tao writes, "What [Xin Xuanzi] says here differs greatly from the preceding [account of Marquis Xun]. Once [Yu Liang] was transferred to become Attendant to the Thearch's Levee, he would have commanded [the Generals] of the Guard. In short, he would be superior to a General of the Central Guard [the rank Marquis Xun gives him]." (*Zhen'gao*, HY 1010, 16.8b6–8; Yoshikawa and Mugitani, *Shinkō*, 589.) And, noting Marquis Xun's entry, he writes, "Xin Xuanzi's revelation is greatly different from this. I fear that either the one precedes the other or that [Yu Liang's] rank was taken from him and he was transferred several times" (see *Zhen'gao*, HY 1010, 16.1b10; Yoshikawa and Mugitani, *Shinkō*, 577.)

84. Marquis Xun had reported only that He Chong had been allowed to leave his position as Censor in the Inner Court of the Northern Thearch of Fengdu to proceed to the Southern Palace for physical refinement. Xun mentions nothing of He Chong going on from there to any further post, but he does mention that this quick release from Fengdu was due to the merit He had accrued through "acts of generosity." (*Zhen'gao*, HY 1010, 15.8b9–10; Yoshikawa and Mugitani, *Shinkō*, 558) This is yet another proof for Tao that Xin Xuanzi's account of the underworld was delivered later than was Marquis Xun's.

85. *Zhen'gao*, HY 1010, 16.9a–9b; Yoshikawa and Mugitani, *Shinkō*, 590. The Japanese translation team even cite a later Lingbao scripture as evidence for the vocabulary employed here.

86. See Mather, *Shih-shuo*, 522, for a brief biography of He Chong, and 420, entry #51, for his family's contributions.

is thus likely that Xin Xuanzi *did* mean to say that He Chong had achieved an early rebirth.

Fourth, and finally, Tao must rationalize Xin Xuanzi's account of Zhou Yi 周顗 (269–322). Xin reports that Zhou had recently been employed as Capital Protector-General 中都護 at the court of the Lord of Western Luminosity, but had been demoted to Capital Protector 中護 for unfairly promoting Deng You 鄧攸 (d. 326). Marquis Xun's assertion that Zhou had served as Commander for the Overseer of Destinies of the demonic offices 鬼官司命帥 but had been replaced by two men for overstepping the charges of his office seems unrelated.[87] Yet Tao Hongjing assumes, on the basis that Xun only gives evidence that Zhou had left a post, that Capital Protector-General must have been Zhou's subsequent appointment.[88]

Lacking any information on the origins of Xin Xuanzi's revelations (who was he? when did he appear? to whom?) and possessing only a single handwritten copy from Xu Hui, Tao has thus labored to construct a plausible story regarding their place in what he sees as a temporally paced flow of information from the underworld.

From our vantage point, it appears that the story might be constructed differently. We have seen enough contradictory accounts of the postmortem duel between Yu Liang and Tao Kan to keep us from trying to make bureaucratic sense of their fates. Yet this is precisely what Tao Hongjing attempts to do. One medium's detected promotions, we now know, are likely to be contradicted rather than supplemented by the next medium to enter the scene, especially if that person has an agenda of his own. We suspect Su Shao and Guo Fan offered flattering portraits of the postmortem achievements of the ancestors of living men with whom they wanted to curry favor. Yang Xi, equally intent on interesting patrons but provided with methods to counter threats from beyond the grave, was disposed to find distressing news in the underworld rather than comforting reports of promotion and success. But Tao Hongjing was not predisposed to notice how such accounts might contribute to such quotidian concerns or conflicts, and so he labors, sometimes with scant success, to find the bureaucratic logic of the unseen worlds.

---

87. *Zhen'gao,* HY 1010, 15.6a8; Yoshikawa and Mugitani, *Shinkō,* 556.

88. Tao further notes that one of the two men who replaced Zhou Yi according to Marquis Xun was said by Xin Xuanzi to be a commander under Xie Kun 謝鯤 (280–322). This would clearly be a demotion, but Tao Hongjing sees it as a "transfer" (*Zhen'gao,* HY 1010, 15.6b1–2; Yoshikawa and Mugitani, *Shinkō,* 556).

The only two points at which Xin Xuanzi's account explicitly parallels those that Yang Xi received from Marquis Xun might, employing Occam's razor, be explained more easily as borrowings of the latter from the former rather than vice-versa. That is to say, Yang Xi's future title of "Overseer of Destinies, with ultimate charge of the spirits and ghosts of Wu and Yue" 司命董司吳越神靈人鬼 might have been inspired by Xin Xuanzi's position as "Overseer of the Ghosts and Spirits of Wu and Yue" 吳越鬼神之司, and the closely similar phrasing of the He Chong entry can only serve to prove that the author of one account likely saw the other. Since we have Tao's assurance that Yang saw both, the likely direction of borrowing is from the Xin Xuanzi account to Yang Xi's "Marquis Xun" account.

Indeed, the modern Japanese scholar Aramaki Noritoshi draws just this conclusion, arguing that the revelations of Xin Xuanzi are a Celestial Master "prototype" for the accounts of the underworld revealed to Yang.[89] As we have seen, such postmortem accounts appear as well in other sources, so there is no need to invoke a single prototype or the Celestial Masters, but Aramaki is correct in noticing the likely dates of these fragments.

My goal here is not to impugn the methods or motives of Tao Hongjing. He brought to his task the wide-ranging erudition, scholarly logic, and habits of careful reading that we know from his work in other fields. As a Daoist, he desperately wanted to understand the ins and outs of the unseen world, so we cannot fault him for failing to see, as we do from our more skeptical vantage-point, that his scholarship reveals some very serious rifts in the unified picture he expected his otherworld informants to relate.

Tao's treatment of the Su Shao and Guo Fan revelations, documents that did not come to his hands through his approved Shangqing sources, reveals as well this inclination to accept unseen authority. Tao wonders at such things as the low underworld rank, in Guo Fan's account, of Xie Shang, given his prominent earthly station and lack of serious misdemeanors, or at the rapidity by which such men as Zhang Heng and Yang Xiong achieved a position among the Five Thearchs, according to Su Shao. Still, he is extremely reluctant to declare that any of these statements might not be true. In the latter case, for example, he opines that there may be a "lesser Five Thearchs" about whom Yang's informants

89. Aramaki Norotoshi, "*Shinkō izen shoshinkō no hennen mondai ni tsuite,* in Yoshikawa Tadao, *Rikuchō dōkyō no kenkyū* (Tokyo: Shunjūsha, 1998), 88–89.

are silent. Only after voicing this possibility does he allow that, on the other hand, the account might not be true 或不然.[90]

The Su Shao revelations, being the oldest and consequently least coherent with regard to the imagined underworld of the late fourth century, prompt three such expressions of doubt from Tao. But Tao clearly does not doubt the Su Shao tale as a whole. He points out none of the political and social benefits that would have accrued to the Su family with the reburial of their forebear. Instead, Tao merely judges certain details to be inaccurate—the number of Gentleman of the Imperial Gates in Fengdu or the identity of Liu Shao as Lord of Taishan (surely he must have been only an assistant!).

What Tao has foregrounded through his investigations are the lineaments of a discourse carried out among the living implicating the revered dead in ongoing power struggles. If the repetition of names and titles from story to story were not sufficiently clear, Tao's scholarly approach to these revelations shows well enough that the promotions and demotions of the otherworldly bureaucracy constitute in fact what these narratives were most significantly about. For Tao Hongjing the mundane, this-worldly power struggles that prompted these tales had vanished like smoke—he seeks the lineaments of an orderly otherworld where none existed for his forebears—but what continues to occupy his attention are individual destinies and their relationship with the recoverable histories of the dead.

CONCLUSION

Although Tao Hongjing strives to read them as one, the Yang Xi revelations are very different than those of Su Shao and Guo Fan. Yang is not a member of any of the families to whom he reports, while the Su Shao and Guo Fan revelations came from younger sons with a very different stake in the reception of their tales. Yang, for his part, receives his revelations on the basis of his own status in the otherworld. We should refrain from drawing evolutionary conclusions on the basis of these facts, however. As Campany has shown, a number of prominent families during this period employed family mages of various sorts.[91]

What is surprising is that, despite (or perhaps precisely because of?)

90. *Zhen'gao*, HY 1010, 16.11a2–4; Yoshikawa and Mugitani, *Shinkō*, 595–96.
91. Robert F. Campany, *To Live as Long as Heaven and Earth: A Translation and Study of Ge Hong's "Traditions of Divine Transcendents"* (Berkeley and Los Angeles: University of California Press, 2000), 93–94.

his status as "outsider," Yang's revelations prove more intimate. He refers to all of the dead by their private names, rather than their public names. The Perfected, lords over the underworld hosts, can do this, while those newly deceased who provided the earlier revelations were still newcomers to the netherworld bureaucracy. Further, while the specific enmities involved in the Su Shao and Guo Fan revelations are relatively clear to us, Yang put people in the underworld for a greater variety of reasons, since he had more hope of gaining patrons than the sons seem to have had. We need to guard against the "documentary fallacy" here, though, in that we have Yang's carrots as well as his sticks. We cannot know what happened to the youngest Su and Guo. Perhaps they went on to successful careers as mediums.

It is likely that this sort of mediumistic practice was occurring at all levels of society, undocumented and thus unavailable to us. Almost without exception, the men whose postmortem fates are given in the accounts that have survived were prominent and powerful in life.[92] They were still recipients of ancestral sacrifice from their equally prominent families. That is one reason these particular records were copied out and thus survived. This means, of course, that we have historical access to only one class of medium, those who worked for, or caught the attention of, the elite.

In this respect, Tao Hongjing has identified for us the context in which Yang Xi worked. Yang Xi's elite contemporaries were concerned about ancestors not only because they might be disease-agents (Su Shao), but also because the unresolved conflicts of the living might be continued beyond the grave (Guo Fan). Thanks primarily to the scholarly efforts of Tao Hongjing, Yang Xi appears to represent the first enduring Daoist conquest of the extended family, with its concern for the afterlife of its forebears. Of course similar interventions had likely been going on all along, unrecorded and so invisible to us. In the next chapter, we follow Tao even more deeply into the imagined community of a single family, the Xus of fourth-century Jurong.

---

92. The exceptions, men who had died earlier and likely did not have surviving family members to provide sacrifice for them, were, like Jiang Ziwen, the subjects of local cults. As Strickmann writes of those Yang Xi found in Fengdu, "The one feature they all shared was that they were receiving sacrificial offerings during the fourth century: In other words, they were all treated by one or another social group, outside the context of Taoism, as gods" (*Chinese Magical Medicine*, 13). We can extend this observation to those discovered in the underworlds by Su Shao, Guo Fan, and Xin Xuanzi.

CHAPTER 4

Doomed for a
Certain Term

The Intimate Dead

The social world constructs the body as a sexually defined
reality and as the depository of sexually defining principles
of vision and division. This embodied social programme of
perception is applied to all the things of the world.

—Pierre Bourdieu, *Masculine Domination*

In this chapter we investigate in detail the progress of one particular underworld lawsuit, similar to the ones Yang Xi found to have embroiled
the father and mother of Chi Yin (chapter 3). The concept may seem to
be an odd one. Remember, though, that familial ancestral practice attests to the ancient and enduring Chinese view that the fates of the living and the dead were intimately, if always uncertainly, connected. Recall too that all of the troubles of the sunlit world were projected onto
the dark world. We have already seen that revolution in the underworld
was a possibility and that the rebels' need to gather a spectral army could
explain the ravages of plague. We have also seen that the bureaucracy of
the underworld might adjudicate plaints brought before them by the
newly dead, as did Tao Kan against his mortal enemy and the murderer
of his brother, Yu Liang. The underworld lawsuit was a frequent explanation for sudden illness and all manner of afflictions brought on the living. As Strickmann has engagingly written, "The land of the dead was
not a cheerful place. It seethed with regrets and complaints, with rivalries, feuds, and intrigues. It appears, too, that the ghosts were especially
given to intricate and protracted litigation. Nothing delighted their
twisted, desiccated hearts more than a nice, drawn-out lawsuit."[1]

The courts of the dead were modeled on the courts of the living in all

---

1. Michel Strickmann, *Chinese Magical Medicine* (Stanford, CA: Stanford University
Press, 2002), 13.

respects except one: the officers sent to apprehend defendants were invisible to normal vision. Thus, all manner of illness could be ascribed to the beginnings of a suit. As spectral litigation proceeded, the unfortunate defendant would inevitably be brought into court to answer charges. This, of course, meant death. More horrifyingly still, one need not have committed any crime oneself. By the law of familial responsibility holding sway in the courts of the quick and the dead, the consequences of serious crimes committed by a family member fell equally on patrilineal descendants. Then, too, an underworld defendant might seek to avoid charges by naming living culprits who might more properly be held responsible.

All of this, of course, occurred beyond the ken of ordinary mortals, who could only surmise that such an illness or such a death might be tied to events transpiring beyond the grave. The uncertainties and anxieties thus produced provided ample room for the creative vision of a Daoist like Yang Xi, as we will see.

· · ·

Among the awe-inspiring glimpses of unseen worlds revealed by Yang Xi to his patron, Xu Mi, one stood out for its horrifying personal immediacy. The Younger Lord Mao 茅, in a communication copied by Yang, revealed that Xu's uncle, Xu Chao 許朝, had long before, in 317 or 318, murdered two men of Xinye Commandery. These two had now brought a complaint before the magistrates of the underworld. As a result, the magistrates had compelled Xu Mi's recently deceased wife, Tao Kedou 陶科斗, to return to her grave. There she languished, "perpetually thirsty, but unable to drink; hungry, but unable to eat."[2] Faced with charges stemming not from her natal family, but from the family she had married into, Kedou proposed "to keep watch for a child in her household due to weaken"—that is, one of her own grandsons in the Xu family—whom she could forward in her stead to satisfy the blood lust of the underworld plaintiffs.

Like the appearance of Hamlet's father, this event resonates with terrifying potential. Clearly the crisis posed by Tao Kedou's postmortem imprisonment and her proposed solution to her dilemma was a defining moment in Yang Xi's relation with his patron Xu Mi. Scholars who have probed the *Declarations of the Perfected* for information on the history

2. *Zhen'gao*, HY 1010, 7.11b4–5; Yoshikawa Tadao and Mugitani Kunio, *Shinkō kenkyū: Yakuchū hen* (Kyoto: Kyōto daigaku jinbun kagaku kenkyūjō, 2000), 262.

of the Shangqing revelations have not been slow to realize the importance of this incident. Strickmann, the first to explore the scene, extracted
from it a wealth of information on the Commanders of the Dead marshaled by Daoist priests to combat disease and other spectral maligni-
ties.[3] Peter Nickerson has several times revisited the story as a vivid illustration of hellish lawsuits and Daoist bureaucratic procedures for settling
the dead.[4] I refer to their important findings concerning the mechanisms
by which Daoist priests like Yang dealt with the "sepulchral plaint," or
lawsuit from beyond the grave, in the footnotes to this chapter. Our focus, as before, is on the family. Our attention is drawn to heroic sons,
errant daughters-in-law, and fatherly negotiations.

As always with the *Declarations,* we owe our understanding of the
events surrounding Tao Kedou's imprisonment in the tomb to Tao
Hongjing, who collected, arranged, and annotated the fragments of communication relating to the event. Tao arrayed most of the records that
will concern us in book 2 of his work, "Transmissions on Discerning Destiny."[5] Finding no evidence as to the year during which these bits of revelation were made, he nonetheless arranged them chronologically, according to the month and day noted on the fragments. Around these
partially dated fragments, he grouped others that were either copied onto
the same sheet of paper or that, by content, seemed to fit the unraveling
of events. There are also a few letters written by Xu Mi that Tao, following his usual practice, relegated to a separate section of the *Declarations,* along with his notes relating them to material properly revealed
by deities. We surveyed some of Tao Hongjing's scholarly methods in
chapter 3, and we will have scant reason to distrust him here.[6]

Our reading strategies will be tested by the material itself, which, with
the exception of the few letters, proves entirely unidirectional. That is to

3. Michel Strickmann, *Le Taoïsme du Mao chan: Chronique d'une révélation* (Paris:
Collège du France, Institut des Hautes Études Chinoises, 1981), 146–69.

4. Peter S. Nickerson, "Taoism, Death, and Bureaucracy in Early Medieval China" (PhD
diss., University of California, Berkeley, 1996), 261–352; and "The Great Petition for Sepulchral Plaints," in Stephen R. Bokenkamp, *Early Daoist Scriptures* (Berkeley and Los Angeles: University of California Press, 1997), 236–37, 248–50.

5. Book 2 covers chapters 11–14 of the Daoist canon edition (HY 1010). See Strickmann, *Le Taoïsme du Mao chan,* 11–12 for the plan of the work.

6. While it does not substantially affect my aim here, I should note that at least one
contemporary scholar has rejected Tao Hongjing's implicit claim that this series of revelations occurred after the sixth month of 365. Aramaki dates these events to 363. For the
most part, I concur with Aramaki's arrangement of the various fragments related to the
Tao Kedou incident; see Aramaki Noritoshi, "Shinkō yizen shoshinkō no hennen mondai
ni tsuite," in Yoshikawa, *Rikuchō dōkyō no kenkyū* (Tokyo: Shunjūsha, 1998), 60–64.

say, we have, through Yang, the instructions, admonitions, and complaints of the Perfected, but little firsthand from the human actors in the family drama we attempt to chart. Nonetheless, if we are attentive, we can hear the echoes of family voices and thus discern something of the tensions that Kedou's unexplained illness and death created among the Xus. The events unravel in terms of a family drama.

The primary dramatis personae follow:

Yang Xi 楊羲 (330–386?), the medium

Xu Mi 許謐 (303–?) Yang's patron

   Tao Kedou 陶科斗 (d. ca. 363–65), his deceased wife

   Xu Quan 許䂮, his eldest son

   Xu Lian 許聯 (328–404), his second son

      Hua Zirong 華子容, Xu Lian's wife

         their son: Xu Chisun 許赤孫

   Xu Hui 許翽 (341–ca. 370), his third son

      Huang Jingyi 黃敬儀, Xu Hui's principal wife

         their son: Xu Huangmin 許黃民 (361–429)

Huang Yan 黃演, Huang Jingyi's deceased father

Ehuang 娥皇, Huang Yan's wife

Secretary Hua 華書吏, Hua Zirong's younger brother

Wei Huacun 魏華存, Lady of the Southern Marchmount, a Perfected being and Yang Xi's preceptress

Consort An 安, Lady of the Right Blossom, a Perfected being who had been promised to Yang Xi as celestial mate

The Lords Mao 茅君, three Perfected beings who serve as Yang Xi's informants

Fan Miao 范邈, aka Middle Watchlord Fan, a Perfected being who was one of Yang's principal informants concerning the underworld

TAO KEDOU'S PLIGHT

News of the underworld lawsuit came on the sixteenth day of the sixth month, almost a year after the death of Kedou.[7] The announcement and Tao's note to it read as follows:

---

7. Since the year during which these events occurred, whether 363 or 365, is not important, I have noted only the Chinese month and day of the dated fragments without attempting to convert these to the Western calendar.

"Xu Chao violently murdered Zhang Huanzhi 張煥之 of the Merit Bureau of Xinye Commandery. He also unjustly killed Qiu Longma 求龍馬.[8] These men have both been waiting for an opportunity and recently have placed an accusation before the Water Official [the most feared of the Three Offices of the underworld]. The Water Official has compelled Xu Dou [i.e., Tao Kedou] to return to her tomb, there to keep watch for a child in her household who is due to weaken."[9] She will take [this child] to nullify [their choice of her] as respondent and release [herself] from constraint 塞對解逼 as a demonstration against those who have brought suit.[10] Kedou will come [to take the child] on the month and day of her death. Since you have received an appointment, you should be able to wipe out the hosts of the dead and control the myriad spirits.[11] I want to observe your skill, that's all. If you wish to avoid further [incidents], you should visit Kedou's tomb on this day to rebuke and bind Huan[zhi] and [Longma] with curses. This will compel the Official of the Left [= the Water Official] to conduct another inquiry and find a new substitute. In this way, we will obliterate the source of the disputes. But do not disclose these [instructions]. You should merely say, "I rely on the might of the Lord." I do not know if it is appropriate for you to be tested by going to bind and destroy them, but evidence of the power to destroy the spirits of the dead will be temporarily granted you in this matter.[12]

Tao provides the following note to this passage:

This orders Lord Yang [Xi] to dispel a sepulchral plaint for the family of Senior Officer Xu [Mi]. Xu Chao was previously [Warden of the] Nanyang Commandery and was made to kill these men of Xinye. . . . That Kedou was of transcendent rank and yet was so pressed by the Water Official was because, during the mourning period, she was still vulnerable to the *qi* of one who had died before her time 喪服中殃氣尚相關涉故也?.[13]

According to Tao, then, it seems to be Yang Xi himself who will be "tested" through the task of addressing the underworld lawsuit. We thus seem to be in the early days of Yang Xi's association with the Xu fam-

8. These two men are otherwise unknown. The Xinye Commandery seat was located at the site of present-day Xinye 新野, He'nan Province.
9. *Zhen'gao*, HY 1010, 7.6a9–b1. The translation to this point is from Nickerson, "Great Petition," 236.
10. Nickerson, in "Taoism, Death, and Bureaucracy," correctly points out the meaning of *dui* here as "respondent" in a lawsuit (271). I do not follow his change of subject, however. Kedou is still the subject of this sentence.
11. Presumably, the "appointment" mentioned here refers to Yang Xi's rank as "Overseer of Destinies of Wu and Yue, with charge of all ghosts and spirits." See chap. 3 of this volume, p. 123.
12. *Zhen'gao*, HY 1010, 7.6a9–6b7; Yoshikawa and Mugitani, *Shinkō*, 254–55. See also the translation in Strickmann, *Le Taoïsme du Mao chan*, 146.
13. *Zhen'gao*, HY 1010, 7.6b7–10; Yoshikawa and Mugitani, *Shinkō*, 255.

ily. This is further evidenced by the Perfected's doubt as to whether it is appropriate for Yang to risk himself on their behalf and by the communication that follows this one, dated the twenty-third of the sixth month, in which Wei Huacun, Lady of the Southern Marchmount, feels the need to explain for Xu Mi the significance of the spirit protectors, generals of the dead whom, as we will see, he will need to call upon in presenting his own petition. This latter announcement ends with the Lady Wei's suggestion that Xu Mi should ingest "five potables pills" to "drive off watery *qi* infusions"—presumably those issuing from the grave of his former wife. Tao Hongjing describes the illness with which Xu Mi suffered as *tanyin* 痰飲, a term that might refer to bronchitis or pneumonia. The pills, Wei instructs, will not cure this illness, but should lessen the symptoms and lengthen Xu Mi's life.[14]

Already in these initial revelations concerning Tao Kedou, we seem to have at least two threads of narrative: the illness of a Xu family member that must be cured through addressing the lawsuit brought by the dead and Xu Mi's own, possibly related, illness that requires additional medical treatment. Following this, as more members of the family become involved and fall ill, matters become even more complex, and the various strands of celestial instruction become difficult to untangle. We will thus find it convenient to observe the series of events from several different angles. First, though, here is an overview of the various revelations as Tao Hongjing arranged them by the month and day of the Chinese calendar (the dashes indicate unknown dates):

6/16   Revelation concerning Tao Kedou's plight.

6/23   Wei Huacun explains the function of the Commanders of the Dead.

6/30   The younger Lord Mao presents lists of offerings for the four Commanders of the Dead who will assist the Xus. He complains that Xu Lian was, on 6.13, already presented with this list in a dream, but failed to pass it on.

——   Lord Mao explains that the minions attached to him and to Lady Wei will also require offerings and suggests that an item of gold jewelry would be appropriate.

7/2   The younger Lord Mao presents information concerning Xu ancestors who also brought a plaint with the Water Office.

14. *Zhen'gao*, HY 1010, 7.7b8–8a5; Yoshikawa and Mugitani, *Shinkō*, 256.

7/26	Lady Wei reminds Xu Mi that the decisive moment draws near and warns that he should stop the quibbling over minor details.
7/27	Xu Lian and his wife Hua Zirong enter the oratory to "defend against what is to come."[15]
8/?	The younger Lord Mao announces that the sixth of the eighth month was when the threatened child Chisun was to die, but that matters have now been satisfactorily arranged.
——	Middle Watchlord Fan says that Xu Lian and Hua Zirong should take their child, Chisun, into the oratory on 8/6. They are told precisely what to expect.
8/2	The discussion of details by the family members has not stopped, so the younger Lord Mao comments on various details concerning the offerings and family representation in the oratory. He reports that Commander of the Dead Fan has threatened to abandon them because the offerings have not yet been received and provides more information on Tao Kedou's condition.
8/6	The younger Lord Mao reports that the local earth-god has complained. Some of Xu Mi's underlings have stolen and cooked dogs, one of which was destined for the earth-god.
——	Tao Kedou herself comes with instructions on further offerings.
——	Xu Lian writes a confession offering himself in place of his sick father and elder brother.
8/24	The Lady Wei warns that Xu Lian should not step in excrement.
——	The younger Lord Mao reminds Xu Lian that the spirits should not be blamed for self-inflicted illness.
——	Tao Kedou returns to remind her husband to cleanse and put away her bed quilts and clothes. She has now moved out of Fengdu to the Palace of Mutation and Promotion.[16]

15. The "oratory" was a small building used since the early days of the Celestial Masters as a ritual chamber for meditation and for communication with the spirits.

16. "Palace of Mutation and Promotion" was the exalted name of a study center for women destined to achieve Perfection after quitting the world. The fortunate few who gained admittance could hope to eventually achieve postings in the highest heavens.

The first thing that we notice in the records of this eventful fall is that the ill members of the Xu family include not only Xu Mi, but also his son Xu Lian and the child selected by Tao Kedou to replace her in the tomb, Lian's son, Chisun. Other members of the family may have been ill as well. For instance, when Kedou finally returns to communicate with her husband through Yang Xi, she warns him that their grandson Huangmin may also be ill from time to time, but will be in no danger.[17] Thus, the threats emanate not merely from Tao Kedou, but from other disease vectors as well. As we will see when we examine these events more closely, various members of the Xu family had invited their own ritual healers, and Yang Xi will identify further underworld threats to the family.

It is frustrating that we do not know how things finally turned out on the sixth of the eighth month when Xu Lian and Hua Zirong took their child into the oratory, where they would present the petition crafted by Yang Xi and Xu Mi. The spirits provide us with no postgame wrap-up or summary report. We do not even have a copy of the petition that was presented on that fateful day.

What we do know is that Chisun lived to the advanced age of seventy-four, that Huangmin lived to be sixty-nine, and that Tao Kedou subsequently visited Yang Xi with wifely bits of advice for Xu Mi, indicating clearly enough that matters had been settled, and she had been freed from captivity in her tomb to move on to the subterranean study center known as the Palace of Mutation and Promotion. From these bits of information, we can only assume that events transpired just as one of the deities, Middle Watchlord Fan, said they should. In modern terms, Yang Xi had succeeded in his intervention.[18]

We shall find that the above outline simplifies the story immensely. Important details appear and then are dropped from consideration. For instance, the initial announcement of Kedou's imprisonment instructs Yang Xi to "visit the tomb" on the anniversary of Kedou's death, but subsequent communications concern solely the actions to be taken in the oratory on that day. Were the plans changed, or was visiting the tomb

---

17. *Zhen'gao*, HY 1010, 8.1b4–8; Yoshikawa and Mugitani, *Shinkō*, 275.

18. Strickmann, who writes of the methods by which Yang Xi and other medieval Daoists cured illness, warns against the indiscriminate application of the language of psychotherapy to premodern religions (see *Chinese Magical Medicine*, 292, n. 87). While I do not intend to draw any connection between the two domains of knowledge and certainly plead innocent to Strickmann's proffered justification ("shock value"), I find the terminology useful at times. The reader will, I trust, understand that Yang Xi's intervention differed radically from that of a modern psychoanalyst.

merely a figure of speech? We have some indication, but no sure evidence. There are several subplots that engage us as well, such as the matter of Xu Lian and his wife's initial recalcitrance to participate in the saving of their child.

Finally, the reader should keep in mind that, for all these reasons, my reconstruction of the events presented below must be at times speculative. Nonetheless, given our goal of understanding the complex web of familial loyalties and interests that a medium such as Yang Xi would of necessity confront in plying his trade, any failure to accurately assess individual details will prove insignificant. What interests us is the picture that emerges despite unavoidable blurring around the edges.

The above outline of events does indicate clearly the number of celestial communications that involve the offerings to be presented, not to the primary deities in charge of rescuing Tao Kedou, but to their minions. As we work through these, the conflicting interests of various members of the Xu family will be thrown into sharper relief.

A MINERAL OF METALS BASE

On the thirtieth of the sixth month, the younger Lord Mao presented to be shown to Xu Mi a list of offerings for the Celestial Master Commanders of the Dead, who were to be repaid for their services in rescuing Kedou. Xu Mi was enjoined to keep secret the nature of his offerings— three hundred sheets of paper, three dippers of oil, thirty feet of blue paper, and three silver hairclasps. In this communication, the Lord further complained that precise information on the offerings had already been given to Xu Lian in a dream on the thirteenth of the month. This dream was given to Lian by the younger Lord Mao himself in the guise of Lian's younger brother, Xu Hui. The reason for this rather strange strategy, we are told, is that while Xu Lian's internal spirits were not yet pure enough to allow him direct concourse with the Perfected, Xu Hui's spiritual attainments were such that he could serve as a "dream conduit" 通夢 for the spirits. Even confronted with this more familiar dream vision in the form of his brother, Xu Lian failed to correctly apprehend this message from the spirits.[19]

Further signs of Xu Hui's spiritually favored status appear throughout the *Declarations*. Of the Xu family members, Xu Hui appears to have

---

19. *Zhen'gao*, HY 1010, 7.6b10–7a7; Yoshikawa and Mugitani, *Shinkō*, 255–56.

been the most eager to undertake the disciplines revealed by Yang.[20] Xu Lian, by contrast, is here accused to his father of either failing to remember or understand his dream, or, worse yet, of concealing it. The younger Lord's specific complaint—"How is it that you have not remembered this and have felt you could inquire again [of others]?"—gives us our first indication that Xu Lian has brought the matter up with other people.[21] Whom did he consult and why?

Earlier, in her announcement on the twenty-third, Lady Wei cites chapter and verse as proof that the offerings must be made: "According to the *Regulations of the Perfected Overseers,* those who employ the strength of the hundred demons or rely on commanding the awesome powers of heaven must also use these offerings."[22] This is the only invocation in the Kedou fragments of textual "regulations." We can conclude that Yang Xi must himself have presented to his patron a list of offerings prior to this time, only to be questioned as to their necessity. This fits as well the complaint of the younger Lord Mao on the thirtieth that the specific list had already, on the thirteenth of the sixth month, been given in a dream to Xu Lian. As we will see, Xu Lian and his wife become the focus of all that we learn about the offerings and, in particular, the offering of women's jewelry. And, as the nature of the offering already hints, the source of resistance is not Lian, but his wife, Hua Zirong.

Sometime early in the seventh month, Xu Mi received from Yang the following, indicating the reason for the silver hairclasps offered to the Commanders of the Dead, but further indicating that gold might be better for this new offering:

> The younger Lord Mao said, "I'm afraid that the functionaries and soldiers subordinate to the two of us also require offerings. They should be presented with precious ornaments that are worn hidden on the body. If not, they will not be willing to help you in the future. They will be Hua Zirong's[23] footsoldiers. Xu Quan[24] will depend on his younger brother;

---

20. See Strickmann, *Le Taoïsme du Mao chan,* 156–59.

21. In translating this phrase, I follow Yoshikawa and Mugitani, *Shinkō,* 255. Tao's note is enigmatic. He writes 餘問謂令與同勿勿勿, which might mean either "'ask of others' means that [Xu Lian?] should be caused to join in. He must not be hasty" or "that [he] should order his compatriots 'don't be hasty!'" Yoshikawa and Mugitani, *Shinkō* choose the latter. In either case, the passage seems to indicate that Xu Lian has taken his problems to others besides Yang and his Perfected.

22. *Zhen'gao,* HY 1010, 7.7b8–9; Yoshikawa and Mugitani, *Shinkō,* 256.

23. The text has Xu Hou 許厚, which is, according to Tao Hongjing, another name for Xu Hui's wife, Hua Zirong. See *Zhen'gao,* HY 1010, 20.12b6.

24. The text has Xu Tuozi 許 子. Tao speculates that Tuozi is the childhood name of Xu Quan, Xu Mi's eldest son. See *Zhen'gao,* HY 1010, 20.12b10.

while Xu Lian will rely on his father. Auspicious events will not be forgotten; neither will inauspicious events. Hairclasps are precious and hidden ornaments and can communicate with those who keep themselves in extreme secrecy.[25] Silver is a precious ornament of secondary importance. Since the present matter is one of great concern, you should be especially scrupulous. Afterwards you should not reflect on your expenditures. This would injure your bodily spirits."[26]

The "two of us" are the younger Lord Mao and Wei Huacun, Lady of the Southern Marchmount, primary among the deities who appeared to Yang Xi. Thus, their "functionaries and soldiers" require an offering more valuable than the paper, oil, and silver jewelry to be offered to the four Commanders of the Dead. Xu Mi, who may have been away at his official post as some of these events transpired, sent several letters that have been preserved, concerning this new request. The likely recipient of the letters is Xu Lian:

> For Lian's offering when he visits the Lady [of the Southern Marchmount] you should use a pair of golden bracelets. If you do not have them, I will give them to you to repay her kindness.

> If Hua Zirong[27] has a golden necklace, she should present it to the Lady [of the Southern Marchmount]. It is said to be for the purpose of thanking her officers and soldiers. Merit Officer Hua 華功曹, with good intentions, privately spoke of this to the new wife [Hua Zirong] so that she would be aware.[28] Be secretive! Be secretive! But if Zirong has no golden necklace, we can use two pairs of golden bracelets for the offering. Do not be stingy! Do not be stingy! To succeed, it is best that we obtain something that is worn on the body.

> Recently, I sent a note to you stating that the two lords should receive offerings. That night there was an announcement that said, "If they do not receive thank offerings, the functionaries and soldiers subordinate to the two of us will not be available for you to command in the future." It was in my mind whether or not we might use hairclasps. The younger Lord [Mao] then approached [Yang Xi] and said, "Hairclasps are that by which one guides and provides passage, so naturally they may be used." If the new wife [Hua Zirong] has golden hairclasps, they may be used, and we need not use the necklace. First we will make offering to the Lady and next to the two spirits. You need to consider this carefully. You should look for

25. This is fairly enigmatic. For Xu Mi's paraphrase, see *Zhen'gao*, HY 1010, 18.9a4; Yoshikawa and Mugitani, *Shinkō*, 653.

26. *Zhen'gao*, HY 1010, 7.8b2–8; Yoshikawa and Mugitani, *Shinkō*, 256–57.

27. Here Hua Zirong's name is given as Hou 厚.

28. We will explore the identity of this "Merit Officer Hua" toward the end of this section.

[a pair of] bracelets as you said in your letter that day. The new wife's silver hairclasps can also be used. If she really does not have any, then you should use the bracelets. I will keep your text [of the memorial]. As to the required and freewill offerings, I will write these in below what you have written when the time comes. You need not write out a new memorial.[29]

In these communications, we see only half of an exchange. Nonetheless, we notice that each stipulation of the Perfected's words refers to requests made by some member of the Xu family. Yang was asked to find out if "hairclasps" were sufficient, rather than other sorts of jewelry, such as necklaces or bracelets that would, by their weight, have been more valuable.[30] The fact that Xu Mi wrote at least three letters on the subject also indicates that familial discussion on this issue was intense.

From these letters, we also learn that it was the "new wife," Lian's wife Hua Zirong, who was reluctant to part with her jewelry. The Perfected beings who appeared to Yang Xi warn in strong terms against stinginess in such matters, but Xu's repeated requests that Lian ask his wife for a golden necklace or, failing that, golden or at least silver hairclasps, show all too clearly her reluctance to part with anything too valuable. Since it was Xu Lian and Hua Zirong's child who was ill, who had been designated by Tao Kedou to bear the brunt of the underworld plaints brought against the Xu family, the duty of providing suitable offerings fell on them. Given the seriousness of the threat directed at her own child, Hua Zirong's concern over the cost of jewelry seems odd.

By the second day of the eighth month, only four days before the scheduled appearance in the oratory, the younger Lord Mao reported that he had even found it necessary to deny the request of Commander of the Dead Fan, who wanted to give up on the matter altogether, since the promised offerings had still not been received. There is also an undated fragment from the Lady of the Right Blossom, Consort An, relaying a message from the younger Lord Mao: "Tell Senior Officer Xu not to worry. Do not fret about these offerings. They can be returned."[31]

---

29. *Zhen'gao*, HY 1010, 18.8b3–9a8; Yoshikawa and Mugitani, *Shinkō*, 653.

30. As Kristofer M. Schipper (personal communication, October 8, 2005) pointed out to me, I have neglected to state that there are clear Celestial Master regulations concerning the ultimate disposal of such offerings. Items not necessary for the support of the priest in his duties are to be distributed to the poor. That said, I have no information on whether or not Yang Xi followed these strictures. That Yang was not motivated by greed is, at any rate, supported by the allowance of his celestial informants that the jewelry could be returned.

31. *Zhen'gao*, HY 1010, 7.8a9; Yoshikawa and Mugitani, *Shinkō*, 256. The Japanese translation team renders 不煩此詭 as "these offerings are not important." I have trans-

Apparently, the family dispute over the jewelry still had not been settled, and Yang's celestial informants were willing to compromise, just as
Xu Mi himself had when he offered to provide the jewelry himself. The
Perfected's answer that the jewelry should be something "worn hidden
on the body" seems to indicate that they desired something from Hua
Zirong herself. The Perfected beings'—or, rather, from our vantage point,
Yang Xi's—final admission that the jewelry "might be returned" thus
seems solid indication of the vehemence of Hua Zirong's refusal to
cooperate.

The fragments of text relating to the offerings highlight the roles in
this affair of Xu Mi's second son, Xu Lian and his wife, Hua Zirong.
More than on Xu Mi or any other members of the family, the threat fell
on them. Yet Hua Zirong's reluctance to donate her personal jewelry is
not the only sign of resistance we see from this couple. The second theme
we trace through the dated and undated fragments, then, is their story.

THORNS IN HER BOSOM LODGE

Following the revelations chronologically, the first we hear of Xu Lian
is on the thirtieth of the sixth month, when the younger Lord Mao presents the list of offerings to the four Generals of the Dead and then
complains:

> The reason this was announced in a dream to Xu Lian is so that he might
> have the couple transfer[32] these four offerings to repay the four generals
> for their actions in apprehending the dead. How is it that you have not
> remembered this and have felt you could inquire again [of others]? Once
> you have rewarded [the four generals], they will always be concerned for
> your welfare. The reason that this was presented in a dream through Xu
> Hui's form is that Xu Lian's cloud and white-souls are not such that he
> can communicate with the Perfected. Xu Hui is pure and cleansed. He
> has purified his white-souls and his heart for a long time and is close to
> transcendence. Thus, I borrowed his image to appear in the dream. One
> who has such a dream and yet remains unaware can be said to lack the
> urge to trustworthiness. Or, if one is aware of it, then neglects to present

---

lated more closely: "do not fret about these offerings." As their repeated mention makes
clear, the offerings were important to all involved.

32. The Japanese translation team (Yoshikawa and Mugitani, *Shinkō*, 255) reads the
term 明輸 to mean "present [the offerings] tomorrow," that is, the day after the list was
proposed. Given the dating of the fragments—Xu Lian's dream was on the thirteenth of
the sixth month, and his visit to the oratory took place on the twenty-seventh of the seventh month—this makes scant sense.

the offerings, they might be said to possess the urge to act with trustworthiness, but lack the proper concern. Once one receives an order, covenant offerings should in all cases be transmitted secretly. Take care that you do not allow others to know of it. As an outside writing says, "I have heard my orders and will not reveal them to others."[33]

Here Xu Lian is accused by the gods of lacking the physical perfection to communicate with the gods even in dream. Thus, they have resorted to the expedient of appearing to him in the form of his younger brother. Yet, Xu Lian has either not comprehended the message he was sent or, worse yet, has "neglected" the information. In the meantime, "others" have been consulted. The Perfected again emphasize, citing powerful words from the *Classic of Poetry,* that the offerings should be kept secret.

To whom have Xu Lian and his wife been leaking information concerning the offerings? We are never directly told. There are, however, enough indications in the text to allow us to form a hypothesis. On the day that Xu Lian and Hua Zirong enter the oratory, the Middle Watchlord predicts, "Secretary Hua 華書吏 will probably be on the well [of the tomb] to aid the [tomb] occupant. He will also come at noon on that day, but will depart in a moment."[34] This person that the Perfected refer to as "Secretary Hua" is likely the same person that Xu Mi, in his letter on the subject of jewelry, called by the more polite title "Merit Officer Hua" 華功曹. That mention of Hua brought forth admonitions to secrecy, indicating that his involvement in the matter may have been considered a breach.

This conjecture is supported by the fact that, as Strickmann notes, "The [Jinling] Huas seem in every way to have been a weak link in the fortunes of the Xus."[35] Xu Mi's father had married a member of this family, as had his son Xu Lian. Another Jinling Hua, Hua Qiao 華喬, after a period of service to profane gods with whom he nightly drank copiously and for whom he identified living men to join their spectral hordes, eventually came to be converted to the true Dao by the Xu family Libationer, Li Dong 李東. For a time, Hua Qiao was visited by some of the same Perfected beings who later appeared to Yang Xi and passed their

---

33. *Zhen'gao,* HY 1010, 7.7a-7b; Yoshikawa and Mugitani, *Shinkō,* 255–56. As Tao notes, this final couplet is close in wording to the final lines of the *Shijing* poem #116, "Yang zhi shui 揚之水" (*SSJZS,* 1:362c).

34. *Zhen'gao,* HY 1010, 7.10b4–5; Yoshikawa and Mugitani, *Shinkō,* 261. The "well" of a tomb, also called the "celestial well," refers to the paintings of the constellations on the center of the tomb's ceiling. See Nickerson, "Great Petition," 248–49.

35. Strickmann, *Le Taoïsme du Mao chan,* 152.

words on to Xu Mi, though none of his revelations survive—probably, as Strickmann points out, because Yang was not eager to elucidate the prehistory of his revelations. By 364 or 365, at any rate, Hua Qiao had died, and Yang was able to report to his former employers that "his head and skin have been transported to the Water Office."[36]

Hua Qiao's most egregious transgression against the Perfected had been that of leaking divine words to the unworthy, a sin that we see repeated here in Merit Officer Hua's well-intentioned divulgence of the offering requirements to his relative Hua Zirong. Noticing this, Tao Hongjing also toys with the notion that this Merit Officer Hua might have been Hua Qiao himself.[37] If Tao Kedou had died in 363, then it is possible that Hua Qiao was still alive. Tao considers it more likely, though, that Yang and Hua did not serve Xu Mi at the same time.

Since Tao Hongjing's information is so much better than ours, his is a solution that we are in no position to second-guess. The best hypothesis, then, seems to be that the "Merit Officer Hua" and "Secretary Hua" mentioned here are a single Hua, following in Hua Qiao's footsteps, who was called by different titles by the Perfected and by Xu Mi. "Secretary Hua," Tao Hongjing states in his editorial supplement to the *Declarations,* was Hua Zirong's younger brother.[38] Whether this was Hua Qiao or not, this Hua was likely the ritual practitioner to whom Xu Lian had been leaking information. "Secretary Hua's" inconsequential action at Tao Kedou's tomb on the anniversary of her death indicates that Xu Lian or his wife employed him independently to deal with the illness that infected their family.

If Hua Zirong was already paying for the services of another ritual practitioner, and a relative at that, her reluctance to part with jewelry in service of Yang Xi's ritual activities makes a certain sense. This is not the

---

36. *Zhen'gao,* HY 1010, 7.6a6–7; Yoshikawa and Mugitani, *Shinkō,* 254. For one account of Hua Qiao, see Strickmann, *Le Taoïsme,* 152–55. Strickmann does seem to implicitly identify "Secretary Hua" with Hua Qiao.

37. *Zhen'gao,* HY 1010, 18.8b9–10; Yoshikawa and Mugitani, *Shinkō,* 653. Tao's reasons for rejecting the identification are a bit hard to follow. He writes only "Merit Officer Hua seems to be Hua Qiao, but later Yang writes 'it was on my mind,' so I fear it is not [the same person]." Tao's reasoning seems to be that Yang Xi must have had using hairclasps "on his mind" because this substitution had been suggested by Hua Zirong herself after she had been told of the purpose of the offerings by Merit Officer Hua. This would have implied an unseemly coordination between Yang and Hua Qiao, so Merit Officer Hua must be someone closer to Yang. But this is conjecture about a conjecture. What is clear is that Tao Hongjing finally discounts the possibility that Merit Officer Hua is Hua Qiao and that his evidence is slender.

38. *Zhen'gao,* HY 1010, 20.12b7; Yoshikawa and Mugitani, *Shinkō,* 711. This person was also known as "Marquis Hua" 華侯.

only failing that was charged to Hua Zirong, however. As we shall see, every woman associated with the Xu family was, in one way or another, a source of potential disaster. To understand this, however, we need to trace the deeds of that paragon of the family, Xu Hui.

O WONDERFUL SON!

In a revelation Tao Hongjing dated to sometime early in the seventh month, requesting additional offerings for the "two Lords," we find the following statement concerning the mortal whom their footsoldiers should serve: "They will be Hua Zirong's footsoldiers. Xu Quan will rely on his younger brother; while Xu Lian will rely on his father."[39] That is, the oldest Xu son will rely on the spiritual protection of the youngest of the Xu brothers, Xu Hui, and the second brother, Lian, on Xu Mi. The spirit-soldiers and officers who require further offerings of golden jewelry are required solely for the protection of Lian's wife, Hua Zirong.

It is striking that, while male Xu family members might rely on one another, the "new wife" needs special spiritual protection. It was, after all, a male Xu ancestor whose misdeeds had resulted in the underworld lawsuit that embroiled the family.

This request, as we have seen, prompted further queries from family members, though it is again worth noting that we are privy only to the answers provided by the Perfected. One of the most enigmatic of these replies is a sarcastic retort from the younger Lord Mao on the second of the eighth month: "As for the matter of the younger replacing the elder— what do you hope to accomplish by repeating the request? Why not [simply] request the Most High to stop [the plaint]?"[40] This plea to "replace the elder with the younger" had, it seems, been previously broached. Tao Hongjing has identified the relevant fragment, spoken by the younger Lord Mao:

> If we allow the young to stand in for the old, what will this do for the
> father? If the young and the old come together, what will this do for the

---

39. *Zhen'gao*, HY 1010, 7.8b3–5; Yoshikawa and Mugitani, *Shinkō*, 256. As normal for these intimate transcripts, family names are used in this passage. I have standardized names throughout. Xu Hou 許厚 is Xu Lian's wife, Hua Zirong. Tao Hongjing speculates that "Tuozi 子" is yet another family name for Xu Mi's eldest son, Quan 卹, though he does not figure anywhere else in these proceedings. (On these two names, see *Zhen'gao*, HY 1010, 20.12b6; Yoshikawa and Mugitani, *Shinkō*, 711.) Xu Lian, as usual, is known here as "Ya 牙," a shortened form of his familiar name "Huya 虎牙."

40. *Zhen'gao*, HY 1010, 7.11a3; Yoshikawa and Mugitani, *Shinkō*, 262.

mother? The weakness arises from your own bodies. The plaint arises
from your own family members. The Three Officials have their established
procedures. You may be vexed about it, but there is no way to bypass
them. If one has not reached complete attainment, both within and without,
one would not be able to avoid being startled and fearful [at what is to
happen].[41]

Neither fragment clarifies just who among the Xus wanted to replace
whom, and Tao Hongjing offers no opinion on the question. The Japanese research team that has studied and translated the *Declarations* has
taken both of these references to signify "replacing Xu Lian with Chisun,"
but it makes scant sense that anyone in the family would have suggested
this, since it is the youngest Xu who was primarily threatened in the first
place.[42]

Admitting that we lack the data to make certain identification, there
is one puzzle piece left to us that does seem to fit here. Among the fragments Tao Hongjing has associated with these events is a rare document
from this period in Daoist history, Xu Hui's petition to sacrifice himself
for the transgressions that have caused the illnesses of his father and older
brother.[43] Here, addressed to the deity Wei Huacun, is a likely offer to
"replace the elder with the younger."

Tao Hongjing's copy of this document, written out in Xu Hui's own
hand, reads in its entirety as follows:

> The male student Yufu [Xu Hui's personal name] confesses: I, Yufu, a
> mortal of defiled corpse, have received the mercy and salvation of the
> sages. Each time they provide their commands and instructions, it is indeed
> to the glory of my sons and grandsons, who will always taste spiritual
> grace and forever rely on celestial care.

---

41. *Zhen'gao*, HY 1010, 7.9b7–10; Yoshikawa and Mugitani, *Shinkō*, 259–60.

42. See Yoshikawa and Mugitani, *Shinkō*, 262 and 259 for this identification.

43. The paradigmatic act of self-sacrifice in Chinese history is the "Metal-bound casket" section of the *Shangshu*. According to this legend, the Duke of Zhou offered his own
life to the ancestral spirits as a replacement for the ailing King Wu, who was on the point
of death. Subsequently, he sealed the documents containing his oath in a metal-bound casket, and the King recovered. The duke, by the way, was not required by the spirits to give
up his life. His sincerity was enough to achieve the desired outcome. See Burton Watson,
Early Chinese Literature (New York: Columbia University Press, 1962), 34–36, for a translation. This sort of scapegoat ritual became ubiquitous in later Chinese religion. See Stephen R.
Bokenkamp, "Sackcloth and Ashes: Self and Family in the Tutan Zhai," in *Scriptures,
Schools, and Forms of Practice in Taoism*, ed. Poul Andersen and Florian C. Reiter (Wiesbaden: Harrassowitz Verlag, 2005), 33–48; and the historical examples given by Kuo Li-
ying, *Confession et contrition dans le bouddhisme chinois du Vᵉ au Xᵉ siècle*, Publications
de l'Ecole française d'Extrême-Orient, no. 170 (Paris: École française d'Extrême-Orient,
1994), 7–16.

But I am obtuse and stupid, by nature hard to instruct. Although I urge myself on day and night, I am plagued with error. Tonight I was enlightened by a dream. Contemplating its meaning, I have come to understand that this is all retribution for my transgressions. At this, shame and fear simultaneously arise within me, and there is no refuge for me.

The numinous way is exalted and void. Fleshly beings have not yet attained its Perfected doctrines, but can only control their hearts, maintain reverence, and practice its precious secrets. Sometimes I fear that, its numinous instructions being lofty and distant, its instructions subtle, I in my obstinate ignorance will never be able to become enlightened. Transgressions such as these, accumulating over the months and days, violate the doctrines and precepts and must by now number in the thousands and tens of thousands. The divine mother [Wei Huacun] is a humane protectress and always willing to pardon. Thus today, with intense apprehension, my inner organs churning, I search within and contemplate my transgressions. There is no repairing the faults of the past. Were I to lay them all before you, they would be extremely numerous, and I hope you will allow that this is not the occasion to do that. At the same time, with fear and trembling, I, Yufu, with full sincerity beg to make the following oath: From today, I will make a new start. Cleansing my heart, with sincerity I make a covenant with heaven and earth. Preserving my body in stillness, I obediently receive instructions and reprimands. I beg that you absolve my father Mu [Xu Mi] and elder brother Huya [Xu Lian] of interrogation for crimes great and small. Though I am of no account, I beg that I personally receive the punishment, so that you can absolve and [grant] amnesty [for all of their] great and small [crimes]. If the divine mother accordingly shows compassion, I, Yufu, will contemplate my transgressions and repair my faults so that the whole family might equally receive your grace. Thus they might ever gaze on the sun, moon, and stars and receive a mandate to renew their lives. Respectfully submitted.[44]

The self-effacing language of Xu Hui's formal confession might obscure for the modern reader the spiritual confidence that regularly informed such offers of self-sacrifice. In early Chinese history, ritual proposals of self-immolation typically emanate from kings, loyal officials, and holy thaumaturges who fully expected that the merit of the offer itself would move the gods to mercy, providing the needed rain, averting the death of a sick monarch, or the like. There is every indication here that Xu Hui expected his offer to be accepted in the same fashion. The deities had already declared him a fitter vessel for their communications with the family than his elder brother, Xu Lian. And, indeed, Xu Hui did seem to be the one member of the family who most fully gave himself to the entice-

---

44. *Zhen'gao*, HY 1010, 7.12b–13a; Yoshikawa and Mugitani, *Shinkō*, 264–65.

ments of the Perfected. His offers of self-sacrifice should, then, be understood as an attempt to barter his spiritual attainments for the welfare of the family.

If Xu Hui was indeed the "younger" who so selflessly offered to replace the "older" Xu Lian in the oratory, the Perfected reject his request on reasonable (and expected) grounds. If Xu Hui were to be allowed to do this, what of the father of the child (Xu Lian)? And, if Xu Hui and Xu Lian were to appear together in the oratory, what would that do for the mother of the child (Hua Zirong)? Further, if Xu Hui, as he allows in his petition, has not yet fully achieved "complete attainment, both within and without," he would surely be "startled and fearful." Why? As it turns out, his own deceased mother-in-law will appear in the oratory on that fateful day.

This apparition of the mother-in-law is perhaps the most enigmatic feature of the series of events we here attempt to trace. Why does Xu Hui's mother-in-law figure at all in these events? With this question we come close to the heart of Xu family dynamics as Yang responded to them—rather, as he portrayed them.

FRAILTY, THY NAME IS WOMAN!

According to Tao Hongjing's history of the Xu family, Xu Hui married Huang Jingyi, daughter of Huang Yan, Governor of Jiankang, and of his own aunt, Ehuang. After giving Hui a son, Huangmin, Huang Jingyi was sent back to her family and eventually married the Governor of Yuanling 宛陵, Dai Qizhi 戴耆之.[45] We know no more of moment about any of these individuals from outside sources. We do not even know when Xu Hui sent his wife back to her family, or why. Xu Hui's father-in-law, Huang Yan, is, however, mentioned together with his wife in this series of revelations. In the angry words of the younger Lord Mao, delivered on the second of the eighth month:

> Xu Lian (Huya) as well? Do not be in a hurry! Huang Yan 演 is a low
> fellow. What has Lian to do with him? Why does he dare to continue

45. *Zhen'gao*, HY 1010, 20.10b2–5; Yoshikawa and Mugitani, *Shinkō*, 707. The *Jinshu* contains only one reference to Dai Qizhi. When Wang Gong 王恭 (d. 398) was captured just before his murder, he met Dai, his former officer, who was by then Governor of Hushu 湖孰 (roughly modern Jiangning County 江寧縣 of Jiangsu Province), and secretly asked him to deliver his son by a secondary wife to his ally Huan Xuan. See Fang Xuanling et al., *Jinshu* (Beijing: Zhonghua shuju, 1974), 84.2187.

pursuing him? [Yan's wife] Ehuang and Hua Zirong have documents with the Water and Fire Offices. Recently, I received orders from the Southern Perfected [Wei Huacun] to take them under control in shackles 推縛盡執. If that leader of the little demons has not yet submitted, how is that anything to worry about? This is also something that can be overcome if the Senior Officer [Xu Mi] will apply himself.[46]

These are strong words indeed. Lacking the query that prompted this violent reply, we have no way of identifying "the leader of the little demons." Clearly Xu Hui's in-laws numbered among his followers (if Huang Yan himself is not the "leader").

Our information concerning Xu Hui's wife and her parents consists only of these unsatisfactory hints. We cannot know for what crimes or family involvements Xu Hui's mother-in-law was to be brought under guard into the oratory, nor can we know what Xu Lian might have had to do with his younger brother's father-in-law. Behind these events must lie a family event of some moment, but only its echoes reverberate in the records that have come down to us. It does seem likely, though, that Xu Hui's confession and offer to replace his father and elder brother in accepting responsibility for the illnesses that beset the family had something to do with his wife and his in-laws. What is clear is that Xu Hui's offer, though not accepted, was a virtuous response, while his brother Xu Lian continues his involvement with Hui's father-in-law or with another ritualist who had served them both.

As if the situation were not dire enough, the revelations of the second of the eighth month, so soon before the scheduled visit to the oratory, contain further information that cannot have been comforting concerning Xu Lian's wife, Hua Zirong. Not only, as we have seen above, does she, along with the unfortunate Ehuang, "have documents with the Water and Fire Offices," she also finds herself named in yet another underworld lawsuit. The younger Lord Mao's communication of the second of the eighth month continues as follows:

Hua Zirong is herself accused by her father. This charge has also arrived [at my office?]. The accusation does not concern [Xu] family affairs, but it has caught the attention of a passing guest.[47] Moreover, I think that [the plaint] will be successful. Why is it always this way, you ask? It has to do with the

---

46. *Zhen'gao*, HY 1010, 7.11a5–8; Yoshikawa and Mugitani, *Shinkō*, 262.
47. Presumably, the "passing guest" 往來之賓 was a transcendent official uninvolved in these events who has informed Lord Mao of the matter.

head of family's instructions and prohibitions, and does not involve me. If you pay attention to dissolving the accusations against Kedou, this problem will certainly also be dissolved.[48]

Hua Zirong's father is unknown to us. Tao notes only that she was the "granddaughter of Hua Qi 華琦 of Jinling 晉陵."[49] Whatever the crisis in the Hua family might have been, none of the Xu clan is to do anything about it. As we have seen, there is some evidence that Hua Zirong and Xu Lian had hired one of her family members to conduct rituals, and the Jinling Hua's were deeply implicated in all of the Xu family travails. Here Hua Zirong is counseled merely to participate in resolving the Xu family crisis, which she might rest assured will also solve her personal problem.

Hua Zirong has clearly not been attending to Xu family affairs. Not only did she hesitate to provide suitable offerings, so that General Fan threatened to excuse himself from dealing with the matter, Zirong also failed to provide normal sustenance for her dead mother-in-law. According to the pronouncements of the younger Lord on the second of the eighth month,

> Just now Commander [of the Dead] Fan wanted no more to do with the matter, since he has not received offerings. I would not permit [his withdrawal]. There is really nothing else to do now. The offerings must be sent immediately in order for the diseases to be cured. Kedou is perpetually thirsty and cannot drink. She is hungry, but cannot eat. Since your son's wife does not pay attention [to these matters], how can I not notify you of her dead father's accusations? Consequently, she should be assiduous in family matters. If she continues in her [present] course of action, she may be brought into the domicile of her father to be taught a lesson.[50]

As the senior woman in the Xu family, after the death of Kedou, it would have been Hua Zirong's responsibility to prepare food offerings for the Xu family ancestors. The title "new wife" that she is frequently given in these fragments indicates clearly that she has ascended to this status in the family.[51] Now, having failed in this, as in all else, she is threatened with the ultimate sanction, death and transport to the underworld Three

48. *Zhen'gao*, HY 1010, 7.11a10–11b3; Yoshikawa and Mugitani, *Shinkō*, 262. The Japanese translation team takes the term *zhangren* 丈人 to mean "uncle." But the term, literally "aged man," was generally used in medieval China to refer to the father of one's wife.

49. *Zhen'gao*, HY 1010, 20.9b4–5; Yoshikawa and Mugitani, *Shinkō*, 706.

50. *Zhen'gao*, HY 1010, 7.11b3–8; Yoshikawa and Mugitani, *Shinkō*, 262.

51. This fact has no bearing on whether or not the younger brother, Xu Hui, has by this time divorced Huang Jingyi or not. These duties would naturally fall on the wife of the eldest son.

Offices, to be "taught a lesson" by her unhappy father! The order of Wei Huacun that she be "taken under control in shackles" along with Ehuang may indicate that she was already ill, and so this threat would have resonated with even greater force.

•   •   •

Looking back over the fragments we have analyzed so far, we realize with some amazement that, even bracketing our conjectures, every single woman involved with the Xu's has proven a source of spiritual and physical malaise. Tao Kedou, held in her tomb due to plaints brought against her in-laws, quite reasonably, if cold-heartedly, seeks a living Xu to repay the debt so she can further her own pursuit of transcendence. Xu Lian's wife, Hua Zirong, boasts the longest list of crimes. A member of the dastardly Jinling Hua family, she has apparently seduced her husband into helping their child through the services of another ritual master. She has consequently withheld the jewelry meant to pay the minions of Yang Xi's Perfected for their services in dissolving the plaints that hold Kedou in her grave. She has further failed to feed Kedou and, for unknown reasons, her own father has brought a plaint against her in the underworld. As a result of all this, she has already acquired a record for herself in the Three Offices. Xu Hui's wife, Huang Jingyi, belongs to yet another ill-omened family. Her father is a rascal and member, if not the leader, of a band of "little demons," while her mother, Ehuang, guilty of who knows what crimes, has been taken into captivity by minions of the Three Offices. Ehuang's sorry figure will, as we shall see, be made to appear before the horrified eyes of her nephew. Beyond Xu Mi's deceased father, the greatest crime Yang Xi's Perfected find among the Xu family men is wavering and irresolution.

All of this is particularly striking in that modern researchers, noting the central role played by goddesses in the Shangqing revelations, have been led to comment on the prominence of women in Yang Xi's visions. With regard to the role of divine women, such as Wei Huacun, who serve as "initiators, preceptors, and possessors of sacred texts and methods," as well as to the later, living Daoist women who would exploit these divine models in support of their own practice, this observation proves quite accurate.[52] But what of the Xu family women? Each of the living has proven a source of possible damnation for the men of the family.

52. See Catherine Despeux, "Women in Daoism," in *Daoism Handbook,* ed. Livia Kohn (Leiden: E. J. Brill, 2000), especially 387–88.

One might argue that Kedou was simply a victim, but, despite her happy prospects, it would be difficult to maintain that Yang Xi meant to present her as a possible intercessor who could work on behalf of her husband, Xu Mi. Her final appearance in the revelations finds her presenting wifely advice and bidding a final farewell to Xu Mi.[53] In fact, we find in the opening pages of the *Declarations* that Yang has in mind for Xu Mi a divine counterpart, the Lady Wang, with whom he was invited to join in a spirit-marriage that would know nothing of the carnal.[54] Nonetheless, in his writings Yang's promised goddesses appeared young, nubile, and enticingly dressed, speaking the language of mystical eroticism. Adept in the poetic language of social intercourse, they put human women to shame, and promised even higher transports of divine intercourse to those lucky men who would leave the world to follow their proffered Way.[55] Can the unmasking of demonic danger among living women in the Xu household be unrelated to the celestial prospects Yang Xi unfolded before the eyes of the Xu men?

The revelations of Yang Xi, as Strickmann first noticed, are full of warnings concerning the danger of the Celestial Master practice of "merging pneumas," a method of sexual congress meant to join the *qi* and bodily spirits of the two practitioners.[56] We know that Wei Huacun, in life a Celestial Master Libationer, obtained her own status in part through these methods, but, as a goddess represented by Yang Xi, she refuses to recommend the procedure for those to whom Yang ministered. We know, too, that Xu Mi had practiced the rite with his wife. Other members of the Xu family may have been initiated into it as well by their Libationer, Li Dong. But this is one Celestial Master practice that Yang Xi obviously

---

53. Tao Kedou does, at one point, offer through the Perfected the advice that petitions should also be sent to Lady Wei and two of the Mao brothers (*Zhen'gao*, HY 1010, 7.12a9–12b3; Yoshikawa and Mugitani, *Shinkō*, 264). This is, however, her only intervention in the affairs we have been tracing. For the "wifely advice," see *Zhen'gao*, HY 1010, 8.1a8–2a6; Yoshikawa and Mugitani, *Shinkō*, 275–76. The passage is replete with warnings about Xu Mi's and Huangmin's health and provisions for a woman who seems to have been one of her servants.

54. Strickmann, *Le Taoïsme du Mao chan*, 188–91.

55. Yang Xi described his own celestial mate, Consort An, as follows: "Her garments flashed with light, illumining the room. Looking at her was like trying to discern the shape of a flake of mica as it reflects the sun. Her billowing hair, black and long at the temples, was arranged exquisitely. It was done up in a topknot on the crown of her head, so that the remaining strands fell almost to her waist. There were golden rings on her fingers and jade circlets on her arms. Judging by her appearance, she must have been about thirteen or fourteen"; see Stephen Bokenkamp, "Declarations of the Perfected," in *Religions of China in Practice*, ed. Donald S. Lopez Jr. (Princeton, NJ: Princeton University Press, 1996), 171.

56. See Bokenkamp "Declarations," 168, 177–79.

wished to reform, for his Perfected criticize all of those who undertake "merging pneumas." It is difficult to escape the suspicion that, in order to ensure that his patrons heeded the warnings the Perfected now saw fit to deliver, Yang Xi understood the value of convincing the men of the family that their current mates were, at the very least, not fit companions for this dual practice.

Before we accuse Yang Xi of simple misogyny, we should recall the environment in which he worked. For a medium wishing to gain access to the men of a powerful family, what could be more powerful than channeling the twin allures of sex *and* the heightened spiritual aptitudes of women—whom some, in that time and place, held to be closer to the divine by virtue of their *yin* nature?[57]

MORE QUESTIONABLE SHAPES

We have no final report on the visit of Xu Lian, Hua Zirong and their infant son to the oratory on the sixth of the eighth month. We know only that Chisun lived to the ripe age of 74. Among the undated fragments, however, is a report to Yang Xi from the younger Lord Mao that all is in readiness:

> The sixth of this month is when Chisun was to die. We have previously arranged matters. [The plaint] has been stopped, and there is nothing further to fear, but the four generals have already reported the matter ahead of time to the Palace Officer of Proscriptions.[58] On that day they will escort the corpse [of Kedou], kill the messengers, and watch over [Kedou] on your behalf. Thus you need not be concerned. On that day, take the mother and father into the oratory. If the illness breaks out in the oratory, there will still be no harm. I will also be watching over you on that day.

Prior to the event, Yang Xi's informant on the underworld, Watchlord Fan, detailed for the couple precisely what was to happen during their visit to the oratory. At the risk of excessive citation, I give this account in its entirety, for it reveals an aspect of Yang Xi's methods that has hereto-

---

57. For demonstration of the erotic allure of some female mediums, see Suzanne E. Cahill, *Transcendence and Divine Passion: The Queen Mother of the West in Medieval China* (Stanford, CA: Stanford University Press, 1993); and Donald Holzman, "Songs for the Gods: The Poetry of Popular Religion in Fifth-Century China," *Asia Major*, 3rd series, 3, no. 1 (1990): 1–20. This appeal to competition is, I know, a very shallow defense of Yang Xi's practice.

58. The Palace Officer of Proscriptions, my speculative translation of Dujin 都禁, was the officer responsible for maintaining ledgers of life and death for the Three Offices. See *Zhen'gao*, HY 1010, 16.13a10.

fore escaped scholarly comment. In brief, we see Yang in the role, which he might only have played this once, of thaumaturge. Like the younger sons of Su Shao and Guo Fan, Yang will perform a play for doubting mortals. Both gods and the dead will be made to appear:

> On the sixth of the eighth month, the parents should take the child into the oratory, burn incense, face north, and offer their entreaties to the two Lords. There will then be something that they see, but what they see will definitely not harm them. On noon of that day, that person from before, wearing a dark blue upper garment and flower-patterned trousers, will appear to stand, then walk back and forth, before the oratory. This will be the younger Lord Mao. You may approach him to offer your entreaties.
>
> At noon on the sixth of the eighth month, there will be a person with very long sideburns, wearing a flat-topped head cloth and trousers of purple leather, who will bring Ehuang with him. This will be the Commander of the Dead Wang Yan. As a human, Yan made some contributions and thus was made general. Ehuang[59] will appear to you. It will perhaps be the case that Ehuang will on that day be swaddled in cloth. On that day, Secretary Hua will probably be on the well [of the tomb] to aid the [tomb] occupant. He will also come at noon on that day, but will depart in a moment. Thus, you should make every effort to submit the Petition for Wind Infusion and Sepulchral Plaints to drive off the flowing vapors and poisons. Once you have submitted it three times, those who have been adjudged will be hidden away. Whenever blindness abounds and inquisitions become widespread, it is always because people do not announce their illnesses. Therefore, they become fearful, and their essences and fetus struggle within them so that the disease breaks out to infect more than one person.[60] The reason you are now ordered to submit the petition is also for the purpose of finally ending Xu Lian's indecisiveness.[61]

The visualization methods Yang Xi taught, by which deities appeared to human sight in precise dress and appearance, have been studied in some detail. The visions promised here are most certainly more immediate, for they concern the appearance of the shades of family members. We are not dealing here with guided meditation, but with human vision. Xu Lian, who could not even be trusted to see the gods in dream, would hardly

59. Huang E 黃娥 is, according to Tao, also known as Ehuang 娥皇. She was the wife of Huang Yan 黃演, the governor of Jiankang and father of Xu Hui's first wife, Huang Jingyi. See *Zhen'gao*, HY 1010, 20.13a5–6. She was clearly dead by the time of these events.

60. "Essences and fetus" refer to members of the pantheon of gods residing within the body of each person. For the account of these gods in one scripture revealed by Yang Xi, see Bokenkamp, *Early Daoist Scriptures*, 314–31; for much more on the inner gods of Shangqing, see Robinet, *Taoist Meditation: The Mao-Shan Tradition of Great Purity*, trans. Julian F. Pas and Norman J. Girardot (Albany: State University of New York Press, 1993).

61. *Zhen'gao*, HY 1010, 7.10a–10b; Yoshikawa and Mugitani, *Shinkō*, 261.

have been so readily suggestible as to see all of these details precisely as described. And there is no mention that his wife had been offered any instruction whatsoever. Further, Ehuang, Xu Lian's aunt and a person he might well have seen in life, will be wrapped in cloth, a detail that gives away the show. For this event, at least, with all its resonances of family drama for the Xu family, Yang doubtless used confederates to represent the Perfected. There is, to my knowledge, nowhere else in the *Declarations* where Yang might be suspected of having done so. Clearly this was a matter of some importance to him and to his future relations with his patrons.

Finally, as I said, we do not know what transpired. Given Yang's continued employment with the Xu family, though, the recalcitrance of Xu Lian and his wife must have been worked out to the mutual satisfaction of Yang Xi and Xu Mi.

CONCLUSION

In dealing with the writings of Yang Xi, it is difficult to avoid the documentary fallacy, whereby historical documents are taken unproblematically to present the events they putatively record. Given the immediacy of the sources Tao Hongjing has collected, it is all too tempting to read them as accurate accounts of what transpired that fall. Further, this is the closest we get to a full "family drama" during this period of Chinese history, so it is difficult to know how typical Yang Xi's work with the Xu family dead might have been. It is thanks to the scholarly efforts of Tao Hongjing and the vicissitudes of preservation that we have even this window into a family's affairs, so it is perhaps ungracious to complain. Still, we must treat the material with a certain caution.

Strickmann, whose study of the *Zhen'gao* informs the present chapter at many points, concluded his work with these words:

> The appeal of the Mao Shan revelations did not only lie in the concessions that they made to worldly activities. Their most important aspect was the message of salvation transmitted by the Perfected. So far we have made use of the texts in the *Zhen'gao* in order to describe the immediate milieu of the Xus and their mundane concerns. For this purpose we have naturally chosen material having a worldly bent. Yet running through the *Zhen'gao* texts is also a pure and undiluted otherworldly strain.[62]

62. Strickmann, *Le Taoïsme du Mao chan*, 208.

I am less convinced that the Chinese religion of this time included a "pure and undiluted otherworldly strain" that was innocent of the quotidian demands of society and the family. If we could know enough, I believe, we would find "mundane concerns" lurking behind all Chinese scriptures.

Yet we must remember that, despite all we stand to learn of other-worldly lawsuits and their anxieties, we are viewing the events as Yang Xi constructed them, and as Tao Hongjing and I have reconstructed them. The blurring filters are multiple. And yet the resulting story seems consonant with what we know from other sources of the understandable tensions in the extended Chinese family. Yang's religious involvement in family issues seems not different in kind from that of his predecessors and contemporaries. Intimate knowledge of family dynamics must have been important to priests and mediums working at all levels of society.

I must admit, however, that the picture of Yang that has emerged from my researches has troubled me. Still in awe of his writing skills, I find myself less fascinated than before with aspects of his religion. In particular, it disturbs me that he seems to have employed confederates and that, despite—or rather because of (?)—the alluring descriptions he provided of celestial women, he seems to have maintained a pronounced animus toward their living counterparts.

As a scholar, I feel that it is important to acknowledge these responses of mine and even more important that I try to see past them. The uneasiness I began to feel in approaching this material seems to me to signal a matter worth investigation. Is it possible that the religion of the Lingbao scriptures, for which we lack social detail concerning its production, would have been less disturbing to modern eyes? I rather doubt it. But there is more to this response of mine than that of a modern repelled at aspects of alien and bygone cultures. We have, through the excellent researches of many scholars, come to see Yang Xi as special, a particularly gifted medium who was able to mold Celestial Master concerns in such a way that they appealed finally to the elite classes. Thus I was at first appalled to find how common he seemed. But we need to remember that while Tao Hongjing regarded Yang Xi as remarkable in many ways, he did not regard him as a unique genius, as his comparisons of Yang's otherworldly reports with that of others shows. Yang, then, seems to me now to be special primarily because we know so much about his work.

Beyond the conjunctions of happenstance, we owe this one intimate picture of a religious practitioner's daily dealings with a family to the fact that relations with the dead changed rapidly in the decades following Yang Xi's death. In many respects, Yang Xi's remarkable revelations represent the end of an era and were preserved in part for that reason. In the following chapter, we chart further the externalist positioning of Yang's view of the otherworld with respect to Buddhism and a few of the remarkable changes that followed.

CHAPTER 5

Rebirth Reborn

The Chinese looked to Buddhism for questions that they
found apposite—they approached Chinese translations
of Buddhist texts not as glosses on the Indic originals, but
as valuable resources that addressed their own immediate
conceptual, social, and existential concerns.

—Robert H. Sharf, *Coming to Terms with Chinese Buddhism*

One of the most detailed expositions of any Chinese individual's former
lives comes from a Daoist text, part of the Lingbao scriptures composed
in the late fourth and early fifth centuries.[1] According to the opening of
one Lingbao text, originally known as *Trials of the Sages,* the Duke Transcendent Ge Xuan 葛玄 gathered thirty-two of his disciples on Mount
Laosheng 勞盛山 on February 11, 240, to answer their queries concerning his practice.[2] Ge's disciples especially wished to know why it was
that, though they had practiced for hundreds of years, none of them could
match the attainments of the Duke Transcendent, who was able to ascend to the highest heavens to attend the court of the most exalted gods.
Ge Xuan reveals that their fault lies in only seeking transcendence for
themselves through such practices as those found in the Shangqing scriptures, an enterprise he characterizes as the "lesser vehicle," while he has
worked for the salvation of all. Still they press him, wanting to know
what he had done in previous lives to merit his high station. To this, he
responds as follows:

> I could speak until the end of the day about the transgressions and merits,
> the transmigrational processes, and the various bodies I have passed

1. The *jātaka* accounts of Śākyamuni's numerous prior existences constitute the most
detailed account of "individual" samsaric experience.
2. The location of Mount Laosheng is unknown.

through in my previous existences and still not tell all. Since you wish to know, I can but relate one corner of it:

(1) Of old I was born as a rich man, but I ignored the poor, supported the strong, and suppressed the weak. Thus I died and entered the earth-prisons.

(2) Then I was born as a commoner, destitute and sickly; orphaned and without support. At this time I thought, "What have I done in past lives to reach such suffering? And what merit have those others accomplished in their past lives to attain such good fortune and riches?" I determined to do good deeds, but did not understand why, so my anxiety was difficult to express. When I died, I ascended into the halls of the blessed and was reborn into a wealthy family.

(3) Treasures were not lacking, and there was nothing I could want, but yet I was violent with our slaves and servants and died to enter [again] the earth-prisons. There I suffered servitude and beatings in the Three Offices until my transgressions were at an end.

(4) Then I was born as a lowly functionary, attendant on others' every breath and laboring at every sort of service. Yet, for each move I was beaten. I labored through the mud and ashes [of societal disorder], experiencing every sort of suffering. Then I thought, "What crimes did I commit in former lives to be made a lowly functionary?" So I used my own goods to aid the poor and to respectfully serve Daoists through offerings of incense and oil. I was willing only that I be born into a wealthy family. Then I died and ascended into the Halls of Blessing, where my clothing and food were naturally provided.

(5) Later I was reborn as an esteemed person, but I again slaughtered the myriad forms of life and practiced fishing and hunting. When I died, I entered [again] the earth-prisons. There I experienced the mountains of knives, the trees of blades, boiling in a vat, and swallowing fire. All of the five sufferings were visited upon me.

(6) Once my transgressions were at an end, I was reborn as a pig and then as a sheep to repay ancient grievances [against me].

(7) Then I was born as a very lowly man, extremely detestable, stinking, and despised. I cheated and robbed others of their goods, never repaying them, and died to enter the earth-prisons.

(8) Then I was reborn as an ox, to requite humans with my labor and to feed humans with my flesh.

(9) After that, I received human form as a person of middling worth with treasures nearly enough [to support myself]. At this time, I thought to perform meritorious deeds. I constantly supported Daoists, revered the scriptures, and kept the precepts. With humility, I placed myself below others and gave alms to the suffering and destitute. In all things, I followed the Way. Whenever I heard of a virtue, I followed it. Then, at eighty years of age, I died and ascended straightaway to the hostels of the blest, where I enjoyed food, clothing, from the celestial canteen.

(10) Then I was born into a noble family, where I became practiced at

martial bravery and undertook killing and campaigning. Yet, still, I was reverent towards Daoists and kept faith with the ultimate law. When I died, I entered the earth-prisons and was about to undergo bitter interrogation when the Most High sent down an instruction, saying, "Although this person has transgressed through murder and warfare and has descended into the earth-prisons, when he was alive he kept faith with the law and revered the Dao. He gave to the distressed. Now I desire that, having been interrogated and punished, he be allowed to ascend to the Halls of Blessing and provided for from the celestial canteen."

(11) Then I was born as a noble, and retributions for the grievances [I had caused in my previous lives] were about to be visited upon me. At this, I vowed to keep my mind fixed on the Way and to respectfully receive the scriptures and teachings. Thus I practiced secret virtues, saving the endangered and distressed, conducting governance in accord with the Way, and maintaining a benevolent heart toward all living beings. I supported Daoists, served my lord with loyalty, and treated my officials according to the rites. With constant mindfulness I eschewed glory and official emoluments. In this way, I avoided [the exactments] of those who bore grievances against me [for the transgressions of my former lives]. When I had lived out my full allotment of years, I died and ascended to heaven.

(12) In my next life, I was again a nobleman. My reverence and faithfulness were even more intense. When I was but young, I burnt incense and made a promise that I would later be born with high intelligence that I might comprehend the wondrous principles and thus become a Daoist. When I died, I entered the Halls of Blessing.

(13) Later I was born into a family in the middle lands and became a Daoist Master of the Law. I wore robes of the law and kept the precepts. When I practiced the Dao, I preached the scriptures with intelligence. Because of my actions as Master of the Law, I was revered by all. Then I took an oath, saying, "Since in this life I am unable to obtain the Dao, it would be best to be a woman, and enjoy the advantages of leisured withdrawal from affairs."

(14) When my lifespan came to an end, I was born a woman, fair of face and body, with innate intelligence and mystically distinguished. My speech was like poetry. At this time I practiced Retreats and recited scriptures. Then I determined to be born a man with vast talent and decisive will, so that I could penetrate to the mysterious and vacant. I wished to fully comprehend the "slight and subtle" and be born as a prince who would associate with Daoists. With this as my goal, I went into reclusion in the mountains and took pleasure in music, frequently having the scriptures recited for me. When my life came to an end, I ascended to heaven and was naturally clothed and fed.

(15) After a while, I was born as heir in the family of a prince. I had free recourse to all the palaces and succeeded to the king's throne. I invited Daoists, worthy Ru, and men of learning to conduct rituals and discourse on the Dao. I held Retreats where I maintained quietude. My most cherished concerns were that the kingdom might know peace and the folk

prosperity; that I might [occupy my throne] reverently and without pursuing [mundane] affairs. At this time I took an oath together with officers of my Three Ministries[3] that we would in our next lives be Daoists. I would be a recluse. Shi Daowei and Zhu Falan vowed to become [Buddhist] monks. Zheng Siyuan and Zhang Tai vowed to become Daoist Masters. We all desired to rise in transcendence and cross over the generations, so we ceased carrying out the business of kingly governance. At death, we ascended immediately to heaven, where we were clothed and fed at the celestial canteen.

(16) In my next life, I was a recluse. Zhu Falan and Shi Daowei were monks, and Zheng and Zhang were Daoists. We all entered the mountains to study the Dao and seek transcendence. Later, I became the master of them all, with my will fixed on the Great Vehicle. I carried out lengthy Retreats, practiced the precepts, recited scriptures, and gave away all my treasures. I paid my respects to a great Master of the Law and received from him the great scriptures of the Three Caverns and the rituals for observance. Vowing to conduct retreats and practice the Dao, I practiced ingesting, inhaling, and exhaling [celestial *qi*].

(17) Since my [karmic] causes and conditions were not yet exhausted, at the end of my lifespan I passed through Grand Darkness and was born into a worthy family. Again, we became Daoists and monks and studied together as master and disciple. Again, I received the great scriptures and practiced the Dao with Retreats and the precepts. For this reason, the higher Sages glimpsed my deeds and sent the Perfected to descend and instruct me.[4]

Ge Xuan here displays one of what the Buddhists know as the "five [or six] penetrating powers," specifically the one known in Chinese as "spiritual penetration into past lives" 宿命神通.[5] How is it that a Daoist sage came to be depicted this way? Why is it that, in the Lingbao scriptures, we suddenly find Daoists ready to fully embrace the concept of cyclical rebirth, even to the extent of allowing for rebirth as an animal, when Daoist scriptures composed scant decades before are innocent of the notion?

---

3. The text here reads "three attendant ministers," *san shichen* 三侍臣, but both versions mention four persons. I thus take the reference to be to the *sansi* 三司, which would have referred to the high officers of the Ministries of Education, Defense, and Works.

4. HY 1107, 3a–5b; with corrections drawn from P 2454, lines 45–96. The added numbers in parentheses are my own.

5. These powers are generally known as the *liutong zhihui* 六通智慧 (Six [Types] of Penetrating Wisdom [Sanskrit: *abhijñā*]). The Buddhist list, as found in the *Avataṁsaka-sūtra,* includes, simply expressed, (1) supernatural vision, (2) supernatural hearing, (3) the ability to know the minds of others, (4) the ability to know the past lives of oneself and others, (5) the ability to travel anywhere at will, and (6) knowledge of the exhaustion of *kleśa* or "defilement." The Daoist list, by contrast, coincides only with the first two, the remainder being, again simply expressed, (3) supernatural sense of smell, (4) supernatural taste, (5) supernatural heart/mind, and (6) supernatural sense of touch and ability.

The changing attitudes toward the dead and familial anxieties we have surveyed in the preceding chapters prepare us to provide plausible answers to these questions. Before we attend more closely to what the Lingbao scriptures have to say of rebirth, however, we must clarify several points. Proclaiming theirs the "religion of life," Daoist writers held out the possibility of continued life both in the heavens and on earth. Among the startling variety of metaphors employed to describe these possibilities, early Daoists sometimes wrote of something that bears a resemblance to Buddhist ideas of rebirth. The differences are worthy of our attention.

DAOIST AND BUDDHIST REBIRTH

When we explore the concept of rebirth as it appears in medieval Daoist texts, we need to distinguish two paths, as it were, both of which were employed at various times to work out concepts similar to those current among contemporary Buddhists. The first path, rebirth into paradisiacal realms or other favored modes of transcendent existence, goes back to the earliest days of the Daoist religion and could be taken only by those who underwent a regimen of physical and spiritual practice, including moral practices. In most cases, this transit into other modes of existence is not described as a rebirth at all. Yet Daoists occasionally employed alchemical metaphors to describe a postmortem "smelting" or "refinement" of the body that would render it suitable for existence in the heavens or other paradises on and below the earth.[6] Such paths, while sometimes described as a rebirth [gengsheng 更生 or fusheng 復生] seem to owe little to Buddhist doctrine.[7]

The second path, elaborated in Ge Xuan's account of his previous lives, stipulates that all mortals as a matter of course undergo rebirth into the world as human beings or animals. The goal then becomes not rebirth itself, but the securing of a favorable rebirth. This second path is almost certainly traceable to the various Buddhist ideas of samsara.[8] Of course,

---

6. Isabelle Robinet, "Metamorphosis and Deliverance from the Corpse in Taoism," *History of Religions* 19, no. 1 (1979): 135–38; Stephen R. Bokenkamp, "Death and Ascent in Ling-pao Taoism," *Taoist Resources* 1, no. 2 (1989): 1–20.

7. See, for instance, the description in the *Nüqing guilü,* an early Celestial Master text, of the benefits the Dao bestows on the "people of Heaven." They are able to avoid disease and, "having died, be born again 天民死而更生." But, as the text later clarifies, they are "reborn" with the sun and moon into a rejuvenated world after the destruction of the end-times (HY 789, 1.8a10 and 5.2a5–2b2).

8. I say "almost certainly" because there have been suggestions that pre-Buddhist China also had a concept of rebirth according to which the *hun* of departed ancestors could be re-

properly understood, Buddhist samsara does not involve the rebirth of an individual ego at all, but only a karmic residue of causes and conditions that remained in solution, as it were, from one life to the next. But Chinese Buddhists had a difficult enough time accepting the nonperdurance of the ego. For Daoists of the fourth and fifth centuries, the clarifications forwarded by the famous translator Kumārajīva (d. 413) were of no moment; thus, we can safely ignore these refinements and follow our sources in understanding samsara as the requisite rebirth of all beings.

The two paths might be called specialized and generalized rebirth, respectively.[9] Descriptions of the path of generalized rebirth appearing in the Lingbao scriptures commonly employ images of circularity. The underlying metaphor is that of a wheel that rolls on as inexorably as the revolution of the seasons. The inevitable rebirth of all beings finds full characterization in the Lingbao scriptures as *lunzhuan* 輪轉 ["cycling" through births and deaths], a locution that was certainly drawn from the translations for samsara, *lunzhuan shengsi* 輪轉生死 or *zhanzhuan shengsi* 展轉生死, employed by early Buddhist translators.

We need to distinguish these two paths because, on occasion, a transcendent being whose form has been remade through Daoist practices can reappear in the world. The sage Laozi, who according to legend was reborn into the world nine or more times as the "teacher of emperors," served as a paradigmatic example. In addition, early Celestial Master texts described how the "seed people" who followed its Dao would survive the cataclysms at the end of the world to be "reborn" into a new age of Great Peace.[10] Tales of the transformative rebirths 化生 achieved by Laozi

---

born into the family. The evidence for this belief, though suggestive, is scant. See Michel Strickmann, *Chinese Magical Medicine*, (Stanford, CA: Stanford University Press, 2002), 43–44.

9. This is, of course, a very rough distinction. What I am characterizing here as "generalized rebirth" supposes an unchanging system in which all individual deeds are directly and causally linked to future states of being. This corresponds to what Wendy Doniger O'Flaherty, citing A. K. Ramanujan, presents as the three basic elements of karma theory: "(1) causality (ethical or non-ethical), involving one life or several lives; (2) ethicization (the belief that good and bad acts lead to certain results in one life or several lives); [and] (3) rebirth" (*Karma and Rebirth in Classical Indian Traditions* [Berkeley and Los Angeles: University of California Press, 1980], xi). What I characterize as "specialized rebirth" lacks such a system for all beings. Instead, it is a sort of "rebirth" into the heavens or other future state of being that is granted, usually by the deities, as a special reward for select individuals who earn it. The primary distinction I wish to make is that "generalized rebirth" is described for all, while "specialized rebirth" is reserved for the few. (I would like to thank Stephen F. Teiser for suggesting the terms *generalized* and *specialized* instead of the terms *passive* and *active* that I first employed.)

10. See fn. 7 above for one example. Also see Yoshioka Yoshitoyo, "Rikuchō dōkyō no shumin shisō, in *Dōkyō to Bukkyō* (Tokyo: Kokushō kankokai, 1976), 3:221–84. While

and other sages, or accorded to the Celestial Master faithful, formed one matrix for the reception of Buddhist ideas of rebirth, but because such transformational skill was reserved for those who had achieved high levels of religious attainment, we should keep this path distinct from that which regarded rebirth as normal for all.

In the writings of Yang Xi, as in the Daoist texts that preceded him, we find only the more traditional path of specialized rebirth. Still, Yang's texts reveal awareness of Buddhist ideas in interesting ways. For this reason, the scattered references to rebirth that we find in them are well worth a brief excursus.

"SPECIALIZED REBIRTH" IN SHANGQING TEXTS

The methods Yang Xi received from the Perfected (or from earlier texts) for the Daoist path of rebirth into the heavens have been thoroughly studied. Here I note only the ways in which these methods respond to the anxieties concerning family and death that we have explored in the previous chapters. These responses also involved ideas adapted from Buddhism, though transfigured in various ways.

Isabelle Robinet has explored a number of Shangqing meditations for remaking the person.[11] Several of these methods taught techniques for creating the perfected embryo that involved the ingestion of celestial emanations, the merging of these with bodily forces, and the accomplishment of generative tasks in key parts of the body, all accompanied by precise visualizations.[12] The *Taijing zhongji,* for example, contains a method for untying the "embryonic knots," twelve sources of death that take root in the human body as it comes to life in the womb.[13] Here is Robinet's summary of the practice:

Yoshioka wishes to show the Buddhist provenance of ideas relating to the "seed people," even he admits that such favored beings were held to enjoy extended life, not rebirth (see especially pp. 263–65).

11. Isabelle Robinet, *La révélation du Shangqing dans l'histoire du taoïsme,* Publications de l'Ecole française d'Extrême-Orient, no. 137, 2 vols. (Paris: École française d'Extrême-Orient, 1984), 1:102 ff.

12. Isabelle Robinet, *Taoist Meditation: The Mao-Shan Tradition of Great Purity,* trans. Julian F. Pas and Norman J. Girardot (Albany: State University of New York Press, 1993), 139–42, *inter alia.*

13. The scripture has the full title *Shangqing jiudan shanghua taijing zhongji jing.* See HY 1371 and Robinet, *Taoist Meditation,* 140–43. It seems that this scripture, or a version of it, may have preceded the Shangqing revelations of Yang Xi. See Robinet, *La révélation du Shangqing,* 2:171–74.

[It] consists in making the adept relive his embryonic life in relation to the divine and cosmic model. . . . Starting from the anniversary of his conception, the adept will, therefore, relive his embryonic development by receiving, month by month, the breaths of the nine primordial heavens. During each of the nine monthly periods, the adept invokes the Original Father 元父 and Mysterious Mother 玄母 while visualizing, simultaneously, the King of the [appropriate] primordial heaven. . . . Having received the King's breath, the adept now reactualizes it. At the same time, the King descends into the [appropriate] bodily cavity.[14]

The somatic aspects of such meditations are fascinating and complex, but our focus here remains on their social and familial implications. Through remaking his or her body in this way, the adept allies with cosmic forces but seemingly repudiates natal ties to any human father and mother. The texts are quite explicit about this. The reason people, whose true being emanates from the pneumas of the Nine Heavens, come to grief is that "they forget that which gave birth to them."[15] The birth parents serve as mere matrix for the celestial forces that engender the person; they "only know the beginnings of parturition and are unaware of the spirits who come to take residence within."[16] Through return to the original purity of one's origins, we suppose, one might avoid familial implication in underworld lawsuits, or indeed any hereditary guilt, through tracing one's true ancestry to an Original Father and Mysterious Mother in the Dao. This proves not to be the case.

In asserting that a person's ultimate source of being derives not from the natal parents, the Shangqing texts approximate Buddhist notions of rebirth as these were presented in early translations.[17] Buddhist karma entailed the idea that one's birth parents are not the true source of one's being, that there is no such thing as collective guilt within the family, and that one suffers the consequences of one's own deeds from previous lives. These were difficult pills to swallow, and Yang Xi did not ingest them all.

While the Shangqing scriptures contain methods for bypassing natal parents to reconnect with one's original source of being, they are quite explicit concerning collective responsibility within the family. Salvation

14. Robinet, *Taoist Meditation*, 141.
15. HY 1371, 2a.
16. HY 1365, 1.2b; P 2751, ll. 220–21 (Ōfuchi, p. 387).
17. See Erik Zürcher, "Buddhist Influence on Taoist Scripture," *T'oung-pao* 66 (1980): 138–40; and Stephen R. Bokenkamp, "Simple Twists of Fate? The Daoist Body and Its *Ming*," in *The Magnitude of Ming: Command, Allotment, and Fate in Chinese Culture*, ed. Christopher Lupke (Honolulu: University of Hawaii Press, 2005), 151–68.

depends ultimately upon the actions of the individual, but the adept was also, as we have seen in the cases of Chi Xin and the Xu family, implicated in the merits and transgressions of his or her ancestors. Robinet succinctly maps this alignment of forces working on the individual: "The adept is invited to assume a triple destiny: as a humane and social being, attached to his or her lineage; as a cosmic immortal; and as a lone individual."[18]

When Yang Xi comes to write of those who achieve rebirth, the full weight of these conflicting demands still applies. Through externalist statements that position his views clearly and serve to discourage any of his disciples from seeking solace in the Buddhist way, Yang Xi describes a few special individuals as undergoing a sort of generalized rebirth. But these favored few always prove to bear particularly heavy familial responsibilities. Either they are beneficiaries of their ancestors in the seventh generation, or they separate themselves from the family to their own detriment. The "triple destiny" Robinet describes remains in force for every individual. Those who discover their original source in the Dao must still guard against entanglements from previous generations. Those who seek to escape such entanglements through rebirth or other methods of leaving the family find themselves still bound.

For example, Yang's informants on the underworld provided him with a list of the merits by which underworld lords might advance in Fengdu. Among these we find the following category:

> Those whose ancestors have achieved merit with the Three Offices sufficient to flow down to their descendants might in some cases move across generations by refinement and transformation [of their bodies] or be reborn, changing their family. This is all due to the hidden virtues of their seventh generation ancestor, [whose merit] reaches them as [nourishment reaches from] the roots to the leaves. Once they die, they are compelled to leave a bone of their foot with the Three Offices. The rest of their bones stay with their bodies as they pass over. Males are to leave behind [bones] from the left foot and females from the right.[19]

As Tao Hongjing emphasizes, it is precisely because these fortunate individuals achieve rebirth through the achievements of their seventh-generation ancestors rather than by their own merit that they must leave a foot bone forfeit with the Three Offices. This personal token ensures

---

18. Robinet, *La révélation du Shangqing*, 1:103; my translation.
19. *Zhen'gao*, HY 1010, 16.12a; Yoshikawa Tadao and Mugitani Kuniō, *Shinkō kenkyū: Yakuchū hen* (Kyoto: Kyōto daigaku jinbun kagaku kenkyūjō, 2000), 596–97.

that they do not fully "leave the family." While this brief reference does not specify which individuals might achieve this state, the passage may well serve to explain why contemporary Buddhists claimed to achieve rebirth. "Leaving the family," as we saw in the introduction, was also the term used to describe those who entered the Buddhist *sangha,* or religious community.

But, for Yang Xi, rebirth is still not something for everyone. Indeed, in that it depends on the merit of an ancestor, rebirth inevitably involves a measure of debt, symbolized by the ransom of bone that must at some point be redeemed if the individual is to achieve wholeness. In this respect, we find Yang Xi describing an intermediate space between active and generalized rebirth, one that is not the common lot of all, yet not the actively sought goal of the individual.

Michel Strickmann has discussed another important passage in Yang Xi's writings that helps to illuminate his attitude toward rebirth. In the writings Yang passed on to his patron Xu Mi, we find the Perfected constantly concerned that, despite their best efforts, Xu Mi would not retire from public life, that he persisted in sexual practices, and that his son Hui was actually making better progress than he. On a more mundane level, Xu Mi's continued interest in official advancement likely threatened Yang Xi's ministry.

Among the stimuli the Perfected applied for the benefit of Xu Mi was the following cautionary tale. There lived during the reign of King Wu of the Zhou (trad. 1169–16 BCE) one Xue Changli 薛長里, who attained the Dao. His younger brother, Xue Lü 薛旅, was not so adept. Though he had retired to the mountains, Lü failed to pass the seven trials set for prospective Perfected precisely because he was given to carnal desires. Nonetheless, his kindness and his fondness for music saved him. In particular, Lü's bodily spirits were kept from departing entirely only by his ability to whistle in imitation of the phoenix. Observing Lü's liminal condition, Xue Changli petitioned the Most High that his younger brother be allowed to profit from the merit accrued by Xu Jing 許敬, Xu Mi's seventh-generation ancestor, by being reborn into the Xu family so that he could work off the more regrettable aspects of his character. And so Xue Lü came to be reborn as Xu Mi.

Xu Mi's destiny was thus "doubly determined." He inherited both the inclinations of his former self—Xue Lü—and the merit of the seventh-generation ancestor of his natal family, Xu Jing. Now, the Perfected elucidated, this not only explains the recalcitrance of Xu Mi's character, it also provides him with ample reason to be enlightened 悟 as to the importance of repairing these shortcomings. He should in no wise betray his various benefactors![20]

Strickmann concludes from this that the Shangqing revelations of Yang Xi merged, at least in this instance, both the traditional Chinese familial etiology by which one's fate was governed in part by the deeds of one's ancestors—particularly the seventh-generation ancestor—and aspects of the Buddhist doctrine of karma. He writes,

> The sophisticated Daoists of Mao Shan were able to synthesize both systems. Like Xu Mi, they stood at the intersection of two discrete strands of destiny, two separate "genealogies of morals." Xu Mi embodied not only a morally charged biological destiny but a comparably weighty pseudo-Indian "past life" as well. Their convergence had framed his present existence, and both channels of fate depended on his current course of behavior for their future outcome. This is heavy moral overdetermination indeed.[21]

Indeed it is, but such "moral overdetermination" seems to have been necessary only in the particularly difficult case of Xu Mi himself, for we find no other individuals who were said by Yang Xi to have such redoubled karmic pasts.

From the perspective of our own investigations, we can see that this is not yet quite the second path of rebirth so forcefully enunciated in Ge Xuan's narration of his past lives. Xu Mi's "rebirth" is granted through the intervention of others and special dispensation; it is not the common lot of humankind. While we are not told whether or not Xu Mi had left a foot bone with the Three Offices, he certainly found that his status as one to whom the Perfected revealed their truths was a precarious one, due not only to the virtues of his seventh-generation ancestor, but also to his elder brother from his former existence.

The interfamilial weight of rebirth finds emphasis in yet another tale given to Yang Xi by the Perfected, the story of Bao Jing 鮑靚 (fl. 322–25?). This story relates to Xu Mi's interests in a different way. Xu Mi was in the process of composing his own biography of transcendent figures, apparently modeled on Ge Hong's *Traditions of Divine Transcendents,* and came to regard Yang Xi's celestial sources as invaluable "fact checkers" for materials he had gathered from local sources. Bao Jing, already given

---

20. *Zhen'gao,* HY 1010, 3.13b–14b; Yoshikawa and Mugitani, *Shinkō,* 126.
21. This story of Xue Lü is discussed in Strickmann, *Chinese Magical Medicine,* 44–46. The passage cited here appears on 46.

an entry in Ge Hong's earlier work, was a figure of local renown, but the Perfected had little praise for him. Among their allegations was that Bao and his sister were in fact reincarnations of their seventh-generation "ancestors" Li Zhan 李湛 and Zhang Lü 張慮. These two had reportedly performed secret acts of merit and, as a result, been allowed to "change their clans and be reborn" 改氏更生 into the same "target" family. The two—Bao Jing and his sister, that is—are now underworld lords. Nonetheless, the Perfected go on, Bao's study in the underworld proved shallow, and his progress has been slight.[22]

Yang Xi's reasons for this report from beyond the grave are not far to seek. Ge Hong had written that Bao Jing was adept at "escape by means of a simulated corpse," another technique that often required one to change one's clan allegiances.[23] This aspect of the method was one of which Yang Xi's informants particularly disapproved. They list rebirth among the grisly outcomes awaiting those who employ methods other than the alchemical drugs and meditations they themselves prescribe. Some "die and are reborn, some already dead with their heads broken emerge on the other side, some have their corpses disappear before they are enshrouded, in some cases the body remains, but without bones." None of them, however they might have escaped death, can ever go home again, "for they are seized by the Three Offices."[24] Therefore, methods of escape from familial responsibility by simulating a corpse and changing one's name or by rebirth into another family ultimately prove futile. The celestial and subterrestrial record keepers are not to be avoided.

Yang Xi's descriptions of the reborn, in short, are not attractive. Aware of the Buddhist notion, he yet describes rebirth as other-directed; somehow distinct from specialized rebirth as a desirable goal, yet not quite the passive and inexorable cycle of rebirth found in Buddhist scripture.

22. Zhen'gao, 12.2b5–3a2; Yoshikawa and Mugitani, Shinkō, 437–38. It may be that Yang Xi is here playing upon a preexisting legend of Bao Jing. According to this tale, as a youth Bao reported to his parents that he had originally been a youngster named Li who fell into a well and died. See Fang Xuanling et al., Jinshu (Beijing: Zhonghua shuju, 1974), 95.2482. The Jinshu is known for collecting earlier legends, but I have not traced this one.

23. It is likely that Yang Xi's information on the postmortem doings of Bao Jing was meant to supplement, and contest, Ge Hong's account in the Shenxian zhuan. See Robert F. Campany, To Live as Long as Heaven and Earth: A Translation and Study of Ge Hong's "Traditions of Divine Transcendents" (Berkeley and Los Angeles: University of California Press, 2000), 295–97; and see 52–60 for a full discussion of "escape by means of a simulated corpse."

24. Zhen'gao, HY 1010, 4.17a; Yoshikawa and Mugitani, Shinkō, 176.

Yang resorts to the notion of rebirth in order to find some explanation—
and cure—for his patron Xu Mi's continued reluctance to leave the quotidian world for full-time devotion to the Daoist path. It is hard to argue, as Strickmann does, that this single gesture represents a fully
articulated system. At the same time, Yang's other references to rebirth
show clearly enough that he regarded it as somehow shameful and its
recipients (for such he regards them) as thereby debt-ridden.

This aspect of Yang Xi's thought comes to the fore most starkly when
we compare his writings on rebirth with the *Essentials of Upholding the
Way* 奉法要, composed by his contemporary Chi Chao 郗超 (336–77).
Chao was a fervent upholder of Buddhism, and his treatise, which is a
sort of "catechism" or introduction to Buddhist doctrine as he understood it, nowhere directly mentions—a point Yang Xi emphasizes—that
rebirth entails leaving the family. Instead, he focuses on the inevitability
of karmic retribution as an individual matter and includes a lengthy section arguing that karma does not involve families. He cites a Buddhist
sūtra to the effect that "when the father has done wrong, the son will not
suffer in his place; if the son has done wrong, the father will not suffer
either," concluding, "How perfect are these words! They agree with the
heart and accord with reason!"[25]

Given what we now know of Chi Chao's family trials, as elucidated
by Yang Xi, it is not difficult to see against whom he is arguing. Chi Chao's
father, Chi Yin, as we saw in chapter 3, had been taken into the inner
circle of Yang Xi's initiates and promised a celestial mate. At the same
time, he had been made aware of the lawsuits from beyond the grave
brought against him because of his father's actions and told of distant
ancestors that could bless or curse his future pursuit of the Dao. It is
difficult to imagine that Chi Chao would not have been aware of Yang's
account of these postmortem familial lawsuits as related to his father.
They would have threatened him equally. It is no wonder, then, that the
message of Buddhist karma should agree with his innermost heart! They
must have seemed "perfect words" indeed to one so burdened with postmortem familial entanglements.

Though we lack such intimate familial detail concerning those who
wrote and promulgated the Lingbao scriptures, these texts respond to
questions of familial responsibility and ancestral threat in a way that is
more like that of Chi Chao than that of Yang Xi.

25. Erik Zürcher, *The Buddhist Conquest of China*, 2 vols, (Leiden: E. J. Brill, 1959),
168–69.

"GENERALIZED REBIRTH" IN THE LINGBAO SCRIPTURES: THE INVENTION OF A DAOIST SAMSARA

Given our close view of Yang Xi's ministry to the Xu family, it would be extremely convenient if we had comparable evidence concerning the authors of the Lingbao scriptures. What ancestral anxieties must they have confronted to create the salvific path we have seen in the case of their self-constructed sage Ge Xuan (and in the introduction to this volume in the ritual of Lu Xiujing), where mere possession of the Lingbao scriptures that they themselves had written rendered them impervious to underworld lawsuit and all manner of infection from beyond the grave?

Unfortunately, history has not been kind to us on this score. We have only the dismissive remark of Tao Hongjing, who wrote, one hundred years after the event, that the Lingbao texts had been "fabricated" by Ge Chaofu 葛巢甫, a grandnephew of Ge Hong 葛洪 (283–343). Beyond Ge Hong himself, the most notable figure in the Ge family was Ge Xuan, whose rebirths we have traced, and to whom Ge Hong also traced his spiritual lineage.[26]

Now, given the importance of family in such matters, it is highly significant for the claim that Ge Chaofu had something to do with the composition of Lingbao scriptures that Ge Xuan plays such a central role. Yang Xi's revelations had earlier called into question Ge Xuan's local reputation as a transcendent; thus, one impetus for the appearance of the Lingbao texts might well have been the desire to counter this claim. But hypotheses of this sort, compelling enough in themselves, hardly count as sufficient cause for the level of anxiety that would lead to such far-reaching changes in Chinese native religion. We are left to assess the revolutionary claims of the Lingbao scriptures themselves.

The appearance of the Lingbao scriptures is indeed a remarkable event in the history of world religions. Suddenly, at the very end of the fourth and into the early decades of the fifth centuries, Daoist scriptures closely modeled on translated Buddhist *sūtras* began to appear in substantial numbers. Whereas earlier Daoist texts had displayed only scattered and superficial references to Buddhism or its concepts, now recognizable "Bud-

---

26. For what can be known of the authorship of the Lingbao scriptures and what cannot, see Stephen R. Bokenkamp, "Sources of the Ling-pao Scriptures, in *Tantric and Taoist Studies in Honour of R. A. Stein*, vol. 2, ed. Michel Strickmann, Mélanges Chinois et Bouddhiques, no. 21 (Bruxelles: Institut belge des hautes études chinoises, 1983), 434–85; and "The Prehistory of Laozi: His Prior Career as a Woman in the Lingbao Scriptures," *Cahiers d'Extrême-Asie*, 14 (2004): 403–21.

dhist elements" adorned nearly every page, so that one can, with some
certainty, distinguish texts produced before and after this sea change.

The Lingbao scriptures mark this dividing line in the history of Daoism. The event appears to be, and scholars often treat it as, a total capitulation on the part of the Daoist religion, as if one stage in the "Buddhist
conquest of China" was the day Daoists decided to begin practicing a
faulty approximation of the Buddhist religion.

Certainly the appropriation of the concept of samsara in the Lingbao
scriptures might be taken to fit such a picture. Erik Zürcher, in his "Buddhist Influence on Early Taoism," puts the matter this way:

> Like any complicated system of thought, Daoism had its "hard" and "soft"
> areas: "hard" areas where, even before contact with Buddhism was made,
> the ideas had already been elaborated and crystallized to such an extent
> that they were comparatively inaccessible to outside influences, and "soft"
> spaces that were "vulnerable" to outside influence, because in such areas
> ideas were either poorly developed or weakened by internal contradiction.
> It could well be that central areas of Daoist thought such as meditation,
> the human body, and stages of saintliness were immune to Buddhist influ-
> ence precisely because they since the beginning had enjoyed so much
> attention and therefore had crystallized into well-developed "closed"
> structures, whereas other areas—vague and conflicting ideas about life
> beyond the grave; indistinct and shifting representations of the heavens
> and / or paradises; the conflict between collective inherited guilt and
> personal responsibility—were open to the impact of Buddhist ideas.[27]

In the introduction, I stated my reservations concerning such "billiard-
ball" (perhaps here the image of dough balls—or a Daoist dough ball
and a Buddhist billiard ball?—would be more apt) metaphors of "influence." For our present purposes, we note that Zürcher places the "complex of karma and retribution" among the prominent "soft areas" in the
Daoist religion. He finds the Lingbao tradition to be "deeply influenced"
by Buddhism in this regard.[28] At the same time, Zürcher's profound
knowledge of early Buddhist translation literature has allowed him to
identify in the Lingbao scriptures a key passage on samsara that will allow us to refine our understanding of the nature and extent of the Lingbao appropriation of the concept of generalized rebirth.

The following lengthy passage is drawn from the *Precepts of the Three
Primordials,* an exhaustive listing of the celestial record-keepers who
work under the Three Offices (the "Three Primordials" of the scripture's

27. Zürcher, "Buddhist Influence," 121.
28. Ibid., 135–41.

title). This vast celestial bureaucracy, we are informed, gathers before the Celestial Worthy, the highest god of the Lingbao scriptures, on three days of the year to compare the records of the living and the dead. At such times, intercession by humans might be particularly effective. These days, the fifteenth of the first, seventh, and tenth months, by the lunar calendar, thus came to gradually replace the thrice-yearly meeting days of the Celestial Masters.

On one such occasion, the Most High Lord of the Dao, the principal interlocutor of the Lingbao scriptures, asked of the Celestial Worthy a question that we ourselves would like answered:

> I dare ask the Celestial Worthy: There are rankings of meritorious deeds, ranks for those to be saved, and distinctions of high and low, but which aspect has priority? Does the blame incurred by previous generations stop with one person, or does it flow down to infect children and grandchildren? Are the evils one commits visited upon one's own body, or do they obstruct above those who have already died? . . .
>
> Some scriptures and traditions say that the evil committed in one's previous life causes disaster to flow down upon the descendants. Or they say that the major transgressions one commits obstruct above the departed ancestors.
>
> Yet others say that each good or evil deed we do finds karmic retribution; good and bad fortune, life and death, are all due to this root of fate. If this is so, then the retribution for all good and evil is visited through [karmic] causation on a single body. There should thus be no further talk of [evil deeds] "flowing down" or "obstructing above."
>
> But again some say, "If one does not establish merit to rescue the banished cloudsouls, they will have no means to gain release. Once merit has been established, [one's] births and deaths will be unobstructed and peaceful." Now if each misdeed has its karmic recompense, those who have committed evil will upon death sink away for thousands of kalpas, bound into the darkness. How can they have the means to establish karmic merit to redeem themselves? But if descendants establish this merit for them, then there is no difference between this idea and the idea that [demerit] might "flow down" or "obstruct above." This is what, in my ignorance, I really cannot understand.
>
> Since the Celestial Worthy has opened forth the all-embracing transformation, life and death have been made clear. Your proclamation causes the worlds of light and dark to be clearly separated so that none will through ignorance be confused regarding these two discourses.[29]

Here we detect elements of all the struggles with ancestral influence over the living that we have mapped out in the preceding chapters. It will help

29. HY 456, 32a10–33a7.

if we disentangle them and uncover the nature of the question asked here
before we proceed to the answer.

While the "scriptures and traditions [biographies or hagiographies]"
are not further specified, it is clear from the conclusion that we are dealing with two contradictory "discourses" 二論. The first two cited passages deal with the traditional Chinese notion of collective guilt by which
the transgressions of an ancestor might affect the living and, conversely,
the transgressions of the living might affect the dead. Transgressions might
thus either "flow down" from the ancestors or "obstruct above" previous generations.

As we have seen, there is no reason to consider these resonances between the living and the dead as strictly "Daoist." Rather, belief in reciprocity between living and dead family members was the foundation of
pan-Chinese ancestral practice. We recognize in this characterization of
"obstructing above" and "flowing down" the motives behind Su Shao's
and Guo Fan's return from the dead and behind the *hun*-summoners' actions of 318 as much as we do the etiology of the ancestrally induced illnesses diagnosed by Yang Xi. Instead of a sea change in relations with
the dead brought about by interactions with Buddhists, these events represent a shift in focus from the assurance of mutually exchanged blessings to a fixation with how the unseen might threaten the living.

This dark view of relations with the dead is here contrasted with two
further ideas. These comprise the second "discourse"—that of Buddhists—
as the terminology employed shows clearly. Buddhist explanation, the
Most High Lord of the Dao points out, contains an inherent contradiction. It holds that merit and demerit solely reside with the individual,
who suffers the consequences of his or her own deeds in a prior lifetime.
Thus, "there should be no further talk of 'flowing down' or 'obstructing
above.'" And, if that moral solipsism really applies to all, how can Buddhists at the same time talk about the transfer of merit to dead ancestors? Either both good and bad deeds are transferable, as Chinese tradition had always held, or they are not. Buddhists, with their talk of
individual responsibility, could not without contradiction also claim that
merit was transferable.

This is the nature of the question that this passage seeks to resolve.
The underlying issue proves not to be a matter of "soft" areas within
Daoism itself; rather, it is a fundamental contradiction that the author
of the Lingbao scriptures found within Buddhist discussions of relations
with the dead, as he understood them. The "conflict between collective
inherited guilt and personal responsibility" that Zürcher noticed in this

passage proves to be something that the author attributed to Buddhist discourse and not some conflict between imported and native ideas.[30] Let us see how the author will seek to resolve the contradiction.

> Then the Celestial Worthy delightedly answered:
> Heaven and earth turn in cycles like the wheel of a chariot. The life of human beings is obliterated as surely as a shadow follows its form—it is difficult to find the end of such things. Pneuma follows pneuma continuously, each a seed giving birth to causation. Good and evil, good fortune and bad—all have their root of fate. This is not due to heaven, not to earth, and also not to humanity, but is born from the heart. The heart is what is spiritual. The human form is not a property of the self 我. The self emerges from the midst of the empty void and the self-actualized. Due to its karmic causes, it is entrusted to the womb, transforms, and is born. Thus the self's birthing father and mother are not the father and mother that originally gave birth to the self.[31] The self's true father and mother are not to be found here. But the birth parents love their offspring and are thus accorded the highest honor. From them one receives the kindnesses of having a place to entrust one's karma and of nurturance in this life. Thus one repays them with ritual and calls them "father" and "mother."
>
> But the form [= body] the self receives is not the form of the self. The form is just a dwelling place or lodging for the self. The self, in entrusting itself to the form, gives demonstrable presence to what is nonexistent. This is why those who obtain the Dao have no further form. "Were I without form, what trouble would I have? The only reason I have trouble is because I have a body."[32] The myriad troubles arise from the body, while the bodiless enter into that which is so of itself.
>
> When one establishes one's practice and conforms with the Dao, the body and the bodily spirits are unified. When these are unified, this is the true [perfected] body. One returns to the father and mother who originally gave birth to the self and completes the Dao. Within the Dao there will be no further troubles, and one will not die. Even if one is obliterated and crosses over [滅度, nirvana] the spirits depart [with one] and the form is not destroyed. The entire body returns to its origin, never departing from it.
>
> But, when one commits the myriad transgressions and dies, this is called "death." Death is obliteration *and* destruction 滅壞. The self then returns to a father and mother and entrusts itself to the womb. So long as the causes born of these transgressions 罪緣 are not exhausted, one will never return to the true father and mother. [Instead] one's spirits will join the ranks of

30. Zürcher, "Buddhist Influence," 140.

31. Lu Xiujing's ordination ritual (HY 528, 44a9) includes a formula for the disciples' remission of guilt (*Da xie* 大 謝) that mentions birth parents 有 身 父 母, using the same terminology.

32. The author cites the *Laozi;* see Stephen R. Bokenkamp, *Early Daoist Scriptures* (Berkeley and Los Angeles: University of California Press, 1997), 94.

those who labor in the earth [prisons], the body will become dust and
ashes. The dust and ashes will fly up to become flickering ghosts 爽. The
cloudsouls and bodily spirits, released, will eventually merge with these
ghosts, transforming to become one again and being reborn as a human
being. For such as these, neither the body nor the bodily spirits will depart.
In this way, good and evil are both visited upon the body. How can the
blame for this fall on ancestors or descendants?

For the modern reader, steeped in Cartesian notions of the body, the most
surprising part of this response will be its insistence on accounting for
the multipart body, which at death is "obliterated" 滅 and must be reconstituted for any sort of postmortem existence, whether for rebirth in
the world or for return to union with the Dao. Where, in such a view of
the person, will the true "self" be located, we wonder? Perhaps, in the
Celestial Worthy's response, we might begin to see the changes that Buddhist notions of self were beginning to foster. Whereas in early Chinese
thought the self was the aggregate of its parts, now the body seems ex-
cluded from any role in the formation of the self. At the same time, paradoxically, the passage still asserts the traditional notion that the body
is necessary for rebirth.[33] But our interest in such questions should not
blind us to the import of the passage.

The Celestial Worthy seeks, through beginning with the cosmic principles of heaven and earth, to reconcile the Buddhist idea of samsara with
traditional Chinese notions of regular cyclical change. Of particular interest is the Lingbao deployment of the concept of *miedu*, which was used
by early translators to render the idea of nirvana. As I have written elsewhere, whereas early Buddhist translators seem to have intended the term

33. The idea that the body was not the residence of the self was difficult for even those
Chinese thinkers who were positively disposed to Buddhist ideas of rebirth. In his "Essay
on Rebirth," Luo Han 羅含 (ca. 310–380) argued that "the spirit(s) 神 and the bodily substance 質 are naturally paired. In this pairing there occur the changes of separation and
joining, death and life. . . . And again, the spirit(s) and bodily substance are darkly fated
to join again as talismans. People of the world all mourn the necessity of their separation,
but no one thinks to sorrow over the fact that what is separated joins again" (Sengyou,
comp., *Hongming ji*, T 2102, 52:27b27–27c3). Zürcher, following Liebenthal, notes that
Luo was likely not acquainted with Buddhist texts, since "even the concept of karman
[= karma] is not mentioned!" (Zürcher, *Buddhist Conquest*, 136), but we can find the same
point emphasized by other, better-informed Chinese apologists. Sun Chuo 孫綽 (ca.
300–380) argues in his treatise "Admonitions on the Dao" 道論 that "Parent and child
are one body—it is fate that joins them. Thus, when a mother harms her finger, the child's
heart is thrown into a panic. This is the resonance between things of the same *qi*" (see Sengyou, *Hongming ji*, 52:17a28–29). The complex Chinese discourse on the body was not
something easily dislodged by Buddhist thought. Thus, the Lingbao conception expressed
here seems noteworthy and deserving of further study.

to mean "transit into extinction," the Lingbao author takes the term literally as a compound verb meaning "to be obliterated (die) and cross over [in salvation]."[34] This destiny, reserved for those of high spiritual attainment, is here directly contrasted with the destinies of those who really die, who *miehuai,* are "obliterated and destroyed." But both outcomes involve a sort of rebirth: the one into the heavens for coexistence with the Dao and the other a reassembling of the vital parts of the body for continued existence in the world. While this text does not specify, we know from other Lingbao texts that one who is "obliterated and destroyed" will be reborn in a new body—either one marked by disease and poverty, or that of an animal (as was Ge Xuan). Ritual intervention, specifically addressed to "all sentient beings" but prominently aimed at the salvation of ancestors, was considered necessary for favorable rebirths, "in the family of a Prince or Marquis."[35]

Notice, too, the reduced but still substantial role accorded birth parents in this system. Their role is reduced exactly as is the role of the body. While "skin and hair," to use the *Xiaojing (Scripture of Filiality)* formulation, are of one substance with the substance of human parents, the self is here no longer seen as an original property of the body. The "true parent" of the self is the Dao. But Lingbao Daoists, like Yang Xi, did not follow those of their Buddhist neighbors who radically relativized the phenomenal world.[36] Like the body, parents are seen (paradoxically perhaps) as vital to the project of salvation. As the Dao is immanent in creation, and human parents contribute positively to this creation through loving and nurturing their offspring and providing a locus for the working out of karmic burden, they are entitled to ritual recompense 禮報—a term heavily charged in Confucian discourse on ancestral practice. Thus space is left for bonds of reciprocity between living and dead, the heart of sacrifice to the ancestors.

The Celestial Worthy then goes on to explain how such "erroneous views" as those that prompted the original question arose. He begins his tale in the imaginative space of prior world-systems, known in the Lingbao texts by exalted reign-titles:

34. Bokenkamp, "Death and Ascent," 8.
35. The Lingbao *Benxing suyuan jing* (HY 1106, 12b) explains that the vow that one's ancestors be reborn "in the family of a Prince or Marquis" 王侯之家, a regular part of Lingbao penitential ritual, represents "the way of supreme filiality."
36. I do not in any way mean this as a critique of Buddhism. For a discussion of some positive social effects of such relativization of the empirical world, see Peter L. Berger, *The Sacred Canopy: Elements of a Sociological Theory of Religion* (Garden City, NY: Doubleday, 1967), 97–101.

From prior to the kalpa cycle of Draconic Magnificence to that of Red
Clarity, according to the old texts, birth and death [= samsara] entirely
resulted from [the actions of] a single person. There was no "flowing
down" or "obstructing those above." Good and evil stopped with the
individual, and each put his own body as forfeit. But, after the age of
Red Clarity and into the age of the Upper Luminary, people's hearts
became evil.[37] Men and women were impure. Envy, strife, and mutual
injury arose among them. Since their hearts were not in themselves depend-
able 心不自固, they began to call upon their ancestors above and their
descendants below for surety as hostages in making oaths to one another
before the spirits.[38] When they did not keep faith and broke their oaths,
[their family members] were bound and taken before the Three Offices, to
sink down among the demon officials 身沒鬼官.[39] Above, their deceased
ancestors were obstructed; while below it [their transgressions] flowed
down upon descendants, bringing calamity on all. Old and young implicated one another, so that they were not released until the heavens came
to an end, thus causing calamity to descend upon entire lineages.

These evil persons brought great calamity upon themselves. They are
eternally unable to accord with the enlightened words of the Ultimate Law.
One who does attain [to the Ultimate Law] and assembles [meritorious]
actions must draw on the Self in all things 諸取我身[40] and not rely on others.
How can the old canons of the Luminous Perfected be false![41]

After all of this patient explanation of individual responsibility, it turns
out that the old laws of collective responsibility are still in force! According to the Lingbao texts, the world age in which we reside was in-
augurated with the "Upper Luminary" reign period. It was thus during
our own fallen times that humans came to call upon the names of their
ancestors in making oaths, and it was this that quite inevitably led the
gods to apply collective punishment. We find reference here to the postmortem trials suffered by those such as Tao Kedou, so graphically described in the visions of Yang Xi. The Ultimate Law 至法 of individual
responsibility, then, applies only to those who take it upon themselves
in order to accumulate merit. With this stroke, the Lingbao scriptures

37. For the world-ages of Lingbao Daoism and its theory of decline, see Bokenkamp,
Early Daoist Scriptures, 380–84.

38. Lu Xiujing makes a similar point in his *Abridged Codes for the Daoist Community* 道門科略. See Peter S. Nickerson, "Abridged Codes of Master Lu for the Daoist Community," in *Religions of China in Practice*, ed. Donald S. Lopez Jr. (Princeton, NJ: Princeton University Press, 1996), 351–52.

39. It is unclear to me whether this means that the ancestors became subject to the
officials of the underworld or that they themselves became officials in the underworld. Perhaps both fates are implied.

40. Following S 6659, ll. 117–18. HY 456 omits the "*wo* 我."

41. HY 456, 33b5–35a5.

ally themselves with Buddhist ideas of individual merit-making, associating the practice with the perfect practice of previous world-cycles. This strategy of engagement is seen throughout the Lingbao scriptures, which describe themselves as versions of primordial scriptures that were later carried by Laozi to "convert the barbarians." Chinese Buddhist scripture, by this account, represents imperfectly understood foreign versions of the original message of Lingbao.[42]

Merit thus can, and should, be transferred. Transgression, unfortunately, still brings recompense to those both above and below, to ancestors as well as descendants.[43] The original question concerned a contradiction that the author of the Lingbao scriptures attributed to Buddhist doctrine. Buddhists hold that merit and demerit are visited solely on the individual, but also that merit is transferable. The Lingbao response is that, yes, merit and demerit were once solely an individual affair in the perfect former world-systems. Now, however, miscreants have involved their relatives, so that transgressions might flow both up and down.

Another aspect of the original question involved those languishing in the earth-prisons for their crimes. From such a station they assuredly could do nothing to save themselves. It is to their sorry plight and to the question of merit transfer that the Celestial Worthy now turns:

> The Celestial Worthy further instructed the Most High Lord of the Dao, saying,
> The way of Great Benevolence gives highest priority to saving others. Only the meritorious are rewarded; only the virtuous are promoted; only the faithful are saved; only those who observe the practices become transcendent. The establishment of merit is for heaven and earth, for the sun, moon, and stars, for the ruler, for commoners, for the ancestors, for those in one's family, for all the myriad forms of life, and only finally for one's

---

42. See Stephen R. Bokenkamp, "The Prehistory of Laozi"; and "The Silkworm and the Bodhi Tree: The Lingbao Attempt to Replace Buddhism in China and Our Attempt to Place Lingbao Daoism," in *Religion and Chinese Society: Ancient and Medieval China*, vol. 1, ed. John Lagerwey (Hong Kong: Chinese University of Hong Kong Press and École française d'Extrême-Orient, 2004), 317–39.

43. Maeda Shigeki has argued that this passage was added to the scripture later because, among other things, it is contradicted by a phrase found in the closing paragraph of the scripture mandating that "those who, treating this text lightly, leak its contents incur disaster that will destroy their clans" (*Shoki dōkyō kyōten no keisei* [Tokyo: Kyūko, 2004], 408–10). This seeming contradiction dissolves once we recognize that the laws of corporate responsibility, far from being denied here, are actually shown to be still in force. Demerit is transferred among the families of transgressors, but for those who accept the laws of Lingbao, only merit can be passed on. Had Maeda read on to the final passage cited here, he would have found this distinction spelled out clearly. I should also note here that Erik Zürcher ("Buddhist Influence, 140–41), though he modestly claims that he "can only indicate the general line of the argument," has construed the passage correctly.

self. The scriptures say, "Whoever wishes to save himself must first save others. I vow not to be saved until all persons are saved." This is widespread benevolence, unlimited in scope and admired by the people of heaven. How could it not [reach to] the seven generations of one's own family! Transgression and blessings need not extend to others, but when it comes to merit 功德, if one is favored with good karma and in full sincerity takes the blame on one's self, heaven is moved by this singleness of purpose, and both the human and the spirit world open up. And how could [such deeds] not reach those who have given birth and nurturance to one? Because of the deep love they held, how could one not greatly establish merit in order to save them and to provide recompense to their orphaned souls?

From the era of Draconic Magnificence to that of Red Clarity, none of those who have achieved the Dao, who now appear in grace, their families exalted and whose karmic inheritance will extend to their next lives, has not reached this state as recompense for assembling meritorious actions that have moved all of the heavens.[44] As for those who have achieved release from the extremes of successive retributions in the dark night of the nine infernal regions due to blame for their conduct in previous lives, none has not been redeemed to return among men but by the redemption of meritorious deeds. Their names are all registered in the Vermilion Palaces of the Southern Mount and the upper records of the Nine Metropolises. The standards of recompense are never in error. Dated and cross-referenced 相推, [the records] are very clearly delineated.[45]

Since the bulk of the *Precepts of the Three Primordials* is devoted to outlining the vast otherworldly system that oversees the deeds of mortals, assigns blame and blessing, and assures proper disposition of the dead, it is no wonder that the passage ends with a reaffirmation of bureaucratic infallibility. The notion of bureaucratic infallibility, as we shall see, proves to be an anodyne to the troubled relations between the living and the dead that we have been examining.

This passage from the *Precepts of the Three Primordials* provides us with a concise statement of Lingbao innovations on the subject of corporate responsibility: "Transgression and blessings need not be extended to others, but when it comes to merit 功德, if one is favored with good karma and in full sincerity takes the blame on one's self, heaven is moved by this singleness of purpose, and both the human and the spirit world

---

44. According to the Tang-period *Haikong zhizang jing*, the term *jiaobao* 交報 ("recompense" in my translation) refers to an alternating series of punishments in the hells (HY 9, 7.4a2–5). I am grateful to Terry Kleeman for pointing me to this passage. But here the term occurs in a clearly positive sense. I thus take it to mean something like "corresponding reward" in the present case.

45. HY 456, 35a–36a.

open up." While the evil continue to implicate their families, those who heed the message of "great benevolence" have a choice. The phrase also leaves open the possibility that ancestral blessings 福 might still be expected.

This raises the question of the role of ancestral sacrifice in the Lingbao scriptures. The standard sacrificial rites included offerings of meat that were distributed by rank and shared by the family in a banquet once the ancestors had "consumed" them. Such rituals cemented bonds between the living and dead, to be certain, but also reaffirmed social relations through the give and take of meat dishes. The early Celestial Masters heartily condemned meat sacrifices to the ancestors. According to the *Xiang'er Commentary,* an early third-century Celestial Master commentary to the *Laozi,*

> The correct law of heaven does not reside in offering foodstuffs and praying at ancestral shrines. Thus the Dao has prohibited these things and provides heavy penalties for them. Sacrifices and food offerings are a means of commerce with deviant forces. Thus, even when there are "excess food" or implements [left over from sacrifices], Daoists will not eat or employ them. . . . Those who possess the Dao will not stay where there are offerings of foodstuffs or praying at ancestral shrines.[46]

One of the precepts derived from the *Xiang'er Commentary* includes this prohibition: "Do not pray or sacrifice to demons and spirits." The texts of the early Celestial Masters emphasize that their pure gods neither eat nor drink, subsisting instead on *qi.* Nor do Celestial Master priests receive payment for their services. As Terry Kleeman, has shown, this "pure covenant," as it was called, distinguished the Celestial Masters from the priests of the common religion and from the ancestral cults, from those of the imperial household down through the elite families of the realm, who fed their gods or sainted ancestors bloody victuals. When Daoist practitioners began to spread their doctrines widely in the higher strata of society, this stark prohibition against meat sacrifice was one of the first to be relaxed.[47] As Kleeman also points out, Lu Xiujing was one of the first Daoists to explicitly sanction ancestral blood sacrifice, albeit only on specific days of the year.[48]

But the restoration of blood sacrifice did not betoken a capitulation

---

46. Bokenkamp, *Early Daoist Scriptures,* 119–20.

47. Terry F. Kleeman, "Licentious Cults and Bloody Victuals: Sacrifice, Reciprocity, and Violence in Traditional China," *Asia Major,* 3rd ser., 7, no. 1 (1994): 200–211.

48. Ibid., 209.

to the sorts of active ancestral threats that we have traced. Lu Xiujing, for instance, warns in the direst terms of the "bloody cults" to dead "generals" and "ladies" who "lead demon troops . . . roving over Heaven and Earth."[49] Rather, in the scripted interactions of the Lingbao scriptures, the ancestors are once more given specific days when they will receive sacrifice and specific roles to act out, as they had been in the ordered ancestral rites of antiquity.[50]

The passage from the *Precepts of the Three Primordials* demonstrates clearly that the authors of the Lingbao scriptures did not simply accept Buddhist doctrines of rebirth.[51] Instead, they critiqued, modified, and adapted the salient points of the doctrines to their own purposes. Rather than allowing traditional Chinese ideas of postmortem familial responsibility to be eroded by this new doctrine, they asserted that Buddhists had misunderstood the nature of the present world age and thus failed to recognize how relations between living and dead were now to be conducted.

But this is only half of the story. The questions posed at the beginning of the passage also address the problem of infection flowing between the world of the living and the dead—postmortem lawsuits implicating living descendants and ancestors held hostage by the transgressions of the living. The explanation that the Lingbao scriptures provide for all of the postmortem threats, anxieties, and machinations that we have surveyed in these pages proves to be simply the assertion of bureaucratic infallibility. The *Precepts of the Three Primordials* itself stands as testimony to

49. Nickerson, "Abridged Codes," 352.

50. On the "scripted" roles of ancestors in early ancestral practice, see David N. Keightley, "The Making of the Ancestors: Late Shang Religion and Its Legacy," in Lagerwey, *Religion and Chinese Society*, 1:3–64; Martin Kern, *Die Hymnen der chinesischen Stattsopfer: Literatur und Ritual in der politischen Repräsentation von der Han-zeit bis zu den Sechs Dynastien* (Stuttgart: Franz Steiner Verlag, 1997), 17–22; and *"Shi jing* Songs as Performance Texts: A Case Study of 'Chu ci'(Thorny Caltrop)," *Early China* 25 (2000): 60 and 104 ff.

51. Typical scholarly characterizations tend to ignore the creative Lingbao adaptations of Buddhist doctrinal points. Livia Kohn, for instance, writes, "Daoists of the Numinous Treasure (Lingbao) school . . . embraced the Buddhist vision [of rebirth] especially heartily" ("Steal Holy Food and Come Back as a Viper: Conceptions of Karma and Rebirth in Medieval Daoism," *Early Medieval China* 4 (1998): 1–48), while Erik Zürcher ("Buddhist Influence") tends to criticize whatever adaptations Lingbao Daoists made to Buddhist thought as "misunderstandings" (See Bokenkamp, "The Silkworm and the Bodhi Tree," 320–22). In the latter case, simplistic notions of "influence" lead to a mistaken assessment of the data; in the former, they discourage reviewing the data at all. For recent textual studies on Lingbao adaptations of Buddhist doctrine, see Maeda Shigeki, *Shoki dōkyō kyōten*, 371–95; Kamitsuka Yoshiko, "Reihōgyō to shoki kōnan bukkyō—Inkahōō shiso o chūshin ni," *Tōhō shūkyō* 91 (1998): 1–21; and Bokenkamp, "The Prehistory of Laozi."

this principle. It presents a dazzlingly complex otherworldly bureaucracy based on the Celestial Master concept of the Three Offices of Heaven, Earth, and Water, the "three primordials" of the scripture's title. Each of the three is divided into three palaces, and these are further subdivided into three bureaus, each with specified numbers of administrative personnel. In addition, hierarchies, meeting dates, and paperwork procedures for the entire system are specified. It would take a book of approximately this length to properly explore the sources and articulation of the system.[52]

Suffice it then to indicate here that the system of otherworldly control over sin and retribution was designed to be all-inclusive—and presumably to fit any eventuality. The names of the various postmortem destinations we have encountered are included or alluded to, as well as many that we have not. Some of these originated with Buddhist texts. Significantly, as if to rob it of its former might, the administrative offices of Fengdu have been distributed to two distinct offices.

To most modern minds, the bureaucratic density of this solution to perceived threats from beyond the grave is anything but reassuring. But recall that, even in the case of the underworld rebellion that Su Shao encountered, the solution was a bureaucratic reorganization. The Lingbao answer is in line with this. Rather than provide new named personnel, however, our text restructures the entire system.

ONE MOBILIZATION OF LINGBAO SOTERIOLOGY

The foregoing analysis of the *Precepts of the Three Primordials* enlightens us on a few of the motives behind the recourse to "Buddhist elements" in the Lingbao scriptures, but it seems dry and academic compared to the lively stories we encountered in previous chapters. What we need is a flesh-and-blood example of how the "awesome rites of Lingbao" might work in practice to counter anxieties resulting from untimely death and to restore threatened relations with the ancestors.

My example comes from a grave document of the Tang period, composed within decades of the *hun*-summoning rites mentioned in chapter 2 and occasioned by the same imperial violence. I first encountered

---

52. One such weighty tome (646 pages) on the otherworldly bureaucracy imagined in medieval China has already been written; see Xiao Dengfu, *Han, Wei, Liuchao Fo Dao liangjiao zhi tiantang diyu shuo* (Taibei: Taiwan xuesheng, 1989). Pages 419–22 outline some of the peculiarities of the *Precepts of the Three Primordials* addressed here.

this inscribed stone in the basement of the *Beilin* [Forest of stelae] Museum of Xi'an. The curators who kindly showed the stone to me related that it had come to the museum from "a private person." It was thus likely recovered from a looted tomb. The curators failed to mention, however, that the piece had already been published in a collection of *muzhi ming* [biographical inscriptions for the tomb]. Indeed, stone inscriptions such as the one they showed me are comparable to *muzhi ming*, both in size and placement next to the coffin. These two sorts of tomb document differ greatly, however, in content. The main part of the text etched into the stone I was shown was written in a celestial language called the "Hidden Language of the Great Brahmā" that figures in the Lingbao scriptures.[53] This portion of the text is best regarded as talismanic, since it does not bear information readily decipherable by us mortals.

The legible portion of the inscription that I saw in the Forest of Stelae Museum is nearly identical to the Lingbao burial text found in the Ming-period Daoist canon, except that the blanks for the names of the beneficiaries and the place of their interment have been filled in (the italicized portions below). It reads as follows:

> In accordance with authenticated orders of the [Celestial Worthy] of Primordial Origins, it is announced to all the spiritual officers of the earth bureaus of the limitless subterranean worlds of the white heavens of the west: *The former parents of the Empress Concordant with Heaven, the Prince of Feng and his Consort Cui,* have now entered obliteration and salvation. The five transcendent ones will entrust their bodies to Grand Darkness. Now they reside in their original village, *Honggu Township of Wannian County,* where we have established a hall and rooms, entrusting their corpses to the Guardians of Earth. In enlightened accordance with the Correct Law, you are to comfort and aid them. The White Spirits should feed them with white efflorescences of the seven *qi*. Fill them with essence and light. Refine their forms so that their bones and flesh are fragrant, never to decay for a million kalpas. The Western Mount Hua is to open the nine Gloomy Halls of Eternal Darkness to raise up their cloudsouls.[54] These should be bathed and capped and transferred above to the Southern Palace.[55] They will be garbed and fed to eternally reside in brilliance. Demons will not dare to encroach upon them. They are to be guarded and secured by all the spirits in accord with the old canons

53. On the "Hidden Language," see Bokenkamp, *Early Daoist Scriptures*," 385–89.
54. HY 369, 13b1, indicates that the names of the deceased should be entered here as well. In the Empress Wei inscription, this has not been done.
55. HY 369, 13b2, has "Celestial Bureau" instead of "Southern Palace." The HY 369 formulas for the east, south, and center all read "Southern Palace," while those for the

of Luminous Perfection and the documents of *nuqing* [mandated by]
the [Celestial Worthy] of Primordial Origins.

Before attending to the purposes of this document, we need to know
what we can of those who caused it to be created. Who was the "Empress Concordant with Heaven" who provided this means of salvation
for her parents? We do not know her given name. For reasons that will
soon become clear, she is known to the histories as "Commoner Wei,"
an appellation that indicates that she was stripped of her title.[56] As one
of the several elite women who sought to succeed Wu Zhao, the only
woman ever to rule in her own name in all of Chinese history and who
in her turn was thoroughly castigated by the officials who constructed
the historical record, the Empress Wei has been characterized by one
modern historian as a "lewd and ambitious woman."[57] Since this is the
image inscribed by Tang historians for us to find, we are unlikely to see
beyond it. Nonetheless, examining this record enables us to learn something of the bloody and contentious struggles for power in which she
took part. Family prestige, and the family dead, were as closely involved
in these quotidian struggles as they had always been. As we have seen,
this was precisely the world for which the soteriology of the Lingbao
scriptures was intended to provide an anodyne, and so the case of Empress Wei can provide a glimpse of one way in which this might work
out in actuality.

Empress Wei, a member of the powerful Guanzhong Wei clan, entered
the palace as the principal wife of the Crown Prince Li Zhe (posthumously
known by his imperial title Zhongzong, 656–710). The historians report
that, like her mother-in-law Wu Zhao, the Empress controlled her weak-
willed husband. It is for this reason, we are told, that soon after he took
the throne in 684, Li Zhe appointed the Empress's father, Wei Xuanzhen
韋玄貞, to the rank of chief minister. This act led Wu Zhao, who saw it
as a threat to her own control, to depose her son in favor of his younger

---

west and north read "Celestial Bureau." Lingbao texts all describe the transmutation of
the spiritual components of the person as occurring at the Southern Palace, so this is
likely the correct reading. I have no theory as to the reasons for this change in our received text.

56. Her brief biographical entries appear in Liu Xu et al., *Jiu Tangshu* (Beijing:
Zhonghua shuju, 1975), 51.2171–75; and Ou-yang Xiu, Song Qi, et al., *Xin Tangshu* (Beijing: Zhonghua shuju, 1975), 76.3486–87.

57. Richard W. L. Guisso, "The Reigns of Empress Wu, Chung-Tsung and Jui-tsung
(684–721)," in *The Cambridge History of China*, vol. 3, *Sui and T'ang China, 589–906*,"
ed. Denis Twitchett (London: Cambridge University Press, 1979), 322.

brother.[58] Li Zhe and the Empress were banished to Fangzhou (modern Fangxian, Hubei), in the south.

Wei Xuanzhen fared much worse. His wife, four sons, and two daughters were banished to Lingnan, the untamed south (corresponding to the present-day provinces of Guangdong and Guangxi).[59] Edward Schafer, who has written engagingly of the perils faced by Tang travelers in this "pestilential land," notes that the specific area to which Wei and his family were banished had been secured only in 622, when the Ning tribes submitted to Tang rule. Schafer describes the journey there as follows:

> Along with soldiers, administrators, and colonists, [merchants] journeyed westward from Canton through the richly mineralized but dangerous province of Rong [where Wei's sons were banished]. Its administrative town was on the Yu (. . . the name means "jungly") River, now called simply "West River." The settlement was much troubled by rampant waters until part of the flow was diverted by Sima Lüren in 710–11. This hazardous road led to the Vietnamese lands (not yet distinguished as such), and above them to the Tibeto-Burmans of Nanzhao, in deadly rivalry with the Tang men for the control of the southwest. Many northern visitors must have found it a frightening experience to pass through the Gate of Ghosts, a gap, thirty paces wide, between two crags in Yulin ("Jungle Forest") County. . . . The lands beyond this portal reeked with deadly miasmas. An eighth-century folk-saying about them went: "The customs barrier at Ghost Gate—Ten men go out, Nine men return.[60]

Lingnan and adjacent Annam were not just places of banishment for Wu Zhao—she had many of her enemies murdered there.[61] Even if they escaped assassination orders from the central government, disease and even cannibals threatened the lives of citified Tang exiles. The Man people were not always amenable to Tang rule, as the lengthy list of reported rebellions during the course of the dynasty that Schafer has collected testifies.[62]

Not surprisingly, given their political enemies and the perils of their journey, Wei Xuanzhen and the male members of his family all are re-

58. Ibid., 290–91.

59. Wei Xuanzhen and his wife were banished to Qinzhou, modern Qinxian in the far south of modern Guangdong Province. His sons are reported to have died in Rongzhou, in the northeastern part of modern Beiliu Xian in Guangxi Province, perhaps on the journey into the region. See Ou-yang Xiu, Song Qi, et al., *Xin Tangshu*, 206.5843; and Liu Xu et al., *Jiu Tangshu*, 183.4743.

60. Edward H. Schafer, *The Vermilion Bird: T'ang Images of the South* (Berkeley and Los Angeles: University of California Press, 1967), 31.

61. Ibid., 39.

62. See ibid., 61–69.

ported as having "died" during their banishment. Perhaps the historians were unable to determine the manner of their deaths. Certainly the fact that the two daughters were able to survive and return to the capital makes us suspicious. Only in the case of his wife, surnamed Cui 崔, do the standard histories specifically mention murder. Madame Cui was killed by Ning Cheng 寧承, a Man 蠻 tribesman, and his brothers.[63]

In 698, Li Zhe and his Empress Wei were recalled to the capital, and Li was reinstated as heir-apparent.[64] In 705, Li Zhe and his supporters moved to depose Wu Zhao and succeeded by force in restoring the Tang dynasty. They did not, however, succeed in blocking all women from what had by now become a bitter, bloody struggle for power.

The following year, the Empress Wei took steps that she hoped would result in her ascent to the throne in her own name, in imitation of Wu Zhao, the remarkable "Child of Heaven" who had died the previous year. The Empress Wei brought her parents' bodies back to the capital for burial. She also had her mother's murderers, including Ning Cheng, executed and their heads brought back to display before the caskets that bore her parents' remains.[65] She then, we know from the inscribed stone, provided for Daoist rituals that would ensure her parents' favorable rebirth or entry into the heavens. Not incidentally, the stone engraved with Lingbao celestial script that she had placed in the grave to accomplish this spiritual transfer also announced a new and exalted title for her father, Prince of Feng, a suitable rank for the father of a future "Child of Heaven."[66]

The Empress's wishes for her parents were satisfied—at least insofar as their names are remembered by us—but her personal desires were not. These were years of swift reprisal within the palace. Empress Wei's head ended up, not crowned in glory, but on a pike in the Eastern Market of the capital Chang'an. Still, despite the failure of her ambitions, we can see the uses to which she hoped to put Daoist ritual. Through her ritual act, ensuring the salvation of her parents, she provided for them a suitable pedigree that would bolster her own aspirations to rule all under heaven.

63. Liu Xu et al., *Jiu Tangshu*, 183.4743; Ou-yang Xiu, Song Qi, et al., *Xin Tangshu*, 206.5843.

64. Guisso, "The Reigns," 317.

65. Liu Xu et al., *Jiu Tangshu*, 183.4744; Ou-yang Xiu, Song Qi, et al., *Xin Tangshu*, 206.5843.

66. The title of "Prince" was usually rewarded only to sons of Emperors or to "unusually distinguished military officers." See Charles O. Hucker, *A Dictionary of Official Titles in Imperial China* (Stanford, CA: Stanford University Press, 1985), 562.

The ritual accompanying the burial of the Empress's inscription is described in the Lingbao scripture entitled *Transit through Extinction by the Refinement of the Five for the Revivification of the Corpse* (HY 369; hereafter, the *Scripture for Revivification*). Here the priest is instructed to write the celestial text known as the Perfected Script in yellow on a white stone and to bury it while pronouncing its powerful words together with the charge translated above.[67]

This charge is a command 符命 (literally: "orders [authenticated by] talisman") emanating from the Lord of Heaven, known by the awesome title Heavenly Worthy of Prime Origin in our scriptures, through the western celestial powers and directed to the underworld officers within their jurisdiction. The purpose of the charge is in one respect the same as that of the Han-period sepulchral documents studied by Seidel and others: to arrange bureaucratic procedures on behalf of the dead.[68] The underworld officials are informed of the precise location of the body in the tomb, where a "hall and rooms" have been set up for them. This characterization recalls the fact that, throughout the ages, Chinese tombs were indeed constructed on the model of palace residences.

Further notification is given that the Five Transcendents, lords at once of the five "naked-eye" planets and of the five viscera, will descend to take charge of the cadavers, bearing them to the Palace of Supreme Darkness, where the White Spirits will rejuvenate them, refining their flesh and bones in alchemical fashion and preparing them for life.

Meanwhile, we are given to understand that one of the spiritual dimensions of their bodies—their cloudsouls, are now under the jurisdiction of the appropriate one of the Five Marchmounts, Mount Hua. Our document commands the officials of this realm to open their earth-prisons (the nine Gloomy Halls of Eternal Darkness) to release their cloudsouls. These constituents of the self will ascend to the Southern Palace where they will also be nourished and garbed in such a fashion as to prepare it for continued existence.[69]

---

67. In fact, while the stone could be described as "white," I saw no evidence that the incised words had ever been colored in yellow.

68. See Anna K. Seidel, "Tokens of Immortality in Han Graves," *Numen* 29, no. 1 (1982): 79–114; and "Traces of Han Religion in Funeral Texts Found in Tombs," in *Dōkyō to shūkyō bunka* [volume in honour of Professor Akitsuki Kan'ei] (Tokyo: Hirakawa, 1987), 21–57.

69. On these visions of postmortem refinement of the various constituents of the self, see also Stephen R. Bokenkamp, "Death and Ascent," and "Stages of Transcendence: The *Bhūmi* Concept in Taoist Scripture," in *Chinese Buddhist Apocrypha*, ed. Robert E. Buswell Jr. (Honolulu: University of Hawaii Press, 1990), 119–47.

So much the document tells us. It appears at this point as if the understanding that separate destinies await the spiritual and the bodily constituents of the person at death holds true here. The Palace of Supreme Darkness is known from Daoist texts predating this one to be the palace where the bodies of the righteous dead were refashioned.[70] The cloud-souls, on the other hand, are here sent to the Southern Palace. With one part of the self going north and the other south, so to speak, the separation could be no more complete.

But the matter does not end there. Along with this imperial command, the Daoist presiding over this burial is instructed to pronounce words of incantation which, while they largely reiterate the directives of the command, further specify that the cloudsouls of the deceased are to be reunited with the body. The whole person is then readied for continued existence in the heavens or for rebirth after a certain number of years, depending on the merits of the deceased.[71] In the words of the text, "Those who should cross over [to the celestial realms], will cross over; those who should be reborn will be reborn; those who should cycle [into a new existence] will cycle; and those who should return [to the Dao] will return."[72]

This burial ritual was crafted for precisely the sort of situation that Empress Wei confronted. What this ritual intends to celebrate, in short, is a reuniting of that which has been separated. Bodies fragmented and threatened are rejoined. The dangerous dead—and all dead were regarded as potentially dangerous—are stripped of the alienation that constitutes their primary reason for resentment. Taxonomic boundaries between the living and the dead are reestablished, and orderly, ancient means of occasional contact through ancestral practice can resume.[73]

But what the ritual story wants to conceal, it gives back in the telling.

70. See Bokenkamp, *Early Daoist Scriptures,* 46–48.

71. Other scriptures of the Lingbao corpus confirm this and further lay out a system of advancement in merit by which a Disciple of Unsullied Belief such as the one in our sepulchral text might expect an improvement both in spiritual status and in worldly status as a result of this rebirth. Through unstinting practice of the Way of Lingbao, he or she can expect nine further "refinements" of body and soul, analogous to the nine-times-recycled elixir of the alchemists, until becoming a "Disciple of Ten Cycles" (*shizhuan dizi* 十轉弟子), ready, both physically and spiritually, to ascend to heaven for the final time to dwell forever among officials of the stellar bureaucracy. See Bokenkamp, "Stages of Transcendence," for the ramifications of this system.

72. This formula is enunciated twice in the text, albeit in slightly different forms; see HY 369, 1b2–3, and 2b4–5.

73. Robert F. Campany, in *Strange Writing: Anomaly Accounts in Early Medieval China* (Albany: State University of New York Press, 1996, 266–71) discusses the disturbing nature of such boundary-crossings in *zhiguai* literature.

Separation remains the fundamental fact about death, and that division is projected onto the dead themselves. The spiritual constituents of the person—the ground of the ancestors' memory and concern for their descendants—are "fed." Decomposing bodies—locus of primal fear for the living—are made whole and "fragrant." But relating the mechanisms by which this was believed to take place, off of the ritual stage, so to speak, reveals to us the fundamental fears that the separation of death, and especially violent death, still occasioned.

Not unexpectedly, then, the persistent anxieties of the living, their projections into the realms of darkness, suffuse this new ritual program. The opening of the *Scripture for Revivification* portrays the Celestial Worthy instructing 7,240 youths in a celestial garden. As the ceremonies are nearing completion and the great Way has been promulgated, two of the assembly, the Youth of Highest Wisdom and the Heaven-turning Youth, approach with a question. The salvation that the Celestial Worthy has promulgated is for all. Even those in the dark cells of the earth-prisons and wandering ghosts have obtained release. But what is to become of them now? Since they have not yet entered again into the revolutions of samsara, "their corpses and spirits flee so that their rotted frame is no use to them, and they sink back into the nine [stygian] realms where they might cross the Earth Officers. Their flying spirits dart about in hesitation, unable to return to earth."[74] But it is not solely compassion for the dead that prompts the request that this situation for the two youths continue with more specific explanations: "Those unable to return to the old residence in their bodies will be unbearably oppressed by the myriads of spirits in the [subterranean] nine springs. With no place to lodge their flying cloudsouls, they will return to infect their descendants."[75]

These concerns are strikingly similar to the ones that motivated those under Sima Rui who wished to conduct for their ancestors *hun*-summoning burials or that prompted Yang Xi's interventions into the Xu family illnesses. Only the solution differs. The Lingbao response was arguably more effective. In the case of Empress Wei, the ritual might have worked as follows: Her father and mother had been separated from her first by banishment and then (at least in the case of her mother) by violent death. This rupture, in the society of her time, represented a double loss of status. Alive, her parents were stripped of prestige; dead they lacked not only the power ascribed to ancestors but became a possible source of un-

74. HY 369, 1a8–9.
75. HY 369, 1b4–5.

seen threat. The Lingbao ritual she commissioned repaired both of these losses. But first it reiterated them in ritual structure with its account of spiritual faculties separated from bodies. In our terms, it attends to both the spiritual and the physical with its account of special "feedings" for both aspects of the person. In a society so concerned with the physicality of the dead, this solution reassures in a way that the burying of simulacra in the case of *hun*-summoning burials cannot. And remember, even Yang Xi's rescue of Tao Kedou, Xu Mi's deceased wife, was nearly sabotaged when the daughter-in-law Hua Zirong failed to keep up with the schedule of ancestral feedings.

In the case of the Empress Wei, we know that her father's status was restored. He was given the title of Prince of Feng, as reported on the stone that once rested in his tomb. And we know that her parents were once again elevated to the status of powerful ancestors. Wei Xuanzhen and his wife were buried in a tumulus called "Glorifying the Ancestors," and their tablets were placed in an ancestral temple with the exalted title "Celebrating Virtue." Their final residences were provided with one hundred persons to guard and cleanse them.[76] For the moment, harmony had been restored.

CONCLUSION

Despite the large numbers of his contemporaries who practiced the faith, when the author of the Lingbao scriptures mentions Buddhism, he invariably states or implies that it is a "foreign" religion. It is remarkable, then, that in Lingbao accounts of rebirth, we find no trace of anxiety concerning the undeniable fact that the mechanisms of rebirth derive from Chinese Buddhism. We do find defensive gestures with regard to other clear adaptations from Buddhist scripture. When the scriptures mention the "bodhisattvas of the ten directions," exotic otherworldly locales, and other identifiable bits pilfered from Buddhist texts, they commonly invoke the supposed antiquity of the Lingbao texts as warrant and state forthrightly some version of the formula "all of this issues from Lingbao."[77] But we find no such disclaimer with regard to the idea of rebirth. Instead, in the only specific reference to Buddhist ideas of individual responsibility, from the *Precepts of the Three Primordials* analyzed above, the strategy is more forthrightly offensive. Buddhist texts have gotten it

76. Liu Xu et al., *Jiu Tangshu,* 183.4744.
77. For the examples given here, see Bokenkamp, "Sources of the Ling-pao Scriptures."

wrong. Personal responsibility has been there all along, but familial responsibility and involvements across the boundary between life and death are an inescapable fact of this fallen age.

This is a feature of the Lingbao message that we noticed in Lu Xiujing's account of the *Retreat of Mud and Ash*. His citation of the ancient *Shijing* poem that contains the lines "If one has no father, on whom shall one rely? If one has no mother, on whom shall one depend? Abroad, one harbors grief; at home one has no one to whom to go," together with his thoroughgoing concern with parents in his conduct of the ritual, represent perhaps the clearest Chinese critique of Buddhist ideas of rebirth. And, indeed, the Lingbao scriptures are almost obsessively concerned with rituals designed to rescue ancestors from the underworlds, restoring fathers and mothers to their sacrificial families.

Postscript

This book, while it deals with the Chinese reception and deployment of the Buddhist ideas of rebirth, karma, and samsara, is not finally about Chinese Buddhism. Rather, as I have tried to make clear at each stage, the texts we have examined are not Buddhist. Further, the "Buddhism" that appears in them is not an accurate, historical reflection of the faces of Chinese Buddhism, but a projection of the authors, who sometimes construe the Buddhism of their compatriots as "other" and sometimes ignore it altogether.

And yet, I have argued, the story our authors tell is all the more valuable for that. These struggles beyond the walls of the monastery with ideas introduced by Buddhism provide us with a very different picture than that presented in Buddhist writings. While I cannot hope to have dislodged the prevailing scholarly notion that Buddhist ideas easily swept all before them in a sort of "Buddhist conquest of China," I do hope to have brought new voices into the conversation and to have introduced novel ways to recover these forgotten voices. I have argued that it will not do to continue searching for *the* Chinese reception of Buddhist ideas only in texts specifically marked as Buddhist, in those writings assembled in Buddhist accounts of the adoption of their faith, or in philosophical works.[1] Engagement with the new notions surrounding re-

---

1. I am thinking here primarily of the Japanese scholars such as Tsukamoto Zenryu, Nakajima Ryūzō, Michihata Yoshihide, and those who follow their lead, who take the trea-

birth took place on the individual level, within the context of families, and was subject to all the evasions, negotiations, and reconfigurations we have charted, and many more we have not.

To keep this locus of change firmly in mind, I began with the idea that the texts I assembled are "arguments" of various sorts, and, adopting rubrics from Campany, portrayed them as "externalist statements," arguments that function to set the ideas of a speaker or writer in opposition to certain prevailing societal values and presuppositions. I argued that these externalist statements do not simply equate with belief systems, but represent one of the many possible cultural repertoires.[2] Thus, the ways that medieval Chinese made their dead to talk, like other sorts of statements, were meant to answer precise questions and concerns and to address specific anxieties. These motives are most often to be found not in abstract systems of thought or doctrines, but in the quotidian conditions of those making the statements, and they are more often personal and familial than ideological.

In the case of those who animated Su Shao and Guo Fan, who argued for a specific configuration of the underworld bureaucracy (one that would privilege their relatives and serve their own interests), the "others" who held different views are easily imagined, and the differences between the two stances rather slight. Primarily at issue was a matter of personnel rather than fundamental structures. As we learned from the 318 debate over *hun*-summoning burials, however, these seemingly slight differences could have for those involved immediate, and dire, real-world consequences.

But, at the same time, these positionings can tell us something of how segments of Chinese society received and deployed Buddhist ideas of rebirth. All of these accounts of the underworld were composed well after ideas of rebirth were rather widely known in Chinese society. None of

---

tises, records of debate, and correspondence between Buddhist monks and the laity, all collected in such Buddhist works as Sengyou's *Hongming ji* (*T* 2102, 52:1–97), to be an accurate record of China's adoption of the Buddhist faith. While their work contains much of value, in this case they are, it seems to me, merely reading the record left for them to find.

2. Several recent studies have emphasized the ways in which cultures are never simple or unitary. Every culture offers a range of possibilities, and actors tend to draw promiscuously on this "toolkit" of sometimes conflicting repertoires in justifying and describing their actions. See Ann Swidler, *Talk of Love: How Culture Matters* (Chicago: University of Chicago Press, 1999), esp. 24–40; and Robert F. Campany, "The Meanings of Cuisines of Transcendence in Late Classical and Early Medieval China," *T'oung Pao* 91 (2005): 1–57.

them mention it at all. In fact, the only references we find in them to Buddhism are ornamental and meant to draw on the prestige of the religion in oblique ways. This is indeed striking, given the spread of the Buddhist religion in the second and third centuries, and its rapid growth in popularity in the elite salons of the Jin, which began in the third century and reached an apex in the fourth.[3] But I would argue strongly against reading this as evidence that ideas of rebirth were not widespread, not only because *ex nihilo nihil fit,* but also because texts exactly like them were written well after we know from other sources that ideas of rebirth were generally known.

Only in the writings of Yang Xi, toward the end of the fourth century, do we begin to encounter explicit references to the idea of rebirth. In Yang's writings we do not, however, detect acceptance of a generalized rebirth, reincarnation as the common lot of all, but a very specialized and provisional deployment of the idea. Yang refers to rebirth to explain the deep-seated recalcitrance of his patron Xu Mi to leave office and pursue fully the Daoist path or to elucidate the reputed success of some practitioners whose methods, they claimed, allowed them to "leave the family" and thus avoid postmortem familial entanglement. In all cases, however, he takes care to emphasize that celestial oversight and the laws of corporate familial responsibility are not to be abrogated.

In his reports from the underworld, Yang Xi positioned himself not against contemporary Buddhism, but primarily with respect to other Daoists and mediums who had reported on the promotions and demotions of the shades in their new bureaucratic offices. While much of the context to which Yang's externalist statements responded has undoubtedly not survived, Tao Hongjing, who sought to trace the procedures of the underworld, provides us with enough evidence to gauge the extent to which this is true. Tao's careful collation of the Yang/Xu manuscripts with other documents thus bears witness to how Yang Xi deployed postmortem reports in his efforts to gain elite converts to his Daoist path. Like those with whom he entered into dialogue on the placement of specific individuals, Yang Xi's Fengdu was not punitive. While he had better prospects to offer, and we see clear signs that contemporaries were beginning to find the bureaucracy there too unpredictable and troublesome, Fengdu was still, like the other Chinese underworlds we traced, a

---

3. See Erik Zürcher, *The Buddhist Conquest of China,* 2 vols. (Leiden: E. J. Brill, 1959), 18–179; and Tsukamoto Zenryu, *A History of Early Chinese Buddhism: From Its Introduction to the Death of Hui Yüan,* trans. Leon Hurvitz (Tokyo: Kodansha, 1985).

desirable destination. In this respect, Yang distinguishes even this lesser afterlife from the Buddhist hells, with their brutal punishments.

Having traced Chinese ideas of the underworld and its tenuous and contested staffing during the third and fourth centuries, and surveyed at least cursorily how the dead were employed to fulfill the desires of the living, we are perhaps prepared to recognize the preciousness of the gift Buddhism represented to those Daoists who wished to reform the religious scene of medieval China. It is not that any of the previous repertoires, the multifarious ways of dealing with and speaking for the dead, were totally abandoned. Rather, with the appearance of the Lingbao scriptures, we can see clearly what appealed to many non-Buddhists in the particular mix of ideas surrounding rebirth. According to the externalist arguments voiced in these scriptures, I have argued, one idea seems to have been especially useful: merit-transfer, the ability to rescue one's ancestors from service in the underworld.

Recall that Yang Xi, while stressing the importance of one's ancestors' place in the underworld, could not offer to pluck them out of Fengdu. All he could do for the dead (and their living relations) was to intervene in underworld lawsuits, bringing to bear the full weight of celestial officialdom, to make things turn out better. The case of Tao Kedou shows this clearly. She was already destined for a position in the subcelestial study center, the Palace of Mutation and Promotion, and had been blocked by entanglements with the unfortunate dead of the Xu family. Yang was able to resolve the lawsuit and thereby allow her to move on to her predestined goal. For the living, men such as Xu Mi and Chi Yin, Yang could hold forth the possibility that they might avoid Fengdu altogether and move on to infinitely more desirable postmortem destinations; once they were dead, however, there was little he could do for them.

The case is very different for the authors of the Lingbao scriptures. They took over one Buddhist idea above all—the notion that one could transfer the merit of ritual action not merely to appease or bargain with the dead, but also to rescue them from unfortunate postmortem fates. The ubiquity of soteriological ritual scripts that are preserved in the early scriptures attest to the centrality of this concern. At the same time, a key passage specifically contesting what the author(s) of the Lingbao scriptures took to be the Buddhist stance on merit-transfer reveals clearly the extent to which this was not simply a case of "Buddhist influence." Rather, the Lingbao scriptures steer a middle course between radical individual responsibility and corporate implication in the misdeeds and dilemmas of the family dead. They accomplish this through a rather ingenious cosmological argument: In past world-systems, individuals were entirely responsible for their own deeds. But humans made oaths on the heads of their dead ancestors, involving families in corporate responsibility and abrogating the old order, so that now the worlds of the living and dead are indeed joined along family lines. The postmortem lawsuits and anxieties about the family dead evident in the stories of Su Shao, Guo Fan, and Tao Kedou are thus still a problem, but only for those who do not accept the message of Lingbao. The scriptures and their practices, it is promised, can make one again an individual agent, no longer vulnerable to the threats of the dark world. And, of course, such a free agent will, through the meritorious practices of Lingbao, work for the salvation of his or her family dead—further assurance that the grateful dead will no longer seek to harm the living.

Further modifications of Buddhist doctrine are entailed by the Lingbao reception of the idea of merit-transfer. Now, for the first time, Daoist texts begin to speak of the regions of the underworld as true hells—places of unremitting torture and suffering. As we saw in the writings of Lu Xiujing, the ancestors are in need of help and must be converted once again into sources of blessing for the living.

The criticisms in this passage directed against Buddhist solutions show the extent to which, at least for some, Buddhist ideas of rebirth and merit-transfer did not seem to solve the problem of infection from beyond the grave. For the author(s) of the Lingbao scriptures, Buddhist dealings with the dead did not sufficiently provide for families and did not account for the very real ways that the dead influenced the living through underworld lawsuits and spectral disease. Of course Chinese Buddhists did attend to these problems, developing their own rituals specifically for the family dead and increasing their emphasis on procedures meant to direct merit to specific recipients.[4] These developments respond to some of the same concerns that are first expressed in the Lingbao scriptures.

Whether presented explicitly or implicitly, the Lingbao critique di-

---

4. See Hou Xudong, *Wu, liu shiji beifang minzhong fojiao xinyang* (Beijing: Zhongguo shehui kexueyuan chubanshe, 1998), for the fifth- and sixth-century stelae often dedicated to share the merit of their construction with specific family members. For ritual solutions, see Stephen F. Teiser, *The Ghost Festival in Medieval China* (Princeton, NJ: Princeton University Press, 1988); and *The Scripture on the Ten Kings and the Making of Purgatory in Medieval Chinese Buddhism* (Honolulu: University of Hawaii Press, 1994). While I concede Gregory Schopen's point that Indian monks transferred merit specifically to their ancestors as well (see his *Bones, Stones, and Buddhist Monks: Collected Papers on the Arche-*

rected at Buddhist ideas of individual responsibility and rebirth outside the family does not—and could not—constitute a motive for adopting the idea of rebirth. Instead, the arguments we have reviewed represent one aspect of the Lingbao authors' modifications of the concept of rebirth—modifications necessary to make the idea a suitable answer to the various threats to ancestral practice that we have traced throughout this book. We would not, I think, have noticed the strength and perdurance of this threat had we not spent time ourselves with the unhappy shades of China's various underworlds.

---

ology, Epigraphy, and Texts of Monastic Buddhism in India [Honolulu: University of Hawaii Press, 1997], 56–71), it remains true that the evidence so far presented by scholars of Buddhism shows a marked increase in such rituals in China beginning in the fifth century. The numerous Buddhist *sūtras* composed in China on the subject of filiality and family merit-transfer also show that this was a societal concern to which Buddhists had to respond.

Abbreviations

Scriptures in the Daoist canon 正統道藏, are cited using the abbreviation HY (for Harvard-Yenching) along with their number in the *Combined Indices to the Authors and Titles of Books in Two Collections of Taoist Literature* 道藏子目引得, ed. Weng Dujian 翁獨健, Harvard-Yenching Institute Sinological Series, no. 25 (Beijing: Harvard-Yenching Institute, 1925). In the list below, I have appended after the title the number of the scripture according to Kristofer M. Schipper's *Concordance du Tao Tsang* (Paris: École française d'Extrême-Orient, 1975), preceded by the abbreviation *CT*.

HY 9	*Taishang yisheng haikong zhizang jing* 太上一乘海空智藏經. *CT* 9.
HY 369	*Taishang dongxuan lingbao miedu wulian shengshi miaojing* 太上洞玄靈寶滅度五錬生尸妙經. *CT* 369.
HY 388	*Taishang lingbao wufu xu* 太上靈寶五符序. *CT* 388.
HY 421	*Dengzhen yinjue* 登真隱訣. *CT* 421.
HY 456	*Taishang dongxuan lingbao sanyuan pinjie gongde qingzhong jing* 太上洞玄靈寶三元品戒功德輕重經. *CT* 456.
HY 528	*Taishang dongxuan lingbao shoudu yi* 太上洞玄靈寶授度儀. *CT* 528.
HY 615	*Chisong zi zhangli* 赤松子章曆. *CT* 615.
HY 789	*Nüqing guilü* 女青鬼律. *CT* 790.
HY 1010	*Zhen'gao* 真誥. *CT* 1016.
HY 1026	*Yunji qiqian* 雲笈七籤. *CT* 1032.

HY 1106   *Taishang dongxuan lingbao benxing suyuan jing* 太上洞玄
             靈寶本行宿緣經. *CT* 1114.

HY 1107   *Taishang dongxuan lingbao benxing yinyuan jing* 太上洞玄
             靈寶本行因緣經. *CT* 1115.

HY 1268   *Dongxuan lingbao wugan wen* 洞玄靈寶五感文. *CT* 1278.

HY 1365   *Shangqing taishang dijun jiuzhen zhongjing* 上清太上帝君九
             真中經. *CT* 1376.

HY 1371   *Shangqing jiudan shanghua taijing zhongji jing* 上清九丹上
             化胎精中記經. *CT* 1382.

The Dunhuang manuscripts collected by Paul Pelliot and Aurel Stein and cited
in this work are collected in Ōfuchi Ninji 大淵忍爾, *Tonkō dōkyō zurokuhen*
敦煌道經圖錄編. (Tokyo: Fukubu shoten, 1979). Those collected by Pelliot
are cited with the initial *P*; those collected by Stein are cited with the initial *S*.
The works cited are listed below, followed by their page numbers in Ōfuchi's
work:

P 2454   *Taishang dongxuan lingbao xianren qingwen benxing*
             yinyuan zhongsheng nan jing 太上洞玄靈寶仙人請問
             本行因緣眾聖難經, 89–92.

P 2751   *Ziwen xingshi jue* 紫文行事訣, 382–94.

S 6659   *Taishang dongxuan lingbao miaojing zhongpian xu zhang*
             太上洞玄靈寶妙經序章, 93–103.

SSJZS   *Shisan jing zhushu* 十三經注疏, ed. Ruan Yuan 阮元 (1764–
             1849) (Beijing: Zhonghua, 1979). Works are cited from this
             edition by their short titles:

Shangshu   *Shangshu zhengyi* 尚書正義.

Shijing   *Maoshi zhengyi* 毛詩正義.

Zhouli   *Zhouli zhushu* 周禮注疏.

Yili   *Yili zhushu* 儀禮注疏.

Liji   *Liji zhengyi* 禮記正義.

Zuo zhuan   *Chunqiu Zuo zhuan zhengyi* 春秋左傳正義.

Lunyu   *Lunyu zhushu* 論語注疏.

Xiaojing   *Xiaojing zhushu* 孝經注疏.

T   *Taishō shinshū daizōkyō* 大正新修大藏經, ed. Takakusa
             Junjirō 高楠順次郎, 100 vols. (Tokyo: Daizō shuppan kai,
             1922–33). Works in this collection are cited by their assigned
             numbers, preceded by the initial *T* and followed by the volume
             and page number. Appended to the page number is the letter

a, b, or c, to indicate the register. To this, I have added line
numbers when it seemed a kindness.

T 152 *Liudu ji jing* 六度集經, by Kang Senghui 康僧會 (fl. 250 CE).

T 2102 *Hongming ji* 弘明集, edited by Sengyou 康僧會 (435–518).

T 2122 *Fayuan zhulin* 法苑珠林, compiled by Daoshi 道世 (d. 683).

T 2149 *Da Tang neidian lu* 大唐內典錄, by Dao Xuan 道宣 (596–667).

Bibliography

Abe, Stanley K. *Ordinary Images*. Chicago: University of Chicago Press, 2002.

Anderson, Benedict. *Imagined Communities: Reflections on the Origin and Spread of Nationalism*. London: Verso, 1991.

Aramaki Noritoshi 荒牧典俊. "Shinkō yizen shoshinkō no hennen mondai ni tsuite 真誥以前の編年問題について." In Yoshikawa, *Rikuchō dōkyō no kenkyū*, 55–100.

Ban Gu 班固 (32–92), et al. *Hanshu* 漢書. Beijing: Zhonghua shuju, 1962.

Bargen, Doris G.. *A Woman's Weapon: Spirit Possession in the Tale of Genji*. Honolulu: University of Hawaii Press, 1997.

Baxandall, Michael. *Patterns of Intention: On the Historical Explanation of Pictures*. New Haven, CT: Yale University Press, 1985.

Bell, Catherine. *Ritual: Perspectives and Dimensions*. Oxford: Oxford University Press, 1997.

Benn, Charles D. *The Cavern-Mystery Transmission: A Taoist Ordination Rite of A.D. 711*. Honolulu: University of Hawaii Press, 1991.

Berger, Peter L. *The Sacred Canopy: Elements of a Sociological Theory of Religion*. Garden City, NY: Doubleday, 1967.

Bloom, Harold. *The Anxiety of Influence: A Theory of Poetry*. Oxford: Oxford University Press, 1973.

Bokenkamp, Stephen R. "Answering a Summons." In Lopez, *Religions of China in Practice*, 188–202.

———. "Daoism: An Overview." In *Encyclopedia of Religion*, ed. Lindsay Jones, 4:2176–92. 2nd ed. New York: Macmillan Reference, 2005.

———. "Death and Ascent in Ling-pao Taoism." *Taoist Resources* 1, no. 2 (1989): 1–20.

———. "Declarations of the Perfected." In Lopez, *Religions of China in Practice*, 166–79.

————. *Early Daoist Scriptures*. Berkeley and Los Angeles: University of California Press, 1997.

————. "The Prehistory of Laozi: His Prior Career as a Woman in the Lingbao Scriptures." *Cahiers d'Extrême-Asie* 14 (2004): 403–21.

————. "Sackcloth and Ashes: Self and Family in the Tutan Zhai." In *Scriptures, Schools, and Forms of Practice in Taoism*, ed. Poul Andersen and Florian C. Reiter, 33–48. Wiesbaden: Harrassowitz Verlag, 2005.

————. "The Silkworm and the Bodhi Tree: The Lingbao Attempt to Replace Buddhism in China and Our Attempt to Place Lingbao Daoism." In Lagerwey, *Religion and Chinese Society*, 317–39.

————. "Simple Twists of Fate? The Daoist Body and Its *Ming*." In *The Magnitude of Ming: Command, Allotment, and Fate in Chinese Culture*, ed. Christopher Lupke, 151–68. Honolulu: University of Hawaii Press, 2005.

————. "Sources of the *Ling-pao* Scriptures." In Strickmann, *Tantric and Taoist Studies*, 434–85.

————. "Stages of Transcendence: the *Bhūmi* Concept in Taoist Scripture." In Buswell, *Chinese Buddhist Apocrypha*, 119–47.

Brashier, K. E. "Han Thanatology and the Division of 'Souls.' " *Early China* 21 (1996): 125–58.

Brown, Miranda. "Did the Early Chinese Preserve Corpses? A Reconsideration of Elite Conceptions of Death." *Journal of East Asian Archeology* 4, nos. 1–4 (2002): 201–23.

————. "Sons and Mothers in Warring States and Han China, 453 BCE—220 CE." *Nan nü* 5, no. 2 (2003): 137–69.

Burke, Peter. 1998. *The European Renaissance: Centres and Peripheries*. Oxford: Blackwell, 1998.

Buswell, Robert E., Jr., ed. *Chinese Buddhist Apocrypha*. Honolulu: University of Hawaii Press, 1990.

Cahill, Suzanne E. *Transcendence and Divine Passion: The Queen Mother of the West in Medieval China*. Stanford, CA: Stanford University Press, 1993.

Cai Yong 蔡邕 (133–92). *Cai zhonglang ji* 蔡中郎集, ed. Sibu beiyao 四部備要. Shanghai: Zhonghua shuju, 1927–1936.

Campany, Robert Ford. "The Meanings of Cuisines of Transcendence in Late Classical and Early Medieval China." *T'oung Pao* 91 (2005): 1–57.

————. "On the Very Idea of Religions (in the Modern West and in Early Medieval China)." *History of Religions* 42, no. 4 (2003): 287–319.

————. "Return-from-Death Narratives in Early Medieval China." *Journal of Chinese Religions* 18 (1990): 91–125.

————. *Strange Writing: Anomaly Accounts in Early Medieval China*. Albany: State University of New York Press, 1996.

————. *To Live as Long as Heaven and Earth: A Translation and Study of Ge Hong's "Traditions of Divine Transcendents."* Berkeley and Los Angeles: University of California Press, 2000.

Cedzich, Ursula-Angelika. "Corpse Deliverance, Substitute Bodies, Name Change, and Feigned Death: Aspects of Metamorphosis and Immortality in Early Medieval China." *Journal of Chinese Religions* 29 (2001): 1–68.

Chen Shou 陳壽 (233–297). *Sanguo zhi* 三國志. Beijing: Zhonghua, 1962.

Chenivesse, Sandrine. *Le Mont Fengdu: Lieu saint Taoïste émergé de la géographie de l'au-delà*. Paris: École Pratique des Hautes Études, 1995.

Chi Chao 郗超 (336–77). *Fengfa yao* 奉法要. T 2102, 52:86a ff.

Chou Chao-ming. "Death, Funerals, and Sacrifices in Wang Ch'ung's Philosophy." *Tamkang Review* 17, no. 2 (1986): 175–95.

Chuci. See Hong Xingzu.

Cole, Alan. *Mothers and Sons in Chinese Buddhism*. Stanford, CA: Stanford University Press, 1998.

———. "Upside Down / Right Side Up: A Revisionist History of Buddhist Funerals in China." *History of Religions* 35, no. 4 (1996): 307–38.

Connery, Chris. "Ts'ai Yung." In *Indiana Companion to Traditional Chinese Literature*, ed. William H. Nienhauser Jr., 787–88. Bloomington: Indiana University Press, 1986.

Deng Ansheng 鄧安生. "Cai Yong zhuzuo bianyi 蔡邕著作辨疑." *Guji zhengli yanjiu xuekan* 古籍整理研究學刊 6 (1966): 31–34.

Despeux, Catherine. "Women in Daoism." In Kohn, *Daoism Handbook*, 384–412.

Dien, Albert E. "Developments in Funerary Practices in the Six Dynasties Period: The *Duisuguan* 堆塑罐 or "Figured Jar" as a Case in Point." In *Between Han and Tang: Cultural and Artistic Interaction in a Transformative Period*, ed. Wu Hung, 509–46. Beijing: Cultural Relics Publishing House, 2001.

Ding Fubao 丁福保, ed. *Quan Han Sanguo Jin Nanbeichao shi* 全漢三國晉南北朝詩. Taibei: Yiwen, 1960.

Dong Gao 董誥, et al., comp. *Qinding quan Tang wen* 欽定全唐文. Taibei: Huiwen shuju, 1961.

Du You 杜佑 (735–812). *Tongdian* 通典. Shanghai: Shangwu, 1935.

Dudbridge, Glen. *Religious Experience and Lay Society in T'ang China: A Reading of Tai Fu's Kuang-i chi*. Cambridge: Cambridge University Press, 1995.

Ebrey, Patricia Buckley. *Chu Hsi's Family Rituals : A Twelfth-Century Chinese Manual for the Performance of Cappings, Weddings, Funerals, and Ancestral Rites*. Princeton, NJ: Princeton University Press, 1991.

Falkenhausen, Lothar von. "Reflections on the Role of Spirit Mediums in Early China: The *Wu* Officials in the *Zhou Li*." *Early China* 20 (1995): 279–300.

———. "Sources of Taoism: Reflections on Archaeological Indicators of Religious Chance in Eastern Zhou China." *Taoist Resources* 5, no. 2 (1994): 1–12.

Fan Ye 范曄 (398–445). *Hou Hanshu* 後漢書. Beijing: Zhonghua shuju, 1971.

Fang Xuanling 房玄齡 (578–648) et al. *Jinshu* 晉書. Beijing: Zhonghua shuju, 1974.

Forke, Alfred. *Lun-heng*. 2 vols. New York: Paragon Book Gallery, 1962.

Gallagher, Catherine, and Stephen Greenblatt. *Practicing New Historicism*. Chicago: University of Chicago Press, 2000.

Gan Bao 干寶 (d. 336?). *Soushen ji* 搜神記. Beijing: Zhonghua shuju, 1979.

Ge Hong 葛洪 (283–343). *Baopuzi neipian jiaoshi* 抱朴子內篇. Ed. Wang Ming 王明. 4 vols. Beijing: Zhonghua shuju, 1980.

Gjertson, Donald E. *Miraculous Retribution: A Study and Translation of T'ang Lin's Ming-pao chi*. Berkeley and Los Angeles: Centers for South and Southeast Asia Studies, University of California, 1989.

Graham, A. C. *The Book of Lieh-tzu: A Classic of the Tao.* New York: Columbia University Press, 1960.

———. *Chuang-tzu: The Seven Inner Chapters and Other Writings.* London: Allen & Unwin, 1981.

Greenblatt, Stephen. *Hamlet in Purgatory.* Princeton, NJ: Princeton University Press, 2001.

Guisso, Richard W. L. "The Reigns of Empress Wu, Chung-Tsung and Jui-tsung (684–721)." In *The Cambridge History of China.* Vol. 3. *Sui and T'ang China, 589–906,* ed. Denis Twitchett. London: Cambridge University Press, 1979.

Guo Maoqian 郭茂倩 (twelfth century), comp. *Yuefu Shiji* 樂府詩集. Beijing: Zhonghua, 1979.

Harper, Donald. "Resurrection in Warring States Popular Religion." *Taoist Resources* 5, no. 2 (1994): 13–29.

Hawkes, David. *The Songs of the South: An Anthology of Ancient Chinese Poems by Qu Yuan and Other Poets.* Harmondsworth, UK: Penguin Books, 1985.

Hinsch, Bret. "Confucian Filial Piety and the Construction of the Ideal Buddhist Woman." *Journal of Chinese Religions* 30 (2002): 49–76.

Ho Wai-kam. "*Hun-p'ing:* The Urn of the Soul." *The Bulletin of the Cleveland Museum of Art* 1, no. 3 (1961): 26–34.

Holcombe, Charles. *In the Shadow of the Han: Literati Thought and Society at the Beginning of the Southern Dynasties.* Honolulu: University of Hawaii Press, 1994.

Holzman, Donald. "Songs for the Gods: The Poetry of Popular Religion in Fifth-Century China." *Asia Major,* 3rd series, 3, no. 1 (1990): 1–20.

Hong Xingzu 洪興祖 (1070–1135). *Chuci buzhu* 楚辭補注. Beijing: Zhonghua shuju, 1983.

Hou Xudong 侯旭東. *Wu, liu shiji beifang minzhong fojiao xinyang* 五, 六世紀北方民眾佛教信仰. Beijing: Zhongguo shehui kexueyuan chubanshe, 1998.

Hucker, Charles O. *A Dictionary of Official Titles in Imperial China.* Stanford, CA: Stanford University Press, 1985.

Hulsewé, A. F. P. *Remnants of Han law.* Leiden: E. J. Brill, 1955.

Hunt, Lynn. *The Family Romance of the French Revolution.* Berkeley and Los Angeles: University of California Press, 1992.

Ikeda On 池田溫. "*Chūgoku rekidai boken ryakkō* 中國歷代墓券略考." *Tōyō-bunka kenkyūjo kiyō* 86 (1981): 193–278.

Kamitsuka Yoshiko 神塚淑子. "*Reihōgyō to shoki kōnan bukkyō—Inkahōō shiso o chūshin ni* 靈寶經と初期江南佛教—因果報應思想を中心に." *Tōhō shūkyō* 東方宗教 91 (1998): 1–21.

———. *Rikuchō dōkyō shisō no kenkyū* 六朝道教思想の研究. Tokyo: Sōbun-sha, 1999.

Karlgren, Bernhard. *The Book of Odes.* Stockholm: Museum of Far Eastern Antiquities, 1974.

Keenan, John P. *How Master Mou Removes Our Doubts: A Reader-Response Study and Translation of the Mou-tzu Li-hou lun.* Albany: State University of New York Press, 1994.

Keightley, David N. "Clean Hands and Shining Helmets: Heroic Action in Early Chinese and Greek Culture." In *Religion and the Authority of the Past,* ed. Tobin Siebers, 13–51. Ann Arbor: University of Michigan Press, 1993.

———. "The Making of the Ancestors: Late Shang Religion and Its Legacy." In Lagerwey, *Religion and Chinese Society,* 3–64.

———. "Shamanism, Death, and the Ancestors: Religious Mediation in Neolithic and Shang China." *Asiatische Studien* 52, no. 3 (1998): 763–828.

Kern, Martin. *Die Hymnen der chinesischen Stattsopfer: Literatur und Ritual in der politischen Repräsentation von der Han-zeit bis zu den Sechs Dynastien.* Stuttgart: Franz Steiner Verlag, 1997.

———. "*Shi jing* Songs as Performance Texts: A Case Study of 'Chu ci'(Thorny Caltrop)." *Early China* 25 (2000): 49–111.

Kieschnik, John. *The Eminent Monk: Buddhist Ideals in Medieval Chinese Hagiography.* Honolulu: University of Hawaii Press, 1997.

Kirkland, Russell. "The History of Taoism: A New Outline." *Journal of Chinese Religions* 30 (2002): 177–93.

Kleeman, Terry F. *Great Perfection: Religion and Ethnicity in a Chinese Millennial Kingdom.* Honolulu: University of Hawaii Press, 1998.

———. "Land Contracts and Related Documents." In *Chūgoku no shūkyō, shisō to kagaku, Festschrift in honour of Makio Ryōkai,* 1–34. Tokyo: Kokusho kankōkai, 1984.

———. "Licentious Cults and Bloody Victuals: Sacrifice, Reciprocity, and Violence in Traditional China." *Asia Major,* 3rd ser., 7, no. 1 (1994): 185–211.

Knapp, Keith. "Heaven and Death According to Huangfu Mi, a Third-Century Confucian." *Early Medieval China* 6 (2000): 1–31.

Knechtges, David. "Culling the Weeds and Selecting Prime Blossoms: The Anthology in Medieval China." In Pearce, Spiro, and Ebrey, *Culture and Power,* 200–241.

———. *Wen Xuan, or Selections of Refined Literature.* Vol. 1. *Rhapsodies on Metropolises and Capitals.* Princeton, NJ: Princeton University Press, 1982.

———. *Wen Xuan, or Selections of Refined Literature.* Vol. 2. *Rhapsodies on Sacrifices, Hunting, Travel, Sightseeing, Palaces and Halls, Rivers and Seas.* Princeton, NJ: Princeton University Press, 1982.

———. *Wen Xuan, or Selections of Refined Literature.* Vol. 3. *Rhapsodies on Natural Phenomena, Birds and Animals, Aspirations and Feelings, Sorrowful Laments, Literature, Music, and Passions.* Princeton, NJ: Princeton University Press, 1996.

Kohn, Livia. "Counting Good Deeds and Days of Life: The Quantification of Fate in Medieval China." *Asiatische Studien* 52 (1998): 833–70.

———, ed. *Daoism Handbook.* Leiden: E. J. Brill, 2000.

———. "Steal Holy Food and Come Back as a Viper: Conceptions of Karma and Rebirth in Medieval Daoism." *Early Medieval China* 4 (1998): 1–48.

Kominami Ichirō 小南一郎. "Shinteiko to Tōgo no bunka 神亭壺と東呉の文化." *Tōhōgakuhō* 東方學報 65 (1993): 225–74.

Kuhn, Philip A. *Soulstealers: The Chinese Sorcery Scare of 1768.* Cambridge, MA: Harvard University Press, 1990.

Kuo Li-ying. *Confession et contrition dans le bouddhisme chinois du Ve au Xe

siècle. Publications de l'École française d'Extrême-Orient, no. 170. Paris: École française d'Extrême-Orient, 1994.

Lagerwey, John, ed. *Religion and Chinese Society: Ancient and Medieval China.* Vol. 1. Hong Kong: Chinese University of Hong Kong Press and École française d'Extrême-Orient, 2004.

Legge, James. *The Four Books: The Great Learning, The Doctrine of the Mean, Confucian Analects, and the Works of Mencius.* New York: Paragon Book Reprint Corp., 1966.

———. *Li Chi: Book of Rites, An Encyclopedia of Ancient Ceremonial Usages, Religious Creeds, and Social Institutions.* 2 vols. New York: University Books, 1967.

Le Goff, Jacques. *The Birth of Purgatory.* Trans. Arthur Goldhammer. Chicago: University of Chicago Press, 1981.

Lewis, I. M. *Ecstatic Religion: An Anthropological Study of Spirit Possession and Shamanism.* Harmondsworth, UK: Penguin Books, 1978.

Lewis, Mark Edward. *Sanctioned Violence in Early China.* Albany: State University of New York Press, 1990.

Li Fang 李昉 (925–96) et al., eds. *Taiping guangji* 太平廣記. Beijing: Zhonghua, 1961.

———. *Taiping yulan* 太平御覽. Beijing: Zhonghua, 1960.

Li Fengmao 李豐楙. "*Daozang* suoshou zaoqi daoshu de wenyi guan <道藏>所收早期道書的瘟疫觀." *Zhongguo wenzhe yanjiu jikan* 中國文哲研究集刊 3 (1993): 417–54.

Li Gang 李剛. "Han Jin Huyong fawei 漢晉胡俑發微." *Dongnan wenhua* 東南文化 3, no. 4 (1991): 73–81.

Li Yanshou 李延壽 (fl. 629). *Nanshi* 南史. Beijing: Zhonghua shuju, 1975.

Liebenthal, Walter. "The Immortality of the Soul in Chinese Thought." *Monumenta Nipponica* 7, nos. 1–2 (1952): 327–97.

Lin Fu-shih 林富士. "The Cult of Jiang Ziwen in Medieval China." *Cahiers d'Extrême-Asie* 10 (1998): 357–75.

———. "Dong Han wanqi de jibing yu zongjiao 東漢晚期的疾病與宗教." *Zhongyang yanjiuyuan lishi yuyan yanjiusuo jikan* 中央研究院歷史語言研究所集刊 66, no. 3 (1995): 695–745.

———. "Toufa, jibing yu yiliao—yi Zhongguo Han-Tang zhijian de yixue wenxian wei zhu de chubu tantao 頭髮, 疾病與醫療—以中國漢唐之間的醫學文獻為主的初步探討." *Zhongyang yanjiuyuan lishi yuyan yanjiusuo jikan* 中央研究院歷史語言研究所集刊 71, no. 1 (2000): 67–127.

Liu Jingshu 劉敬叔 (fl. early fifth century CE). *Yiyuan* 異苑. In *Shuoku* 說庫, ed. Wang Wenru 王文濡. Taibei: Xinxing shuju, 1963.

Liu, Ming-Wood. "Fan Chen's *Treatise on the Destructibility of the Spirit* and Its Buddhist Critics." *Philosophy East and West* 37, no. 4 (1987): 402–28.

Liu Xu 劉煦 (887–946) et al. *Jiu Tangshu* 舊唐書. Beijing: Zhonghua shuju, 1975.

Lopez, Donald S., Jr., "Belief." In *Critical Terms for Religious Studies*, ed. Mark C. Taylor, 21–35. Chicago: University of Chicago Press, 1998.

———, ed. *Religions of China in Practice.* Princeton, NJ: Princeton University Press, 1996.

Maeda Shigeki 前田繁樹. *Shoki dōkyō kyōten no keisei* 初期道教經典の形成. Tokyo: Kyūko, 2004.

Maspero, Henri. *Le Taoïsme et les religions Chinoises*. Vol. 2. Paris: Publications du Musée Guimet, 1950.

Mather, Richard B. *Shih-shuo Hsin-yü: A New Account of Tales of the World*. Minneapolis: University of Minnesota Press, 1976.

Matsumura Takumi 松村巧. "Shinkō ni mieru Rahōdo kikai setsu 真誥に見える羅酆都鬼界說." In Yoshikawa, *Rikuchō dōkyō no kenkyū*, 167–88.

McDermott, James P. 1980. "Karma and Rebirth in Early Buddhism." In O'Flaherty, *Karma and Rebirth*, 165–92.

Michihata Yoshihide 道端良秀. *Chūgoku Bukkyō shisōshi no kenkyū: chūgoku minshū no bukkyō juyō* 中國佛教思想史の研究: 中國民眾の佛教受容. Kyoto: Heiryakuji shoten, 1979.

———. "*Tonkō bunken ni mieru shigō no sekkai* 敦煌文獻に見える死後の世界." In *Tonkō to Chūgoku Bukkyō* 敦煌と中國佛教, ed. Makita Tairyō 牧田諦亮 and Fukui Fumimasa 福井文雅. Tokyo: Daitō, 1984.

Miller, Amy Lynn. "Doing Time in Taoist Purgatory: Annotated Translations, Dating, and Analysis of Punishments in Two Six Dynasties *Ling-pao* Texts on Purgatory." Master's thesis, Indiana University, 1994.

Miyakawa Hisayuki 宮川尚志. *Rikuchō shi kenkyū—Seiji, shakai hen* 六朝史研究—政治, 社會篇. Tokyo: Nihon Gakujutsu Shinkōkai, 1956.

Mollier, Christine. *Messianisme Taoïste de la Chine medieval: Étude du Dongyuan shenzhou jing*. Paris: Université de Paris, 1986.

———. "La méthode de l'empereur du nord du mont Fengdu: Une tradition exorciste du Taoïsme médiéval." *T'oung Pao* 83 (1997): 329–85.

Nakajima Ryūzō 中島隆藏. *Rikuchō shisō no kenkyū* 六朝思想の研究. Kyoto: Heirakuji shoten, 1985.

Nickerson, Peter S. "Abridged Codes of Master Lu for the Daoist Community." In Lopez, *Religions of China in Practice*, 347–59.

———. "The Great Petition for Sepulchral Plaints." In Bokenkamp, *Early Daoist Scriptures*, 230–74.

———. "Taoism, Death, and Bureaucracy in Early Medieval China." PhD diss., University of California, Berkeley, 1996.

O'Flaherty, Wendy Doniger, ed. *Karma and Rebirth in Classical Indian Traditions*. Berkeley and Los Angeles: University of California Press, 1980.

O'Hara, Albert Richard. *The Position of Women in Early China According to the Lieh nü chuan, "The Biographies of Eminent Chinese Women."* Washington, DC: Catholic University of America Press, 1945.

Ou-yang Xiu 歐陽修 (1007–72), Song Qi 宋祁 (998–1061), et al. *Xin Tangshu* 新唐書. Beijing: Zhonghua shuju, 1975.

Ouyang Xun 歐陽詢 (557–641), ed. *Yiwen Leiju* 藝文類聚. Shanghai: Guji, 1965.

Pearce, Scott, Audrey Spiro, and Patricia Ebrey, eds. *Culture and Power in the Reconstitution of the Chinese Realm, 200–600*. Cambridge, MA: Harvard University Press, 2001.

Poo Mu-chou 浦慕州. "The Concept of Ghost in Ancient Chinese Religion." In Lagerwey, *Religion and Chinese Society*, 173–92.

———. *In Search of Personal Welfare: A View of Ancient Chinese Religion.* Albany: State University of New York Press, 1998.

———. *Muzang yu shengsi—Zhongguo gudai zongjiao zhi xingsi* 墓葬與生死—中國古代宗教之省思. Taibei: Lianjing, 1993.

Powers, Martin J. *Art and Political Expression in Early China.* New Haven, CT: Yale University Press, 1991.

Puett, Michael J. *The Ambivalence of Creation: Debates Concerning Innovation and Artifice in Early China.* Stanford, CA: Stanford University Press, 2001.

———. *To Become a God: Cosmology, Sacrifice, and Self-Divinization in Early China.* Harvard-Yenching Monograph Series, no. 57. Cambridge, MA: Harvard University Press, 2002.

Qian Nanxiu. *Spirit and Self in Medieval China: The "Shih-shuo hsin-yü" and Its Legacy.* Honolulu: University of Hawaii Press, 2001.

Riegel, Jeffrey. "Do Not Serve the Dead as You Serve the Living: The *Lüshi chunqiu* Treatises on Moderation in Burial." *Early China* 20 (1995): 310–30.

Robinet, Isabelle. *Méditation Taoïste.* Paris: Dervy-livres, 1979.

———. "Metamorphosis and Deliverance from the Corpse in Taoism." *History of Religions* 19, no. 1 (1979): 57–70.

———. "Les randonées extatiques des Taoistes dans les astres." *Monumenta Serica* 32 (1976): 159–273.

———. *La révélation du Shangqing dans l'histoire du Taoïsme.* Publications de l'École française d'Extrême-Orient, no. 137. 2 vols. Paris: École française d'Extrême-Orient, 1984.

———. *Taoist Meditation: The Mao-Shan Tradition of Great Purity.* Trans. Julian F. Pas and Norman J. Girardot. Albany: State University of New York Press, 1993.

Sawada Mizuho 澤田瑞穗. *Jigoku hen: chūgoku no meikai setsu* 地獄篇: 中國の冥界說. Kyoto: Hōzōkan, 1968.

Schafer, Edward H. *Mao Shan in T'ang Times.* 2nd ed. Society for the Study of Chinese Religions Monograph, no. 1. Boulder, CO: Society for the Study of Chinese Religions, 1989.

———. *The Vermilion Bird: T'ang Images of the South.* Berkeley and Los Angeles: University of California Press, 1967.

Schopen, Gregory. *Bones, Stones, and Buddhist Monks: Collected Papers on the Archeology, Epigraphy, and Texts of Monastic Buddhism in India.* Honolulu: University of Hawaii Press, 1997.

Segal, Robert A. "The Myth-Ritualist Theory of Religion." *Journal for the Scientific Study of Religion* 2 (1980):173–85.

Seidel, Anna K. "Geleitbrief an die Unterwelt—Jenseitsvorstellungen in den Graburkunden der späteren Han-Zeit." In *Religion und Philosophie in Ostasien,* [in honour of Hans Steininger], ed. G. Naundorf, K. H. Pohl, and H. H. Schmidt, 161–83. Würzburg: Könighausen & Neumann, 1985.

———. "Imperial Treasures and Taoist Sacraments: Taoist Roots in the Apocrypha." In Strickmann, *Tantric and Taoist Studies,* 291–371.

———. "Post-Mortem Immortality, or: The Taoist Resurrection of the Body." In *GILGUL: Essays on Transformation, Revolution and Permanence in the*

History of Religions, ed. S. Shaked, D. Shulman, and G. G. Stroumsa, 223–37. Leiden: E. J. Brill, 1987.

———. "Tokens of Immortality in Han Graves." *Numen* 29, no. 1 (1982): 79–114.

———. "Traces of Han Religion in Funeral Texts Found in Tombs." In *Dōkyō to shūkyō bunka* [volume in honour of Professor Akitsuki Kan'ei], 21–57. Tokyo: Hirakawa, 1987.

Sharf, Robert H. *Coming to Terms with Chinese Buddhism: A Reading of the Treasure Store Treatise*. Honolulu: University of Hawaii Press, 2002.

Shen Yue 沈約 (441–513). *Songshu* 宋書. Beijing: Zhonghua shuju, 1974.

Shi Zhicun 施蟄存. *Shuijing zhu bei lu* 水經注碑錄. Tianjin: Guji, 1987.

Shryock, J. K. *The Study of Human Abilities*. American Oriental Series, vol. 11. New Haven, CT: Yale University Press, 1937.

Sibu beiyao 四部備要, compiled and published in Shanghai by the Zhonghua shuju, 1927–1935.

Sima Guang 司馬光 (1019–86). *Zizhi tongjian* 資治通鑑. Beijing: Guji, 1957.

Sima Tan 司馬談 (180–110? BCE) and 司馬遷 Sima Qian (145–86? CE). *Shiji* 史記. Beijing: Zhonghua shuju, 1972.

Steele, John. *The I-li, or Book of Etiquette and Ceremonial*. Taibei: Chengwen, 1966.

Strickmann, Michel. *Chinese Magical Medicine*. Stanford, CA: Stanford University Press, 2002.

———. "The Mao-shan Revelations: Taoism and the Aristocracy." *T'oung-pao* 63 (1977): 1–63.

———. "On the Alchemy of T'ao Hung-ching." In Welch and Seidel, *Facets of Taoism*, 123–92.

———, ed. 1983. *Tantric and Taoist Studies in Honour of R. A. Stein*. Vol. 2. Mélanges chinois et bouddhiques, no. 21. Bruxelles: Institut belge des hautes études chinoises, 1983.

———. *Le Taoïsme du Mao chan: Chronique d'une révélation*. Paris: Collège du France, Institut des hautes études chinoises, 1981.

Swidler, Ann. *Talk of Love: How Culture Matters*. Chicago: University of Chicago Press, 1999.

Tang Yongtong 湯用彤, ed. *Gaoseng zhuan* 高僧傳. Beijing: Zhonghua shuju, 1992.

Teiser, Stephen F. *The Ghost Festival in Medieval China*. Princeton, NJ: Princeton University Press, 1988.

———. "'Having Once Died and Returned to Life': Representations of Hell in Medieval China." *Journal of Asiatic Studies* 48, no. 2 (1988): 433–64.

———. *The Scripture on the Ten Kings and the Making of Purgatory in Medieval Chinese Buddhism*. Honolulu: University of Hawaii Press, 1994.

Tsukamoto Zenryu. *A History of Early Chinese Buddhism: From Its Introduction to the Death of Hui Yüan*. Trans. Leon Hurvitz. Tokyo: Kodansha, 1985.

Verellen, Franciscus. "The Heavenly Master Liturgical Agenda According to Chisong zi's Petition Almanac." *Cahiers d'Extrême-Asie* 14 (2004): 291–344.

von Glahn, Richard. *The Sinister Way: The Divine and the Demonic in Chinese Religious Culture*. Berkeley and Los Angeles: University of California Press, 2004.

Wang Chong 王充 (27–91). *Lunheng jiaoshi* 論橫校釋. Ed. Huang Hui 黃暉. Beijing: Zhonghua shuju, 1990.

Wang Jiakui 王家葵. *Tao Hongjing congkao* 陶弘景叢考. Jinan: Qilu shushe, 2003.

Wang Wenjin 王文錦, ed. *Tongdian jiaodian ben* 通典校點本. 4 vols. Beijing: Zhonghua, 1988.

Wang Wenru 王文濡, ed. *Shuoku* 說庫. Taibei: Xinxing shuju, 1963.

Watson, Burton. *Early Chinese Literature.* New York: Columbia University Press, 1962.

Watson, Rubie S. "Remembering the Dead: Graves and Politics in Southeastern China." In *Death Ritual in Late Imperial and Modern China,* ed. James L. Watson and Evelyn S. Rawski, 203–27. Berkeley and Los Angeles: University of California Press, 1988.

Welch, Holmes, and Anna Seidel, eds. *Facets of Taoism: Essays in Chinese Religion.* New Haven, CT: Yale University Press, 1979.

Wu Hung. "Art in a Ritual Context: Rethinking Mawangdui." *Early China* 17 (1992): 111–44.

———. "Buddhist Elements in Early Chinese Art (Second and Third Centuries AD)." *Artibus Asiae* 47 (1986): 263–376.

———. *Monumentality in Early Chinese Art and Architecture.* Stanford, CA: Stanford University Press, 1995.

Xiao Dengfu 蕭登福. *Han, Wei, Liuchao Fo Dao liangjiao zhi tiantang diyu shuo* 漢, 魏, 六朝 佛道兩教之天堂地獄說. Taibei: Taiwan xuesheng, 1989.

Xiao Tong 蕭統 (501–31), comp. *Wen xuan* 文選. Hong Kong: Shangwu yinshu guan, 1974.

Xu Song 許嵩 (fl. 756). *Jiankang shilu* 建康實錄. Ed. Zhang Chenshi 張忱石. Beijing: Zhonghua, 1986.

Yamada Toshiaki. "The Lingbao School." In Kohn, *Daoism Handbook,* 225–55.

Yan Kejun 嚴可均 (1762–1843), comp. *Quan shanggu Sandai Qin Han Sanguo Liuchao wen* 全上古三代秦漢三國六朝文. 5 vols. Taibei: Hongye, 1975.

Yasui Kōzan 安居香山 and Nakamura Shōhachi 中村璋八, eds. *Isho shūsei* 緯書集成. 6 vols. Tokyo: Meitoku, 1971–78.

Yoshikawa Tadao 吉川忠夫. *Chūgoku kodaijin no yume to shi* 中國古代人の夢と死. . Tokyo: Heibonsha, 1985.

———, ed. *Rikuchō dōkyō no kenkyū* 六朝道教の研究. Tokyo: Shunjūsha, 1998.

Yoshikawa Tadao 吉川忠夫 and Mugitani Kuniō 麥谷邦夫. *Shinkō kenkyū: Yakuchū hen* 真誥研究:譯注篇. Kyoto: Kyōto daigaku jinbun kagaku kenkyūjō, 2000.

Yoshioka Yoshitoyo 吉岡義豐. "Rikucho dōkyō no shumin shisō 六朝道教種民の思想." In *Dōkyō to Bukkyō* 道教と佛教, 3:221–84. 3 vols. Tokyo: Kokushō kankokai, 1976.

Yü, Ying-shih. "'O Soul, Come Back!' A Study in the Changing Conceptions of the Soul and Afterlife in Pre-Buddhist China." *Harvard Journal of Asiatic Studies* 47, no. 2 (1987): 363–95.

Yuan Hong 袁宏 (328–76). *Hou Han ji jiaozhu* 後漢紀較注. Ed. with annotations by Zhou Tianyou 周天遊. Tianjin: Tianjin guji chubanshe, 1987.

Zhang Jiefu 張捷夫. *Zhongguo sangzang shi* 中國喪葬史. Taibei: Wenjin, 1995.

Zhong Laiyin 鍾來因. *Changsheng busi de tanqiu: Daojing Zhen'gao zhi mi* 長生不死的探求—道經<真誥>之謎. Shanghai: Wenhui, 1992.

Zhou Yiliang 周一良. *Wei Jin Nanbei chao shi zhaji* 魏晉南北朝史札記. Beijing: Zhonghua, 1985.

Zhu Dawei 朱大維 et al. *Wei Jin Nanbei chao shehui shenghuo shi* 魏晉南北朝社會生活史. Beijing: Zhongguo shehui kexue chubanshe, 1998.

Zürcher, Erik. *The Buddhist Conquest of China.* 2 vols. Leiden: E. J. Brill, 1959.

———. "Buddhist Influence on Taoist Scripture." *T'oung-pao* 66, nos. 1–3 (1980): 84–147.

Index

Abe, Stanley K., 64
afterlife. *See* rebirth; underworlds
An, Consort (Lady of the Right Blossom), 141
Analects, 8, 22, 24–25
Anderson, Benedict, 95
Anxiety of Influence (Bloom), 18
apocryphal sutras, 9
Aramaki Noritoshi, 127

Bao Jing, 168
Baopuzi (Ge Hong), 44–45
Baxandall, Michael, 11
Bloom, Harold, 18, 19, 23
Bo Ji, 75–76
Book of Odes (Shijing), 6, 22, 78–79
Bourdieu, Pierre, 130
Bu Shang, 43
Buddhism: Daoist adaptation of, 4, 7, 9–12, 20, 23, 30, 158; hell, 5–6, 35, 197; influence on Daoist concept of rebirth, 7, 10, 30, 161, 171–72, 182, 194–95; karma, 163, 165, 170; literary traditions in, 23–25; merit-transfer, 174, 179, 196; monastic practices, 22, 30–31, 40–41; nirvana, 176–77; samsara, 163; self, notions of, 175–76; spread of, 30, 172, 195
"Buddhist Influence on Early Taoism" (Zürcher), 172

Bulletin of the Cleveland Museum of Art, 63
burial. *See* grave; *hun*-summoning burial

Cai Yong, 1–3, 4–5, 6–7, 8
Campany, Robert Ford, 16–17, 33
Cao Cao, 54
Cao Fu, 84, 85
Cao Pi, 49, 54–55
capping ceremony, 3
Celestial Master priests, 181. *See also* Daoism
ceremonies. *See* rituals and rites
Chen dynasty, 109
Chi Chao, 170
Chi Jian, 104, 106, 107–8, 110, 114, 115
Chi Yin: as Celestial Master Daoist initiate, 114, 170; escape from underworld threats, 116–18; underworld threat to, 97, 115–16, 170; Yang Xi's revelations for, 97, 113–14
Classic of Filial Piety, 22
cloudsouls, 176, 184, 188, 190
collective versus individual guilt, 173–76, 178–81, 191–93, 196–97
Coming to Terms with Chinese Buddhism (Sharf), 12, 158
commemoration of dead, 46, 51–53. *See also* filial piety; rituals and rites; sacrifice

Confucius, 8
Cui, Madame, 187
cyclical rebirth (samsara), 17, 162–63,
    172. See also rebirth

Dai Qizhi, 148
Dan (resurrected man), 53
Daode jing, 22
Daoism: adaptation of Buddhist doctrine,
    4, 7, 9–12, 20, 23, 30, 158; Celestial
    Master priests, 181; five phases of
    existence, 33n2, 91; ritual manuals,
    118; social contexts in development
    of conceptualizations, 13, 16, 19–
    20; Three Offices of Heaven, Earth,
    and Water, 115, 183. See also Ling-
    bao scriptures; rebirth
Declarations of the Perfected (Zhen'gao),
    13, 15, 119. See also Tao Hong-
    jing; Yang Xi; specific characters
    and events
deliverance by means of substitute
    corpse, 70
Deng You, 126
Dien, Albert E., 63–64, 89
Discours de Rome (Lacan), 23
disembodied burials, 70–72. See also
    hun-summoning burial
Divina Commedia, 14, 34
diyu, 35
Dou, Empress, 67–69
double-trunk tree, 1, 5
Du You, 65, 72

Ehuang, 148, 149, 151, 154, 155
Eight Princes' Rebellion, 82, 90
"encounter paradigm," 12
Essentials of Upholding the Way (Chi
    Chao), 170
externalist analysis of religion, 16–18, 194

Falkenhausen, Lothar von, 52
familial guilt versus personal responsi-
    bility, 173–76, 178–81, 191–93,
    196–97
Fan Miao (Commander of the Dead;
    Middle Watchlord Fan), 133, 136,
    141, 150, 153–54
Fang Xuanling, 72
Fengdu: bureaucratic administration of,
    33–34, 36, 183; as desirable desti-
    nation, 36–37, 195–96; position
    and rank in, 34, 36; role of tran-
    scendents in, 44–45
filial piety, 1–3, 20, 22, 28, 52, 88
five phases of existence, 33n2, 91
Fu Chun, 64–65

Gan Bao, 74, 79–80, 86–87, 90, 109
Ge Chaofu, 14, 171
Ge Hong, 44–45, 169, 171
Ge Xuan, 158–61
Gong, Duke, 75
Gongsha Xin, 73, 76–77, 80, 91
grave: austerity of, 45, 49, 50, 53–55,
    86, 100; confinement of hun in, 69,
    76, 78–81; filial devotions at, 1–3;
    mortuary jars, 63–64; palatial model
    of, 188; provisioning of, 52, 62;
    versus temple, 64–65, 69, 78, 80–
    81, 85–89; texts and inscriptions,
    57–58, 88, 112, 184
"Great Summons," 51
Greenblatt, Stephen, 19
grievances of ancestors. See underworld
    lawsuits
Guide to the Abhidharma (Sengdu), 27
Guo Cha, 98
Guo Fan: accounts of underworld, com-
    pared with Su Shao's, 96, 100–101;
    earthly life, 96, 98–99, 102; Guo
    Fan biezhuan, 98, 99; political cli-
    mate at time of revelations, 96, 102–
    3, 106–8; rank in underworld, 102–
    3, 106; on Wang Yue's death, 108–9;
    on Yu Liang's underworld status,
    102, 111, 124
Guo Na, 98
Guo Pu, 25
Guo Xun (Guo Xiu), 75
guojia, 60

hair, 22, 28n, 39, 40–41, 177
Harper, Donald, 53–54
He Chong, 125–26
He Lü, 43
hells, 3–4, 5–6, 35, 197
History of the Jin (Gan Bao), 79–80
Ho Wai-kam, 63
Hua, Merit Officer (Secretary Hua), 140,
    143–44, 154
Hua Qi, 150
Hua Qiao, 143–44
Hua Zirong: consultation with others,
    143–44; entrance into oratory, 136,
    137; failure to feed dead mother-
    in-law, 150–51; offering required
    of, 145; problems unrelated to Xu
    family, 149–50, 151; resistance to
    offering, 139, 140–42, 144, 151.
    See also Tao Kedou; Xu Lian
Huan Wen, 107–8
Huang Jingye, 148, 151
Huang Yan, 148, 149, 151
Huijiao, 20

hun: ability to move in and out of tomb, 78–80; dangers faced by, 51; nature of, 62–63; provisions for, 52; resting place for, 69, 76, 78–81; wronged, fear of, 90–92

hunping, 63–64

hun-summoning burial: banning of, 61, 72–74, 81, 85; Confucian ritual classics on, 76–80; construction of grave, 87; *hun*-summoning garment, 61, 68–70; political implications, 85, 88–94; precedent for, 68, 74–76; recipients of, 67–68, 81–85; for victims of violence, 67, 76, 90

hun-summoning rite, 69–70, 77

"Hymn of Praise on the Virtues of My Ancestors" (Cai Yong), 2–3

"Inciting My Determination" (Zhang Hua), 25

internalist analysis of religion, 16–17

Jia, Empress, 90

Jiang, Supreme Marquis, 103

Jiang Ziwen, 108–9

Jin dynasty, 109–10

Jinshu, 72

karma, 163, 165, 170

Keightley, David N., 95

Kleeman, Terry, 181

Knechtges, David, 24

Kong Yan, 72, 75–76, 79, 80

Kumārajīva, 163

Lacan, Jacques, 23

Laozi, 163, 179

lawsuits. *See* underworld lawsuits

Li Dan (Tang Ruizong), 67, 68

Li Dong, 143, 152

Li Wei, 73, 75–76, 78

Li Zhan, 169

Li Zhe (Tang Zhongzong), 67, 185–86, 187

Liji, 77

Lingbao scriptures: as adaptation of Buddhist doctrine, 171–72, 182, 191; composition of, 12–13, 171; inherited guilt versus personal responsibility, 173–76, 178–81, 191–93, 196–97; as means of salvation, 183–91, 196; merit-transfer, 174, 179–80, 196, 197; nirvana, 176–77; samsara, 162–63, 172; sanction of ancestral sacrifice, 181; as turning point in Daoism, 13, 172. *See also* rebirth

Liu, Empress, 67–69

Liu Che, 75

Liu Shao, 48, 59

Liu Xia, 84–85

Liu Xiu, 75, 86

Liu Yuan, 75

Liu Zhuang, 86

Liu-Song dynasty, 109

Lopez, Donald S. Jr., 16

Lord of Mount Tai, 36, 47–48

Lu Xiujing, 3–4, 5–6, 7, 14, 181–82

Lunyu, 77

"Making of the Ancestors, The" (Keightley), 95

Mao, younger Lord: appearance at oratory, 154; arrangements for oratory, 153; at Commander Fan's impatience with Xu family, 136, 141, 150; on offering requirements, 135–36, 138–39, 140–41, 142–43; on underworld lawsuits, 131, 149–50; at Xu Hui's offer of self-sacrifice, 145–46

Martial Marquis of Wei, 41–42

Masculine Domination (Bourdieu), 130

Mather, Richard, 106

mediums: goals of, 46, 106; personators, *shi,* 38, 40; possession by spirit, 99; professional, 96–97; sons as, 40, 112; written transmissions of spirits, 41, 100. *See also* Xin Xuanzi; Yang Xi

memories of ancestors concerning descendants, 38, 46, 51–53, 55, 100

Mengzi, 77

"merging pneumas," 152

merit-transfer, 174, 179–80, 196, 197

"Miscellaneous Poem #2" (Zhang Xie), 25

Mohists, 53

Mount Luofeng. *See* Fengdu

Music Bureau myth, 24

Nickerson, Peter, 118, 132

Nineteen Old Poems, 22, 24

Ning Cheng, 187

nirvāṇa, 29, 176–77

Northern Thearch, 33

offering. *See* sacrifice

otherworlds. *See* underworlds

Pei, Ms., 61, 72, 82, 93

penetrating powers, 161

Peng Jingzhi, 68–69, 75

personators of dead, 38, 40

po, 62–63

poetry, 23–28
political factors: family allegiances, 60;
    in Guo Fan's revelations, 96, 102–5,
    106–11; in *hun*-summoning burial,
    85, 88–94; in plague, 47–48, 60
postmortem lawsuits. *See* underworld
    lawsuits
Precepts of the Three Primordials, 172,
    180, 182–83
Puett, Michael, 17–18

Qian Nanxiu, 105
Qiu Longma, 134

Rebellion of the Eight Princes, 82, 90
rebirth: birth parents' roles, 175, 177;
    body versus self, 175–76; Buddhist
    influence in Daoist concept of, 7,
    10, 30, 161, 171–72, 182, 194–
    95; burial ritual, 188–91; centrality
    of, in Daoist texts, 13; generalized
    versus specialized paths, 162–64;
    in hells, three paths, 4; individual
    versus family responsibility, 165–
    70, 178–79, 191–92; merit-transfer,
    174, 179–80, 196, 197; ritual inter-
    vention for favorable rebirths, 177;
    samsara concept, 17, 162–63, 172;
    social context surrounding develop-
    ment of concept, 16; succession of
    lives, 158–61
*Records of an Inquest into the Spirit-
    Realms* (Gan Bao), 79
Records of Ritual, 37
remembrance of descendants by ances-
    tors, 38, 46, 51–53, 55, 100
Retreat of Mud and Ash, 3, 192
rituals and rites: burial, 188–91; conduct
    of living toward dead, 51; distinction
    between body and spirit in, 64–65;
    for favorable rebirths, 177; manuals
    of formulas, 118; "merging pneu-
    mas," 152–53; personation of dead,
    38; rescue of ancestors from hell,
    3–4; self-sacrifice, 147; shift of,
    from temple to gravesite, 85–89;
    visualization and nourishment of
    ancestors, 37–38. See also *hun*-
    summoning burial
"Roaming in Transcendence, #4" (Guo
    Pu), 25
Robinet, Isabelle, 164–65, 166
Ruan Yu, 56–57

sacrifice: blood sacrifice, 181–82; instruc-
    tions for, 53; negligence of, under-
    world lawsuits and, 57, 90–91; offers
        of self-sacrifice, 147; in reciprocity
        between living and dead, 49, 177;
        site of, 64–65, 78, 86–89
salvation, 3–4, 6, 165–66, 183–91, 192,
    196. *See also* rebirth
samsara, 17, 162–63, 172
Schafer, Edward, 186
Scripture for Revivification, 188–89, 190
Scripture of Filiality (Xiaojing), 22, 177
Scripture of the Arrayed Five Talismans,
    70–71
Seidel, Anna, 57–58
self, Buddhist notions of, 175–76
Sengdu, 20–23, 26–30
Shangqing texts, 116, 132, 151, 164–70
Sharf, Robert H., 12, 158
Shen Sheng, 91
shi, 38, 40
Shi Le, 82, 83, 85
Shiji, 42
shijie, 70–71
Shijing (Book of Odes), 6, 22, 78–79
Shishuo xinyu, 105, 106
Sima Bi, 83
Sima Chi (Huai), 90–92
Sima Chong, 82
Sima Lun, 83
Sima Pi, 82
Sima Que, 83
Sima Rui, 60–61, 63, 85, 89, 94
Sima Shao, 104
Sima Sui, 48
Sima Tao, 83
Sima Teng, 82–83
Sima Xi, 84
Sima Yen, 90
Sima Yu, 90–91, 93, 113
Sima Yue, 72, 82, 84, 91, 92–94
Sima Zhan, 83–84
Sima Zhong, 90
social contexts: in development of Daoist
    conceptualizations, 13, 16, 19–20;
    fallen times, collective familial
    punishment and, 178, 192; political
    climate at time of Guo Fan's revela-
    tions, 96, 102–5, 106–11; politics
    surrounding *hun*-summoning burial,
    85, 90–94; war, separation of
    families from dead by, 56–58
soul: cloudsouls, 176, 184, 188, 190;
    pre-Buddhist notions of, 62–66.
    See also *hun*
soul jars, 63–64
Soushen ji (Gan Bao), 109
Strange Writing (Campany), 33
Strickmann, Michael, observations and
    interpretations: connections between

Hua and Xu families, 143–44; nature of underworld, 130; powers of Commanders of the Dead, 132; relationship between medium and patron, 116; rite of "merging pneumas," 152; salvation transmitted by Perfected, 155; social context, 60; Yang Xi's attitude toward rebirth, 167–68

Su Cheng, 48

Su Jie, 39, 40, 41–43, 45–46

Su Jun, 104–5, 110

Su Shao: accounts of underworld, compared with Guo Fan's, 96, 100–101; contradictions and ambiguities, 55, 58–59; position in underworld, 50; on relations between living and dead, 45–46, 47–48; on remembrance of living by dead, 46, 52; request for reburial, 41–42, 48, 49; return to son in dream, 39; written transmission, 41

"Summons to the *hun*," 51–52

Taijing zhongji, 164–65

Taiping guangji, 99–101

tame animals as omens, 1, 5

Tao Hongjing: acceptance of accounts as fact, 34, 122, 127–28; annotations on Su Shao narrative, 44, 50; annotations on Tao Kedou narrative, 134, 144; background, 118–19; collection and annotation of underworld accounts, 13–14, 33, 119–20; coordination of disparate information, 34, 97; dismissal of Lingbao texts, 171; organization of Tao Kedou records, 132, 135–36; scholarly methods, 121–27

Tao Kan, 96, 103, 104–7, 111

Tao Kedou: imprisonment in tomb, 131, 150; lawsuit, 134; substitution of child for repayment of debt, 131, 134, 151; transcendence, 136, 151, 153, 196

Tao Kedou narrative, 133, 135–36. *See also* Hua Zirong; Tao Kedou; Xu Lian

temple versus grave, 64–65, 69, 78, 80–81, 85–89

tessera, 23

threats from underworld. *See* underworld lawsuits

Three Offices of Heaven, Earth, and Water, 115, 183

three paths of rebirth in hell, 4

tomb. *See* grave

Tongdian, 72

Traditions of Eminent Monks (Huijiao), 20

transcendence, 44–45, 158–61, 162. *See also* rebirth

Treatise on Sacrifices of the Hanshu, 68

Trials of the Sages, 158

underworld lawsuits: bartering of living in exchange for dead, 115–16; bureaucratic infallibility in, 182–83; court proceedings against living, 111, 130–31; delight of dead in, 130; medium's intervention in, 112–18, 134, 196; for neglect of service to dead, 57, 90–91; remedies, 57–58, 91, 112; as threat to descendants, 115, 131; Three Offices of Heaven, Earth, and Water, 115. *See also* Tao Kedou narrative

underworlds: bureaucratic system of administration, 33–34, 182–83; changing portrayals of, 49–50; Chinese versus Buddhist notions of, 35–37; increase in accounts of, 34; variety of possible destinations, 37, 51

unquiet dead. *See* underworld lawsuits

Vimalakīrtinirdeśa-sūtra, 22

visualization of spirits, 37–38. *See also* mediums

Wang Can, 57

Wang Changyu (Yue), 103, 104, 108–9

Wang Chong, 52

Wang Dao, 103, 104, 108

Wang Long, 84

Wang Yan, 154

war, separation from ancestors by, 56–58

Watson, Rubie S., 87–88

Wei, Empress Concordant with Heaven (Commoner Wei), 185–87, 191

Wei Huacun (Lady of the Southern Marchmount), 117, 135, 136, 139, 140–41, 151, 152

Wei Xuanzhen, 185–87, 191

Wilden, Anthony, 23

women, 40, 115–16, 151–53. *See also* specific women

written transmissions, 41, 100

wronged *hun*. *See* underworld lawsuits

Wu, King of the Zhou, 167

Wu Hong, 85–86, 89

Wu Jizi, 43

Wu Qi, 41–42

Wu Zhao (Wu Zetian), 67–69, 185–86

Xiang Liangcheng, 43, 44–45
Xiang'er Commentary, 181
Xiaojing (Scripture of Filiality), 22, 177
Xie clan, 102
Xie Renzu (Shang), 99, 103, 104, 106,
　107–8, 110
Xin Pi, 121–22
Xin Xuanzi: autobiography, 121–22;
　postmortem rank, 123; reports of
　underworld, compared to Marquis
　Xun's, 97, 124–27; Tao Hongjing's
　collection of revelations by, 119–20;
　on Yang Xi's postmortem rank, 123,
　127
Xu Chao, 131, 134
Xu Chisun, 136, 137, 153
Xu Huangmin, 137, 148
Xu Hui, 14, 120, 138–39, 142–43, 145–
　48, 149
Xu Jing, 167
Xu Lian: consultation with others, 139,
　143–44; illness, 137; offer of self as
　substitute for family members, 136;
　petition to spirits in behalf of child,
　137; receipt of offering requirements,
　135, 138–39, 140–41, 142–43; re-
　liance on father's spiritual protec-
　tion, 140, 145. *See also* Hua Zirong;
　Tao Kedou
Xu Mi: illness, 135; involvement in under-
　world lawsuit, 131, 140, 142; offer-
　ings required for rescue of wife, 138,
　140, 142; as patron of Yang Xi, 14,
　113; practice of rite of "merging
　pneumas," 152; rebirth, 167–68; as
　spiritual protector of son, 140, 145;
　transmittal of message from
　Perfected, 114
Xu Quan, 145
Xue Changli, 167
Xue Lü, 167
Xun, Marquis, 114–15, 119, 124–27
Xunzi, 77

Yan Yuan (Yan Hui), 43
Yang Tiaohua, 20–23, 24–25, 26–29
Yang Xi: background, 113; employment
by Chi Yin, 97, 116–18; employment
by Xu family, 14, 112–13; inducements to prospective clients, 116–
18, 195; intervention in underworld
lawsuits, 112–18, 134, 196; as outsider to patrons' families, 128–29;
on rebirth, 164, 165–70, 195; status
in otherworld, 127, 128; visualization methods, use of confederates,
154–55, 156; women, depictions of,
151–53, 156
Yang Xiong, 43
Yellow Springs, 35–36
Yellow Thearch, 68, 74–75, 76
Yili, 69, 77
You, King of Western Zhou, 6
younger Lord Mao. *See* Mao, younger
　Lord
Yu clan, 102
Yu Liang: earthly power, 99, 102; otherworld positions of comrades, 108–
11; rank in otherworld, 102–3, 124–
25; and Tao Kan, enmity between,
96, 104–7
Yu Yi, 99, 107

Zhai Tang, 99
Zhang Heng, 43, 44
Zhang Hua, 25
Zhang Huanzhi, 134
Zhang Jiefu, 86
Zhang Lü, 169
Zhang Xie, 25
Zhao, Empress, 67–69
Zhao Gui, 67
*zhaohun zang. See hun-*summoning
　burial
Zheng Xuan, 69
*Zhen'gao. See Declarations of the
　Perfected (Zhen'gao)*
zhong, 78, 80
Zhou Fu, 114
Zhou Sheng, 73, 74
Zhou Yi, 126
Zhu Sengdu, 20–23, 26–30
Zhuangzi, 22
Zürcher, Erik, 101, 172

Text: 10/13 Sabon
Display: Sabon
Compositor: Integrated Composition Systems
Printer and binder: Thomson-Shore, Inc.